TAX PATH FOR MIDDLE-INCOME HOUSEHOLDS

Explore Income Tax Savings and
Keep More of Your Money

Lisa Bushur, CPA

Copyright © 2015 by Lisa Bushur CPA Team, LLC
All rights reserved
ISBN 978-0-9905808-1-2
Printed in the United States of America

Contents

Author's Preface vii
Disclaimer xi
Chapter 1 1
   My Personal Trek
Chapter 2 5
   Do You Need A CPA?
Chapter 3 15
   Pay NO Income Tax on These Items!
Chapter 4 23
   Strategies for Portfolio Income
Chapter 5 31
   Retirement Plans - First Move for an Employee
Chapter 6 39
   What You Need to Know About IRAs, Non-Deductible IRAs, and Catch-Up Contributions
Chapter 7 45
   Roth IRAs and Roth Conversion Considerations
Chapter 8 55
   Let Your Retirement Plan Help You During Hard Times
Chapter 9 63
   Which Filing Status: Married Filing Joint or Married Filing Separate?
Chapter 10 69
   Head of Household Status
Chapter 11 73
   Maximize the Value of Kids' Exemptions
Chapter 12 79
   Do You Qualify for Grandma's Dependency Exemption?
Chapter 13 83
   The Kiddie Tax is More Advantageous Than You Think
Chapter 14 89
   Which Will Net You the Better Tax Advantage: Dependent Care Benefit or Dependent Care Credit?

Chapter 15 95
    Adoption Credit: Make the Difference in the Life of a
    Child, and Earn a Tax Credit Along the Way

Chapter 16 103
    Force Uncle Sam to Help Pay for College

Chapter 17 127
    Additional Medicare Tax

Chapter 18 131
    The IRS Raised The Bar, and So Must You
    (Itemized Deductions 👍, Medical Expenses 👍,
    & Personal Exemptions 👍)

Chapter 19 137
    Charitable Donations Help You More Than You Think

Chapter 20 145
    Pay Off Your Mortgage or Build More Savings?

Chapter 21 153
    Miscellaneous Itemized Deductions 👍 -
    Gather Enough to Deduct

Chapter 22 159
    Escape Tax on the Sale of a Personal Residence

Chapter 23 165
    Can You Minimize Alternative Minimum Tax?

Chapter 24 173
    Choose Between a W-2 Employee or Independent
    Contractor

Chapter 25 183
    Can You Deduct Moving Expenses?

Chapter 26 189
    How to Manage Hobby Losses to Avoid IRS Issues

Chapter 27 195
    Muscle Up With the Right Hammer to Deduct
    Medical Expenses (Health Savings Accounts
    & Flexible Spending Accounts)

Chapter 28 201
    Minimize Income Tax Even in Divorce

Chapter 29 211
    Think Green to Save Some Green
Chapter 30 217
    What Action to Take in High-Income Years
Chapter 31 227
    What Action to Take in Low-Income Years
Chapter 32 233
    Penalties Are a Waste of Your Money
Chapter 33 245
    Tax Savings Quantified
Appendix A 249
    What to Gather for Your CPA for Tax Preparation Time
Appendix B 269
    Home Office Deduction Information Collection Sheet
Appendix C 271
    Mileage Reporting Form
Glossary 273
About the Author 295

Author's Preface

Do you know what's even more important when it comes to your income taxes than getting them filed on time? Many folks don't even consider this! Strategizing and planning so that you pay the least amount of income taxes is much more important than actually filing your income tax return! These are more important because it takes time and thought to execute effective income tax savings ideas. Here are just a few of the punch lines I've delivered, from throughout this book, relative to both successful and unsuccessful income tax planning:

> "The balance due with your return is $5,400, including the 10% penalty for early withdrawal from your retirement plan. I'm sorry your employer didn't tell you about the early withdrawal penalty on the hardship withdrawal."

> "Dave, if you do that, you'll pay income tax AND the 10% penalty on those funds now. Why don't you keep the funds in the retirement plan. Then when you need them for Sara's college expenses, THEN take the funds out. That way, you postpone paying the income tax and you completely escape the 10% penalty. This will save you $3,520 in income tax and penalty this year."

> "Rodney, we've amended your prior three years' income tax returns, and you will be receiving $11K in Federal and state refunds," I said to a self-employed consultant whose brother missed the Self Employed Health Insurance deduction in preparing the original income tax returns.

> "Gloria, you won the race, and filed your income tax return first; you lowered your Federal tax liability by $21K by filing first!," said to a woman who was estranged from her husband, and needed to file first so she could take her itemized deductions, instead of being forced to only take the Standard Deduction.

> "I'm sorry, the statute of limitations has run, and it's too late to get your $32K in income tax back," I said to a young gal who prepared her own income tax return, and incorrectly reported cost basis on inherited stocks that she sold.

This book is different from other similarly cataloged books, and the reasons are helpful to you. First, the book is specifically for middle-income households. The focus is on how to save income tax just for this group, and no other. No time is wasted on a discussion about buying and selling companies (perhaps like a wealthy person may want to learn) or the Earned Income Credit (which is only applicable to lower-income families). Your time is not wasted wading through information that has no relevance to you.

The second reason this book is different from others is that this book isn't as perishable as others. My website will be updated as various income tax rates and thresholds change, so even if you are reading this book several years after it is written, you can still find relevant tax planning ideas in the book, and the updated income tax facts on my website, www.LisaBCPA.com.

U.S. income tax planning is a somewhat dry subject. But let me put it in perspective for you. Have you ever bought life insurance? Have you ever bought a new HVAC system for your home? I hope you said "YES" to at least one of those questions, because if so, this book will interest you significantly more! (Sorry to my life insurance sales friends!)

In case you don't know why income tax planning is important, let me make it clear: it's so you can reduce your income tax burden and use the excess cash to build wealth, take care of other obligations for your family, fund your retirement, or spend on fun things. Reducing your income tax burden is important, so that you don't waste dollars that could be put to better use elsewhere.

But income tax planning need not be an all-inclusive, full-throttle event. If you go to the superstore in the neighboring county because the sales tax rate is lower, you've done tax planning! Have you started a Section 529 college savings plan for a child? If yes, then you've done income tax planning too! If you do many small things that save tax, the cumulative effect over a lifetime will be staggering. The whole purpose is to defer or avoid income tax whenever possible, over your whole adult life, and you will have accumulated more cash and wealth, and/or consumed more things that are important to you, in comparison to if you failed to do any tax planning at all.

Let me tell you about Emily, my niece. Emily's high school physical education teacher required all students run two miles. She worried about it for days before the event. She's a little heavy-set and shy, and didn't think she could make it, but the two-mile run was required to pass the course. The day Emily ran her two miles, an athlete who took resource classes with Emily started to run beside her, even though he had already taken his turn.

He repeated her name with every step to encourage her, "Emily! Emily!"

Then several of his athlete friends started running with Emily too. And then they ran circles around her and chanted her name, as she ran her two miles. "Emily! Emily!"

Emily finished her two miles, as she laughed and smiled! She chatted about what happened for a week. Those boys did her a huge favor and gave her a memory that will last forever! I mention this story, because in planning to save income tax, it's okay to take it slow, and find someone to help you, like a CPA. And I hope to be the inspiration running around you, prompting you to not give up.

Any professional will say, take it slow. Tax planning is thick stuff. If you just want to tackle one income tax issue at a time, that's fine, and likely an improvement over your current game plan. For some, if you try to do too much at once, you won't accomplish any of it. And becoming more familiar with income tax savings opportunities is an educational event, which takes time. Pace yourself, so you can take adequate time to consider matters and their effect, for the best result possible.

You likely will want to get an income tax planning checkup often with your CPA or other qualified tax professional. The United States income tax law changes annually, and those changes can affect most Americans. Make sure your income tax plan is still working for you.

Throughout this book, you will see an airplane notation, ✈ and that is important to notice, because those are facts that will be updated periodically on my website, www.LisaBcpa.com. The updates on the website will keep this book from becoming perishable as I already mentioned. You should also confirm key information on www.irs.gov and with your CPA before moving forward with any tax strategies and any transactions that affect income tax.

Also throughout the book, you will see oval callouts:

> IRS Form xxxx is used to calculate and/or report yyyy.

These contain references to specific IRS Form numbers. This is helpful if you want to know exactly which tax form to use for a specific income item, Income Tax Deduction, or Income Tax Credit.

Additionally, Tax Credits are always denoted with a diamond ❖ next to them. Tax Credits are a dollar-for-dollar reduction of income tax, and thus are better than Income Tax Deductions.

Although not quite as helpful as Tax Credits, Income Tax Deductions are denoted with a thumbs up sign 👍 next to them. Income Tax Deductions reduce taxable income, so less dollars are subject to income tax. Also denoted with the thumbs up sign 👍 is any item that reduces taxable income, such as excluded income and exemptions.

I hope you are able to save a lot of income tax by reading this book!

Disclaimer

This book is not a comprehensive reference book on United States income tax law and procedures. I have not listed every income tax law or rule, and I have not listed every potential income tax planning move, in this one book. If I addressed every possible scenario related to every income tax planning point, you wouldn't read the book because it would be thicker than a phone book, and weigh more than my youngest child, Troy. Rather, I have narrowed the subject area to the most common income tax issues related to middle-income households.

My website, www.LisaBcpa.com, is also not intended to be a comprehensive reference source, although I do attempt to update the thresholds and other pertinent information of specific planning points discussed in this book. Your CPA and www.irs.gov are your best authoritative sources for the final word on U.S. income tax law.

In writing this book, I constantly thought of exceptions to the rule, and anomalies that would change the desired result of the income tax planning point being presented. I also worry about the reader that doesn't follow the advice as directed, or has additional circumstances that make the advice not applicable. You will need to seek the final advice of your CPA before making any major moves, because they are familiar with your entire income tax situation and I am not.

Sometimes, if an acquaintance sees me at one of my kids' ball games, they ask me an income tax question. I don't mind answering the question, but I can't help but sense their feeling of disappointment. They usually want a "fast-food" answer, while I prefer to ask questions and get the full picture before I give my "sirloin-steak" answer. Don't consume this book as if it is "fast-food" advice. Major income tax moves need planning and full consideration of your complete situation and needs before any action should be taken. In my CPA practice, I am unwilling to help a client with specific tax planning strategies until I have reviewed their most recent income tax returns. Most of my CPA colleagues feel the same way.

This book's purpose is to point out ideas to save you income tax, so you can keep more of your money for your family. But I respectfully request that you have detailed discussions with your CPA or other qualified tax adviser, before you implement any income tax strategies. If you can't agree with this request, please return this book to me in good shape for a refund. You can locate my current mailing address on my website, www.LisaBcpa.com.

As you read this book, use the tabs below to mark the pages that you want to refer back to later. Mark the ideas that fit your situation, so that you can easily find them when you're ready to implement them.

Happy Tax Savings!

Lisa Bushur, CPA

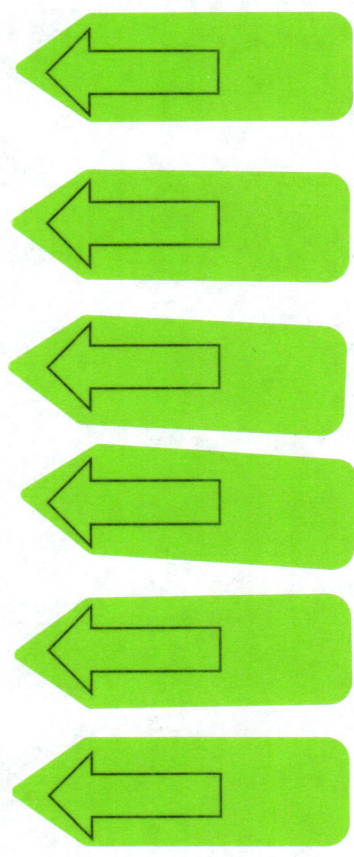

Chapter 1
My Personal Trek

It was in the early 1980s, and I opened the letter without thought or care. I wasn't expecting the letter. Well, maybe I was expecting a letter that started like this, "Thank you for your submission, but unfortunately..." I didn't appreciate until years later, that the receipt of this letter led me down an exciting path like no other could. The letter opened a big door for me, and that opened up into bigger doors and bigger opportunities. And the doors are still opening for me.

I have enjoyed my career as a CPA, and it feels like comfortable, well-fitting shoes, except they are stylish, if only to me. In my late teens, I thought I would be forced into night school to attend college, so I could work to support myself. But thankfully, Wal*Mart sent me the aforementioned letter that awarded me a full ride scholarship to the state college of my choice, and enabled me to attend college full time after high school. I'm so thankful for that. Let this be my grateful salute to the Walton (Wal*Mart) Family Foundation!

I knew I wanted to be a CPA even as a high school junior, because of the wonderful accounting teacher at Pacific High School, Mr. Hughes. He helped me see that accounting clicked in my brain and that I enjoyed it.

Price Waterhouse (now PriceWaterhouseCoopers), a Big Four Accounting Firm, trained me on their training grounds like boot camp for a soldier; structured and disciplined, yet it was fun and intriguing. I left Price Waterhouse to become a controller of a mid-sized corporation. Running day-to-day administration in a mid-sized accounting department also enhanced my experience. These experiences developed my skills for the CPA I am today.

Best of all, after working as a controller, I transitioned back to public accounting, working with individual and small business clients in my own CPA firm. I loved meeting all of the people and hearing about their careers, and I've learned so much from them.

My CPA practice experienced fast-paced growth, sometimes

more than 20% annually. However, I began to feel frustrated if I couldn't personally help every client that walked in the door. My staff grew, and they have been wonderful over the years. Because of the tremendous growth in the client base, once in a while I couldn't remember the name of a client if they dropped in without an appointment. That wasn't the type of firm I wanted to own!

I wanted to be able to help the clients save more income tax, and have detailed discussions about that. Clients needed help on strategizing about real estate purchases, retirement plan options, and charitable donations, to name just a few. But the larger my firm grew, it seemed I spent more time on income tax preparation instead of income tax planning. The two responsibilities pulled me in different directions, like a tug-of-war game, and I was the rope!

I felt ineffective at saving folks tax money. I grew tired of sleeping on the blue suede couch in my office so that I could put in more time at the office. Working so many hours drained me, and I needed to take better care of myself by working out several times per week.

I needed to have more time at home also; in one week I twice ate my morning oatmeal in a measuring cup and with a fork, just because no clean dishes could be found. And I wanted to spend more time with my family.

I often repeated myself, explaining the same income tax or money matters to clients and associates. I started thinking about the tax issues I explained like a recording in my head. For a few years now, I have typed out my little pieces of advice. And this book is the result from part of those notes.

> It hit me: income tax planning ranks more important than income tax preparation!

I decided to write this book because I realized I wanted to be more effective with folks by talking about income tax savings ideas, instead of income tax preparation. At the same time, it hit me: income tax planning ranks more important than income tax preparation! In addition, I could reach more people by writing and speaking, than by preparing income tax returns. And becoming a writer would allow me to be at home more of the time.

A dear friend, and the office manager of my firm, convinced me to stop sleeping at the office and sell my blue suede couch. In October 2013, I merged my CPA firm with a larger CPA firm, and kept very few of the clients myself. I made this move so I could focus on income tax strategy instead of income tax preparation.

I spend my professional time these days helping those few retained clients, and writing about income tax strategies. Having spent about three decades as an accountant, I have learned what I can offer best: tax savings ideas and strategies.

Chapter 2
Do You Need A CPA?

Chapter 2 Trail Route
- Chances of IRS Audit
- Untrained Preparers
- Why Do Some Folks Need Help?
- Amended Income Tax Returns to Correct Mistakes
- Level of Services
- Professional Fees
- Client Responsibilities

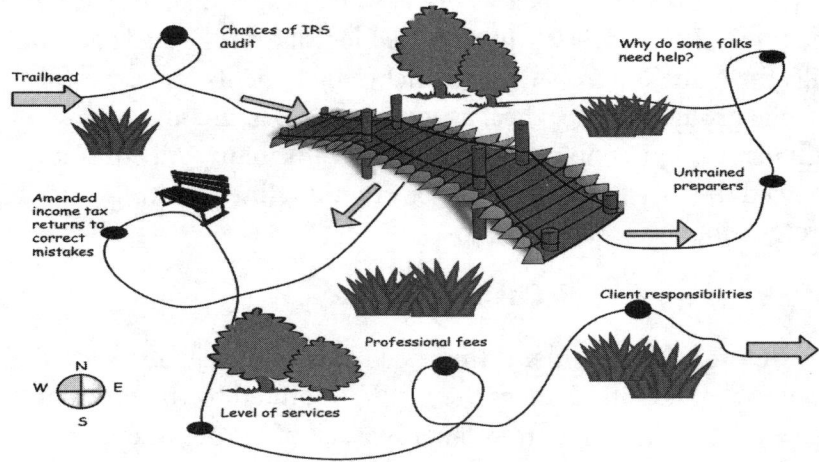

There are times when everybody needs someone to catch them when they're about to fall. When we adopted my son as a newborn, my oldest daughter (age six at the time) wanted to hold him and carry him around. We did let her hold him, but told her she could not walk around with him yet. Tina sat on our deck one day holding two-week old Troy, and something convinced her to get up and carry Troy. Her pants hung too long and caught on a nail sticking up from the floor of the deck. She tripped and fell with Troy in her arms! Tina felt terrified she hurt Troy. But no worries--Tina took great pride in being big sister. She cradled him in her arms, and landed on her forearms. Her elbows looked like fresh cut strawberries, all skinned up, but Troy lay nestled in her arms, oblivious to the fall. You may need a tax professional to watch out for you and catch you when you are about to make an income tax mistake that isn't in your best interest.

It seems inherently wrong that the U.S income tax system is so complicated that a citizen has to pay money to comply with the income tax laws. (And that individual income tax preparation fees are usually not income tax deductible--see Chapter 21 for a more thorough discussion of this matter.) This isn't something that I believe will change in the future. Every time "tax simplification" or "flat tax" is spoke, it's followed by a bunch of proposed exceptions, and then we're back where we are now, with a complicated income tax system. Well-intentioned legislators can't get their tax bills through Congress without including benefits for powerful special groups. The tecÚical aspects of the U.S. income tax law will persist, in my opinion. And that means many will continue to need the assistance of a CPA or other qualified tax preparation professional.

Chance of IRS Audit

Before folks consider if they need help, they usually want to know, what are the chances they will be audited by the Internal Revenue Service? This from Janet Novack of Forbes Magazine, related to IRS audits of personal income tax returns:

Total Income Level	Tax Return Includes Schedule C business?	Tax Return Includes Schedule E Rental or K-1?	Chance of IRS Audit
<$200K	No	No	0.4%
<$200K	Yes, <$25K revenue	Yes, <$25K revenue	1.2%
<$200K	Yes, >$100K revenue	Yes, >$100K revenue	3.5%
$200K - $1Mil			3.2%
$1Mil +			12.1%

Untrained Preparers

We have all heard of someone's brother-in-law who attempted to fix the kitchen water leak, and then came home to a flooded house after vacation. We've also seen in our own neighborhoods the guy who has planned to fix his garage door for three years. Perhaps these folks should have sought professional help. Folks certainly don't do their own dental work.

I've seen some do-it-yourselfers do a fabulous job with their income tax preparation (a couple of them could have been offered jobs as junior tax preparers). Interestingly, when a nonfinancial person is doing a great job at income tax preparation with his or her own income tax return, it's usually someone who works in a highly tecÚical profession, such as an engineer or pharmacist.

But most situations I've seen could force you to tears. It's fairly common for new clients to come to my CPA firm, and once we review their prior income tax returns, we amend them to correct previous mistakes. This is one of my favorite client quotes: "The security guard I was talking to [about IRS tax regulations] was full of hot air." If you follow income tax advice that a security guard or your hairdresser dispenses, you likely need a CPA.

With approximately three decades of experience, these are just a small spattering of do-it-yourselfer critical mistakes I've seen:

- A smart young woman, Samantha, inherited and then sold numerous stocks from her deceased father, Harold. She found her father's cost basis records from when the stocks were purchased in the 1970s and 1980s, and deducted this as cost basis on Schedule D of her personal income tax return. (The cost basis is deducted from the sale proceeds, to obtain the gain on the sale of the stocks.) The problem: she would have been allowed a step up in cost basis on the stocks to Fair Market Value 👍 as of the date of Harold's death. When the cost basis increases, gain and resulting income tax decrease. She overpaid income tax on the sale of the stocks. She didn't come to my firm as a client until more than three years later, after the statute of limitations passed to file an amended income tax return to correct the matter and get her $32K in excess income tax back. "I'm sorry," I said to this young woman. "The statute of limitations has run, and it's too late to get your $32K in income tax back."

- A self-employed computer consultant allowed his brother to do his income tax return for years, and the brother mistakenly included the consultant's health insurance as a medical expense on Schedule A, Itemized Deductions. The medical expenses fell short of being deductible because they never exceeded 7.5% of total income (this threshold increased to 10% effective beginning in January 2013 for folks under age 65). What the well-intentioned brother didn't know is that Self Employed Health Insurance is 100% deductible 👍 on page 1 of the income tax return, and doesn't have to be added to medical expense on Schedule A. The consultant missed out on the Self Employed Health Insurance Deduction 👍 averaging $12K per year for a total of 5 years! We amended the most recent three years of income tax returns, and the consultant received Federal and state refunds related to this matter of over $11K. I delivered this message, "Rodney, we've amended your prior three years' income tax returns and you will be receiving $11K in Federal and state refunds."

- A very conservative couple, Thomas and Maureen, excessively feared the IRS and a potential audit, so they did not claim all of their charity deductions 👍 or their home office deductions 👍. After discussions with the couple, I determined their eligibility for these deductions 👍 for the previous three years. We quantified the charity and employee unreimbursed expenses for the home office, and amended three years of income tax returns. The couple received Federal and state income tax refunds that totaled $14K. They have not been audited by the IRS.

A suggestion for folks who want to know if they need a CPA or not, is to go ask a CPA in tax practice. Go visit a reputable CPA or other tax professional and ask that your previous years' income tax returns be reviewed. Most CPA firms are happy to review prior income tax returns of potential clients, as a courtesy. They will want to do this review outside of their tax season.

I once let my four young children paint my son's bedroom. We painted the room red, and redecorated it with a St. Louis Cardinals baseball theme. No carpet or trim had been installed yet, "So what the heck!"

The kids reveled in the painting, and splattered themselves with more paint than what ended up on the walls. They became little monsters with paintbrushes as weapons. After I cleaned up the kids, I called a professional painter to come and paint the room. A professional in the field was definitely needed. Perhaps you need a professional income tax preparer as badly as we needed a painter.

Why do some folks need help? Ask yourself if the items below are of concern to you:
- *It takes me a lot of time to thoroughly prepare my tax returns.*
- *It is difficult for me to keep up with income tax law.*
- *My background experience has no relevance to income tax preparation.*
- *I don't have a detail-oriented work style.*
- *My income tax return is extremely involved with the types of investments I have, the detail of deductions, etc.*
- *I have anxiety, just thinking about preparing my income taxes.*

These are all very common reasons folks seek help with their income tax preparation.

Amended Income Tax Returns to Correct Mistakes

If the CPA does find mistakes in your prior income tax returns, whether self-prepared or prepared by another tax preparer, you have three years from the original due date (including extension time) to amend an income tax return before the statute of limitations runs out. My firm has often amended prior tax returns of new clients, to get the refunds back, and this is NOT a red flag to the IRS. Amended income tax returns do not increase audit risk.

Even if the CPA confirms your income tax return preparation is without error, and with full tax planning being considered, full information almost always is a key to good decision-making, and receiving this review will put your mind at ease, if nothing else.

Level of Services

One other point about CPAs and other tax professionals; you need to discuss up front what level of service you would like, and let them know if your preferences change. I've lost a client in the past for giving them more attention than they wanted to pay for, and I've lost a client for not giving them enough attention. Both times I should have rechecked with them after a couple years of being their CPA to determine their current level of expectations. If you have a preference, you need to communicate that to your CPA.

Professional Fees

There are times when any professional encounters a client that is fee sensitive. This also needs to be an upfront discussion. Having an understanding of how the pricing works will make for a better business relationship with the CPA. Make sure you know what the fees are going to be for your income tax preparation, and whether or not they include:
- Strategy meetings for tax planning;
- Follow up of any IRS or state notices that are no one's "fault" (IRS misposted estimated tax payment to someone else's account, for example);
- Follow up of any IRS or state notices that are the "fault" of the client (income not reported to CPA for inclusion on income tax return, for example);
- Follow up of any IRS or state notices that are the "fault" of

the CPA (incorrectly reporting taxability of an IRA distribution, for example); and
- Short telephone discussions.

I recently lost a client because she thought she didn't need thorough, professional help anymore. Mildred, in her sixties, procrastinated providing data for us to complete her 2012 and 2013 income tax returns, to the point of both of them being filed late. She never owned her own business in her life, and decided to give it a try in 2012. But she dismissed any idea of bookkeeping help, not wanting to incur any costs. She struggled to compile her business income and expenses.

When we finished her 2012 income tax returns (late) and asked for the 2013 data, she mentioned she went to a retail chain tax preparer to prepare her 2014 income tax return. Because she planned to sell her business in 2015, and had very little business activity in 2014, she thought she'd just skip the inclusion of the business activity on her income tax returns for 2014 and 2015. However, the IRS requires business activity be recorded on an income tax return, especially a sale of a business.

When we finished Mildred's 2013 income tax return (also late), this is the note I wrote to Mildred:

Mildred,

Please see below a list of information your new tax preparer needed in order to accurately and thoroughly complete your 2014 income tax return:

- Long Term Capital Loss carry forward, $142K
- Short Term Capital Loss carry forward, $6K
- 2014 Depreciation Expense on your business assets, $9K
- 2014 Cash receipts from business, no matter how small
- 2014 Cash disbursements from business, no matter how small
- 2014 fixed asset sales from your business (and adjust above depreciation accordingly)
- Home office expenses disallowed in 2013 that carry over to 2014, $1,200

Your 2014 income tax return likely needs amended, because it's doubtful your new income tax preparer would have known all of the above information. If you don't have the 2014 income tax return amended, I'm afraid you will miss out on the Income Tax Deductions listed above, and the related income tax savings.

Respectfully,

Lisa Bushur, CPA

If only Mildred would have discussed this with me, she could have been warned about having the 2014 income tax return prepared before completion of the previous year's income tax return. Her fear of paying professional fees cost her an amount much greater than the professional fees because of all of the lost income tax deductions.

Client Responsibilities

Those seeking a CPA should also keep in mind that they have responsibilities too. CPAs want clients that are forthcoming in discussions, not secretive. And CPAs also want clients that will provide requested information on a timely basis. You won't get as thorough of a result if the CPA does not have access to the necessary information.

Chapter Summary

The majority of middle-income households need a professional preparing their income tax returns in order to obtain a complete and accurate result. Untrained income tax preparers can miss deductions 👍. And it takes a lot of time to keep up with income tax law changes and to prepare an accurate income tax return. Some folks don't have the interest to prepare their own income tax return, or they experience anxiety just thinking about income tax preparation. Having a professional prepare your income tax return will produce the best final result and help save you money. The money from saved income tax, due to additional Income Tax Deductions 👍, I'm sure can be put to better use by you for your family or your retirement fund, than by Uncle Sam.

Chapter 3

Pay NO Income Tax on These Items!

Chapter 3 Trail Route
- Tax-Free Cash
- Tax-Free Goods
- Tax-Free Services

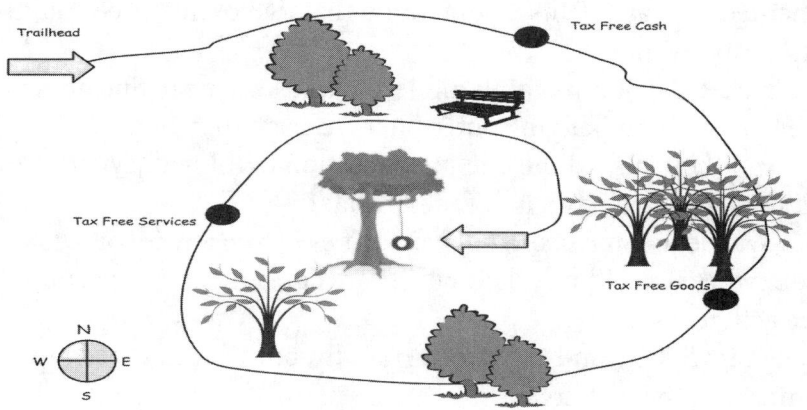

With the high cost of everything, receiving anything that is income tax free is appreciated by all! My kids even get a kick out of getting $10 from recycling aluminum cans.

There's a family in Missouri that pays only pennies on the dollar for their food and household goods. They toil in their garden and own livestock. They produce bio-diesel fuel for their truck from used cooking oil from a local restaurant. They only buy goods at the store if they have a coupon or it's on sale. They trade for car repairs. They bake their own breads. They don't have air conditioning in their home. The father works a part-time job, but otherwise, the parents build, create, fix and manage their property and goods. I met this family by chance, and asked nosey questions such as, "What about computers and cell phones? Do you buy those?"

"No," she said. "We don't consider those to be necessary."

I felt drawn to hear more, and wondered how my family and I could make do without computers and cell phones. "And what about a television?" I asked.

The mother readily answered, "We don't watch TV. We do have radios. Our kids read books. We've home schooled our children through high school, and the kids have benefitted from being very good readers. My oldest is graduating college this month with theology and history degrees."

"Does your daughter pressure you for the cool clothes that other teens wear?" This is something that two of my three daughters always want.

"Nope, she doesn't think modern clothes are neat. She doesn't like her back end hanging out, or her cleavage showing."

And then I asked the one final question that I really wanted to ask first. "Do you pay a lot of income tax?"

"We file income taxes, but we don't ever owe any income tax." From what she told me, their efforts are considered income tax-free activities.

I'm intrigued, and the family friendly, but I am not ready to conform to their lifestyle.

The following list includes many things that are income tax-free. Sometimes an item is tax-free because of the source, not just because of the nature of the item. This isn't a complete list, just the most popular items for middle-income households.

Tax-Free Cash

Life Insurance Proceeds and Annuities 👍

If you receive life insurance proceeds following the death of a loved one, those proceeds are not income taxable. (Most life insurance companies also sell annuities, and if you inherit an annuity, the earnings part of the annuity could be income taxable, even if paid by a life insurance company.)

Cash Inheritance 👍

If you inherit cash or investments upon the death of a loved one, the assets you receive are income tax-free. Any estate or gift tax due is the responsibility of the estate, and not your personal responsibility. (If the investments earn dividends or interest between the date of the death of your loved one and the date you receive the assets, there could be a small amount of income tax on those investment earnings.)

Disability Benefits 👍

These also are usually income tax free, but make sure you check with the payer of the benefits because under certain very limited instances, disability can be taxable. If you paid for your disability coverage with after-tax dollars (defined in the Glossary at the end of this book), or if your employer paid the disability premiums, but then included them as taxable income on your year-end Form W-2, then your disability benefits are likely income tax-free.

Child Support 👍

Child support is nontaxable to the recipient, but alimony is taxable to the recipient.

Dependent Child's Wages 👍

A child who is a dependent of another can earn up to their Standard Deduction 👍 before they pay income tax. For 2015, they can earn up to $6,300 ✈ before any income tax will be due (unless they also have unearned income, in which case the Kiddie Tax may apply; see Chapter 13 for Kiddie Tax rules). An employer is required to withhold FICA and Medicare tax, however.

Interest Income from Municipal Bonds and Municipal Bond Mutual Funds 👍

Interest income from Municipal Bonds and Municipal Bond Mutual Funds is usually income tax free (some bonds don't qualify so check with your investment advisor). Also, municipal bonds from your home state are usually state income tax free (but double check with your investment advisor to make sure your bond qualifies). The rate of return on these types of bonds may be lower than you anticipate, so keep that in mind when determining where to put your investment dollars.

Child's Investment Income 👍

A child's unearned income of up to $1,050 ✈ for 2015 is income tax free, and thereafter is subject to the Kiddie Tax rules discussed in Chapter 13.

Purchase Rebates 👍

Purchase rebates are considered nontaxable. For example, say you buy a Ford vehicle, and upon purchase, Ford sends you a $2K rebate. The rebate is a reduction in your cost basis of the vehicle, but it is not taxable. (Upon selling the vehicle later, if there's a gain on the sale--which is doubtful if you use the car on a regular basis--that gain will be income taxable. The gain is calculated as the resale price, less the original cost of the car, which is the cost less the rebate received.)

Credit Card Rebates 👍

Rebates from credit cards on which personal goods or services are purchased are not income taxable.

Garage Sales 👍

If you sell your personal items at your garage or yard sale, and you originally paid more than what you are selling the items for, then the proceeds from the sale of those items are income tax free. (If you have "collectibles" such as art or antiques, and sell those at a profit, then those are income taxable transactions, however.)

Tax-Free Goods

Prizes & Awards for Length of Service or Safety 👍

Prizes and awards from an employer that are to show appreciation for length of service or for a positive safety record are income tax-free to the employee recipient.

Inheritance of Property 👍

If you inherit real estate or personal property upon the death of a loved one, the assets you receive are income tax free. Any estate or gift tax due is the responsibility of the estate, and not your personal responsibility.

Coupon Savings 👍

Similar to purchase rebates, coupon savings are a reduction in purchase cost, and reduce your cost basis in the purchased item. Because you are likely to consume the items purchased with the coupons, your cost basis doesn't matter.

Tax-Free Services

Employer-Paid Life Insurance Premiums 👍

Life insurance premiums paid by an employer for policies with a face value of $50K or less are excludable from taxable income by the employee. Any eventual proceeds from such a life insurance policy remain income tax-free to the beneficiary.

Frequent Flier Miles 👍

Earn frequent flier miles on personal trips, and use them for personal trips, and that's not income taxable either. (If frequent flier miles are earned on business trips, a case can made that the resulting free airline flight is income taxable, because of the allowed Income Tax Deduction taken for the airfare purchased to earn the frequent flier miles.)

Bartering 👍

If you barter personal services or belongings in exchange for personal services or belongings, that is income tax-free. An example of this would be trading babysitting services with a friend who also has small children, or trading homemade jellies to your neighbor in return for him cutting your lawn. There are websites that are dedicated to helping folks find bartering deals, although I have not used them myself. Bartering can be a very inexpensive way to obtain needed goods and services, especially considering the income tax savings of personal bartering transactions.

I do quite a bit of bartering. I barter with my tax preparation services (a business activity), so I do claim the income. But it's still a good deal for me, because my cost of the goods and services I receive is only the income tax on the value of services I provide. I have prepared income tax returns in return for all of the following:
- Riding lawn mower (traded with the equipment dealer)
- Use of a condo in Branson, MO (traded with real estate agents that own the condo)
- Granite countertops for my kitchen (traded with a contractor)
- Novels for my daughters to read (traded with a teen book author)

College Tuition Discounts 👍

See Chapter 16, were college costs are discussed. Students often receive discounted or free college tuition if:
1. They or their parent work at the educational institution
2. They are in an undergraduate program
3. They are a degree candidate
4. The funds are used for tuition, books, supplies or equipment required for coursework
5. The funds are not used for room and board

College Scholarships 👍

Scholarships, including those from the United States Armed Forces, are income tax free if you meet requirements 3 through 5 above; you must be a degree candidate, and the funds must be used for tuition, books, supplies or equipment required for coursework.

Chapter Summary

You may want to make all members in your household aware of income tax-free items, so in their daily activities, they can keep them in mind and help you identify opportunities where you can take advantage of as many of these as possible. Tax-free cash items include purchase rebates, child's wages up to $6,300 ✈ for 2015, and garage sales, to name a few. Tax-free goods include coupon savings and bartering. Tax-free services include college tuition discounts, scholarships, and frequent flyer miles earned on personal trips, among other things. Saving income tax on goods and services will help you build wealth and/or have more money available for the things you want. You may want to use the savings for your retirement fund, or for your child's college fund. Take control of this excess money, and put it to good use!

Chapter 4
Strategies for Portfolio Income

> Chapter 4 Trail Route
> - Net Investment Income Tax
> - Capital Gains
> - Qualified Dividends
> - Municipal Bonds
> - Passive Activities

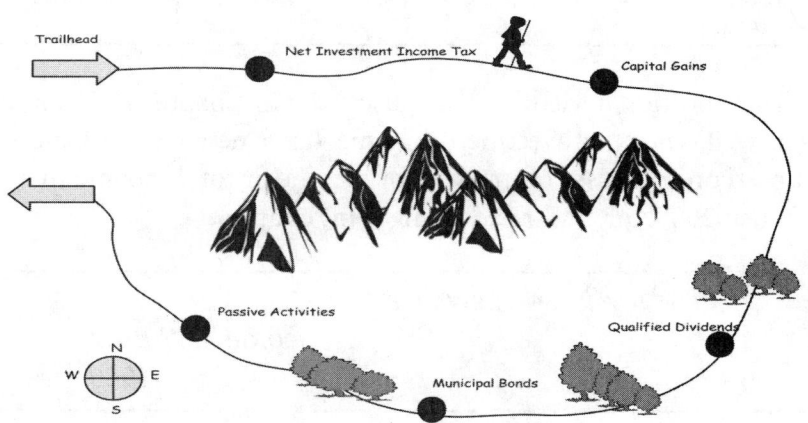

You work hard for a nice portfolio, to provide security for your family, or for retirement. But you have a disappointment with your portfolio. Despite having already paid income tax on your money as you earned it, you are forced to pay income tax again on the earnings from your savings. Despite the harsh reality of income tax, being strategic about investments can at least help lower your income tax.

Net Investment Income Tax

New taxes further complicate the income tax code. As a CPA, new income tax laws and rules should be low hanging fruit, and a source of lots of new potential fees. But to me, completely new income tax rules just further complicate the tax code for the types of folks reading this book. An increase in income tax is one matter, but completely new types of tax seem to add complexity that is excessive.

The Net Investment Income Tax is a 3.8% tax that is new beginning in 2013, and is imposed on the lesser of net investment income or total income over these thresholds:

Filing Status	Married Filing Joint	Single	Head of Household	Married Filing Separate
Total income (AGI)	$250K	$200K	$200K	$125K

The Additional Medicare Tax discussed in Chapter 17 is a new tax as well. The Net Investment Income Tax is new for 2013 and is imposed on the lesser of investment income or total income that exceeds $250K for a Married Filing Joint couple.

> *"Read my lips: No new taxes."*
> *-- George H. W. Bush*
> *1988*

If you have the opportunity to shift income between years, and the Net Investment Income Tax will hit you in a given year but you expect it not to be applicable the following year, this is an opportunity for you to save some income tax by shifting income to the lower-income year. Examples of shifting income to lower-income tax bracket years are discussed in Chapter 30.

After learning of the Net Investment Income Tax, one of my creative clients, Diane, thought that perhaps if she not take her last quarterly interest income check from the mortgage she holds on her son's home until next year, she might escape the Net Investment Income Tax for the current year.

"Oh, Diane, yes, that would help. You would save 3.8% of $4,500. But I won't be able to deduct that interest expense on your son's income tax return until next year, when he actually pays it."

The son subsequently agreed to postpone his last quarterly house payment to his mother, which suited him fine, since he was on a tight cash flow budget anyway.

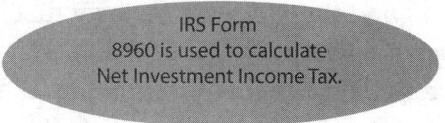
IRS Form 8960 is used to calculate Net Investment Income Tax.

Capital Gains

If you hold a security, mutual fund or other capital asset for more than one year, and then sell it for a gain, you will be taxed at the more favorable (lower) Capital Gain rates, even considering the Capital Gain Rate increase discussed below. So consider the length of time you hold your investments before selling, striving to hold them at least one year, so that they may earn Capital Gain status.

Capital Gain Rate Increase

This increase is only going to hit some of you. If your marginal income tax rate is at 39.6%, then your new Capital Gain rate is 20% ✈, instead of the previous 15%. For 2015, the 39.6% income tax bracket applies to taxable income as follows:

Filing Status	Married Filing Joint	Single	Head of Household	Married Filing Separate
Taxable Income	$464,851	$413,201	$439,001	$232,426

The sounds of the grumbles from the few of you reading this book who will be affected by the higher Capital Gain rate is NOT drowned out by the sighs of relief from everyone else.

Folks in the 25% regular income tax bracket up to but not including the 39.6% regular income tax bracket still have a Capital Gain rate of 15%. And those folks in the 10% and 15% regular income tax brackets still have a 0% Capital Gain rate. When evaluating whether to sell stocks, mutual funds, or other capital assets, it's helpful to know where you stand year-to-date on your net gain or loss from the sale of securities and other capital items. If you are at a net gain, perhaps it's a good time to sell a security that possesses an unrealized loss, in order to offset your gain. If you are at a net loss, perhaps it's a good time to sell a security that has a lot of unrealized gain, because, when offset with the loss, it could be a tax-free transaction for you. Note that you are only eligible to deduct a net capital loss of up to $3K ✈ per year ($1,500 for married filing separate filers), and the remainder carries forward indefinitely to future years until utilized. Said another way, when you add up all gains and losses for the year, if there is a total net loss, only a net $3K loss is deductible in that year, and the remainder is to be reflected on your income tax return for the following year. The remaining loss can be carried forward indefinitely until deducted.

> *The Capital Gain rate increase will only hit those of you in the 39.6% Federal income tax bracket; your new Capital Gain rate for Federal income tax purposes is 20%.*

It is generally assumed you will sell securities on the FIFO basis (First In, First Out); however, you can specifically identify which shares you plan to sell. This is helpful if you want to sell shares with a relatively low cost basis (which will result in more Capital Gain) to take advantage of a lower Capital Gain rate in a given year. Or perhaps you want to create a large gain because you have a Capital Loss carry forward from the previous year. Or perhaps you want to go ahead and take a loss because you have a large gain on another stock trade, and you want them to offset each other. Strategically selecting the stock lots can help you manage your net Capital Gain or Loss.

IRS Schedule D is used to accumulate Capital Gains and Losses from the sale of securities.

Qualified Dividends

Dividends on stocks and mutual funds held for more than 1 year ✈ are taxed at your Capital Gain rate, which as explained above, is lower than your regular income tax rate. So, keep in mind, if you are a busy trader, you may be forgoing the more favorable Capital Gain rate on the dividends for securities not held at least one year.

A couple of years ago, we prepared an income tax return for Steve, a client in my private practice who didn't hold a job. Steve lives on his investment and trust income. This Married Filing Joint income tax return involved quite a bit of time to prepare, only because of the volume of investments and related 1099 forms. When one of the staff members completed a draft of the income tax return, she brought it to me and looked confused. She said, "How can there be no tax liability when he made more than $60K in total (Adjusted Gross) income?!"

I also felt mystified, but then I saw that all of the income was earned from Qualified Dividends and Long Term Capital Gains. This client, with Adjusted Gross Income of just over $60K, qualified for the 0% Capital Gain Rate! He paid NO Federal income tax!

Municipal Bonds

Municipal bonds are income tax-free 👍 for Federal income tax purposes. Some muni bond interest is state tax free when issued from your home state, but you should check with your investment advisor and state regulatory authority before assuming the municipal bond you are purchasing qualifies for the income tax-free status. In addition to the expected return and safety of the bond, some investors select bonds based on what month the bond pays interest, so they can own a variety of bonds with varying payment dates for interest income checks arriving on a monthly basis. Other investors prefer to invest in mutual funds made up of municipal bonds, in order to diversify their holdings.

Passive Activities

Income from passive activities, such as rental real estate or investments in partnerships in which you do not actively participate, are taxable in the year the income is received or earned, as appropriate. Yet passive losses have limitations to the amount that can be deducted each year. Remember these basic rules:

- Passive losses can be deducted to the extent of passive income;
- A passive loss on any individual investment may only be deducted up to the amount you paid for the investment (referred to as cost basis); and
- Rental losses (for those that are not real estate professionals) can be deducted up to $25K ✈ per year, if your total income (Adjusted Gross Income) is less than $100K and the deductible portion of a rental loss is completely phased out at $150K of total income.

Passive losses that cannot be deducted may be carried forward to future years to offset later years' passive income. There is no time limitation in which you must take these losses. In the year of disposition of a passive activity, you can generally deduct the prior passive losses related to that activity if you don't sell to a related party, you have cost basis, and you sell your complete interest in the activity.

One last note on portfolio income: you can encourage your investment advisor and CPA to communicate with each other, and sign releases saying so. That way, when either of them have questions, they can contact the other, without worrying you with the details. This has been helpful in my tax practice when I want the investment advisor to know the amount of Capital Loss carry forward the client has, or I need to know the cost basis of securities in the year of sale. The investment advisors like the arrangement as well, sometimes needing the mutual client's income tax bracket for planning purposes and other needs.

> IRS Form 8582 is used to accumulate passive losses for later offset against passive income.

Chapter Summary

You should try to build your portfolio keeping income tax strategies in mind. The Net Investment Income Tax will encourage taxpayers to shift income to lower-income years when the Net Investment Income Tax isn't applicable. Many will continue to hold investments for more than one year to take advantage of the lower Capital Gain rates and/or they may plan to hold onto the investments, and be eligible to the Qualified Dividend treatment on stock and mutual fund dividends. With the Capital Gain rate increase, folks may prefer to sell capital assets with unrealized gain in a year when they are not in the highest Capital Gain tax bracket. Municipal bonds and municipal bond mutual funds are a good investment for some because they are Federal income tax-free and may be state income tax-free if issued from your home state. Beware, passive losses (from investments in partnerships or real estate, for example) may be limited. Decreasing the income tax burden on portfolio income will allow you to build more wealth in your portfolio or use the extra funds for other family needs. Your family depends on you, and being as tax efficient as possible will help you meet your family's needs.

Chapter 5

Retirement Plans - First Move for an Employee

> ## Chapter 5 Trail Route
> - Tax-Deferred Employer Retirement Plans
> - Tax-Free Employer Retirement Plans (e.g. Roth-type plans)

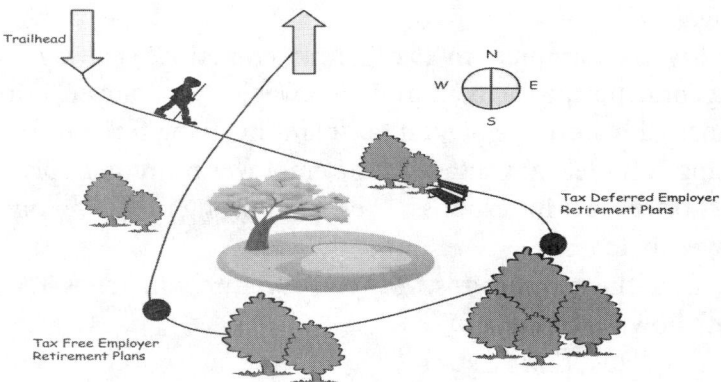

Clients in my private practice, Scott & Mary Ann, often thank me when they see me. They have been clients from very early in my career, about 25 years. Early on, my training reminded me to encourage retirement plan savings, and so I always nudged Scott & Mary Ann to contribute to their retirement plans. In reality, at the beginning of my career, I didn't appreciate the need for saving for retirement. I was young, and thought I would always be young and full of energy. But I saved for my own retirement and encouraged others to do the same, because I trusted my mentors.

When I talk to Scott & Mary Ann, they often say, "Thank you so much! We would never have started our retirement fund without you! It's worth over $1.5 million, all because of you!"

"No," I say, "it's your hard-earned money! You made the call to save it!" When they show appreciation to me, I mentally thank those who taught and encouraged me.

There's an open invitation to clients in my private practice to make an appointment to brainstorm for income tax savings ideas, called a Tax Planning Meeting. This is helpful for clients so they can focus on goals to save income tax, and thus keep more of their dollars in their own pockets. Retirement planning often is the most discussed topic in Tax Planning Meetings. A person needs to plan for a retirement that will last an estimated 15 to 25 years. In retirement, a person needs an estimated 75% to 80% of their preretirement income to live. Meeting these retirement needs takes planning.

My first comment in Tax Planning Meetings is always, "Are you contributing the maximum allowable to employer retirement plans?" I believe the biggest tax-planning bang for your buck is taking complete advantage of the employer retirement plans.

I often hear in response, "Yes, I'm putting in the 4% my employer matches."

Then the spouse adds, "My employer only matches 3%, so that's how much I put in."

I say, "Ok, that's a start."

While desperate folks are searching for Income Tax Deductions ☙, they often pass up an opportunity that's right in front of them. They often miss the opportunity to contribute the maximum allowable to their employer retirement plans. The maximum allowable is much higher than the amount the employer is able to match; see the chart on next page for the maximum allowable contributions ☙ (elective deferrals) for 2015 to various retirement plans.

✈	Under Age 50	Age 50 and Older
SIMPLE IRAs	$12,500	$15,000
401(k) and Roth 401(k) plans	$18,000	$24,000
SIMPLE 401(k)s	$12,500	$15,000
403(b) plans	$18,000	$24,000
457 plans	$18,000	$24,000
Profit sharing plans	100% of compensation, up to a maximum of $53,000	
SEP plans, Self-Employed Person	20% of income (after deduction for self-employment tax) up to a maximum of $53,000	
SEP Plans, Employee	25% of income up to a maximum of $53,000	

Of course, you cannot contribute too much of your earnings, if you won't have any money to live; but you should work toward maximum participation. The income tax deferral of the non-Roth plans is a wonderful tool. The amount of the retirement plan contributions is deducted from your Form W-2 at year-end, so you don't pay income tax on those earnings that you contributed into the retirement plan. When you are retired, and taking money out of your retirement plan to live, you likely will be in a much lower income tax bracket.

Sometimes a person says, "I don't know if I'll really be in a lower income tax bracket at retirement age." The client is concerned that if they will owe income tax on the retirement plan distribution later anyway, then perhaps they shouldn't make a retirement plan contribution now (and take an Income Tax Deduction 👍 for it). Further, they may believe their income tax bracket will not be decreasing at retirement age when they'll be paying income tax on the distribution.

I say, "Ok, let's say you'll be in the same income tax bracket when you retire as you are right now. Now consider the time value of money. Consider the postponement of paying income tax on the amount of your retirement plan contribution. Would you rather pay $6,200 in income tax this year (assumes a $20K retirement plan contribution and a 31% combined Federal and state income tax rate), or in some undetermined future year?" Paying the $6,200 at a later date is obviously more desirable. That usually makes the point, because anyone would rather postpone paying income tax.

Every employee, no matter their age, and no matter how far or near retirement is, needs to be saving for retirement. Like a squirrel hiding acorns for winter, you should be prepping for retirement. If you are tight on cash, at least start with a tiny contribution, perhaps $50 per pay period, until you can afford to contribute more. The uncertainty surrounding how much you will need in savings to retire, and how long you will live, are not reasons to ignore the need for retirement savings.

TAX DEFERRED EMPLOYER RETIREMENT PLANS
(income tax is due upon withdrawal):

401(K) Plans 👍

The most popular employer retirement plan is the 401(k) plan, used by for-profit corporations, LLCs, partnerships and others.

SIMPLE IRAs 👍

The most common retirement plan for small for-profit employers with less than 100 employees is the SIMPLE IRA, and is inexpensive to administer.

403(B) Plans 👍

These retirement plans are in use by public education organizations, 501(c)(3) non-profit organizations and certain cooperative service hospitals.

457 Plans 👍

This type of retirement plan is in common use by state and local governments for their employees.

Profit Sharing Plans 👍

These retirement plans are used by for-profit companies to

further motivate employee performance by sharing a portion of profits with employees based on a predetermined formula. These are often used in addition to a 401(k) plan.

SEP IRA Plans 👍

This retirement plan is used by a self-employed person, with few or no employees, and is inexpensive to administer.

All of the above retirement plans are income tax deferred; you are eligible for an Income Tax Deduction 👍 at the time of (for the income tax year of) your employee contribution.

TAX-FREE EMPLOYER RETIREMENT PLANS (no income tax is due upon withdrawal):

Roth 401(k)s 👍

There is no immediate income tax benefit for contributing to this type of 401(k) retirement plan, but the plan grows income tax-free, which is more advantageous than growing income tax-deferred. More and more clients are selecting this option for at least part of their retirement savings, because:
- They are worried about income tax rates skyrocketing by the time they retire;
- They like the tax free aspect of the Roth 401(k) distributions being income tax free at a time in their life when they will have less cash available; and
- Some already have large regular 401(k) plan balances, and they feel like this gives them some diversity.

Timing of Retirement Plan Contributions

All of the employer retirement plans discussed in this chapter, except the SEP IRA plans and Profit Sharing plans, are funded by employee payroll deductions 👍, thus they are funded during the tax year in which they relate. SEP IRAs, however, can be funded by the employer through the due date of the income tax return for the given year, including extensions. Profit Sharing plans are also funded by the employer, not the employee.

Decision on the Roth Option

One of the investment planner associations which refers clients to me quotes that it takes 14 years of growth in a Roth IRA or a Roth 401(k) to make up for the lost Income Tax Deduction 👍 of the regular IRA or 401(k). To test this assumption, I assumed a person decides to put $18K into a Roth 401(k) instead of a regular 401(k), that money doubles in value every 10 years, which is a somewhat commonly held theory, and that they plan to take the money out in 10 years. The following table tests that assumption.

	Roth 401(k)	Regular 401(k)
A. Income Tax Deduction 👍 on the $18,000 401(k) contribution at 25% Federal +6% state	$0	$5,580
B. Tax savings plus investment growth on the tax savings of the regular 401(k) contribution for 10 years (assuming money doubles every 10 years, the money would double once)	$0	$11,160
C. 10 years from now, assume the original $18,000 401(k) contribution has grown to $36,000 and that it is pulled out of the plan, the tax would be approximately...	$0	$11,160
Bottom line benefit (B minus C)	$0	$0

The assumption that it takes 14 years to break even, if you contribute to a Roth instead of a traditional retirement plan, is within the realm of reasonableness, although it cannot be proved for any definite time in the future. In reality, I'm unsure of assumptions that could be used to calculate the validity of the comment, in this calculation or any other, because there is too much guesswork in these variables:
- Income tax rates of the future;

- Growth rate of the tax savings, if invested;
- Growth rate of the 401(k) assets; and
- Timing of when participant will decide to take the money out of the plan

I could have manipulated this calculation to have any result ... bottom line is, the longer you have to keep the money in a Roth account, the more advantageous it is from the income tax aspect. Now get out your crystal balls, and figure out all of the unanswered variables above! In my personal opinion, if you are age 50 or under, a Roth 401(k) is preferable to a regular 401(k).

Below you will find a table summarizing the tax treatments of tax deferred and Roth type retirement plans:

	Tax Deferred Retirement Plans	Tax Free (Roth-type) Retirement Plans
Income Tax Deduction	In year of contribution to retirement plan 👍	Not allowed
Taxability of Distributions	Fully taxable in year of distribution	Not taxable when Distributed 👍

Chapter Summary

It's of utmost importance that you participate to the maximum allowable extent in employer retirement plans, as soon as your budget allows. Pension plans (funded by the employer) are not as common as they used to be a few decades ago, so folks need to make sure they are contributing enough for retirement in employer retirement plans. You will need to decide whether a tax deferred or Roth-type plan is best for you, based on your age and when you will need those funds. Your comfort (or lack thereof) during retirement is up to you; saving for retirement is each person's individual responsibility, and not the government's or your employer's responsibility. Your spouse may be depending on you to save for an adequate retirement, and you don't want to let your spouse or yourself down.

Chapter 6
What You Need to Know About IRAs, Non-Deductible IRAs, and Catch-Up Contributions

> **Chapter 6 Trail Route**
> - Individual Retirement Accounts (IRAs)
> - Non-Deductible IRAs
> - Catch Up Contributions
> - Cash Flow Planning
> - Timing of IRA Contributions
> - Spousal IRAs

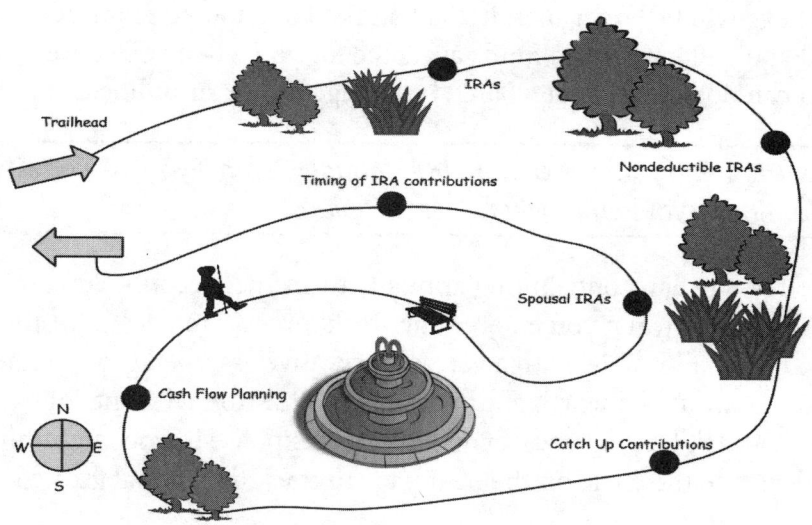

Individual Retirement Accounts (IRAs) are critical tools for a prosperous retirement. As discussed in the previous chapter, because traditional pension plans are much less common than in prior decades, and folks are needing to take more responsibility for their own retirement, IRAs have become a very important piece of retirement planning. This chapter shares facts about IRAs that you need to keep in mind in planning your retirement savings. To contribute to an IRA (or Roth IRA), you or your spouse must have earned income at least equal to your IRA contributions.

Individual Retirement Accounts (IRAs) 👍

You may contribute to an IRA even if you are participating in an employer retirement plan. Many folks are employed and have a 401(k) or other type of retirement plan in which they participate, and that is very important that they do so. Employees should participate in employer 401(k) or other similar retirement plans to the maximum extent allowable. In addition, as discussed in the previous chapter, don't just contribute enough to earn the employer matching contribution. Contribute the maximum allowable by the IRS. At the same time, contribute 👍 annually to your IRA account. Why? You will be thanking me at retirement time because your nest egg will be larger than if you had not contributed to an IRA and you will have more funds available for you when you retire. You can open an IRA at a bank, brokerage house, or online.

> *Contribute to your IRA or Roth IRA annually, even if you are contributing to your employer retirement plan.*

If you began contributing annually to an IRA account 20 years ago (perhaps when you entered the work force as an adult), for the maximum allowable, with a very conservative assumed growth rate of 6%, it would be worth approximately $122K today! Contributing wouldn't be too hard, if you place this expense in your monthly budget. See the chart on the next page to track the annual growth.

	Maximum allowable annual IRA contribution for each year	6% annual growth	Cumulative IRA balance
1995	$2,000	$120	$2,120
1996	$2,000	$247	$4,367
1997	$2,000	$382	$6,749
1998	$2,000	$525	$9,274
1999	$2,000	$676	$11,951
2000	$2,000	$837	$14,788
2001	$2,000	$1,007	$17,795
2002	$3,000	$1,248	$22,043
2003	$3,000	$1,503	$26,545
2004	$3,000	$1,773	$31,318
2005	$4,000	$2,119	$37,437
2006	$4,000	$2,486	$43,923
2007	$4,000	$2,875	$50,799
2008	$5,000	$3,348	$59,147
2009	$5,000	$3,849	$67,995
2010	$5,000	$4,380	$77,375
2011	$5,000	$4,943	$87,318
2012	$5,000	$5,539	$97,857
2013	$5,500	$6,201	$109,558
2014	$5,500	$6,903	$121,961

If your income is too high to contribute to a Roth IRA, consider contributing to a traditional IRA, not taking a deduction, and then converting it to a Roth. If you have no other IRA accounts, the conversion to the Roth is income tax free.

For 2015, you can contribute 🖐 to an IRA or Roth IRA for a maximum of $5,500 ✈ (or $6,500 ✈ if you are age 50 or older), and still take a deduction 🖐 for the IRA, if you fall below these income thresholds:

	Beginning of Adjusted Gross Income phase out of ability to contribute to a deductible ✋ IRA		
	IRA, if taxpayer or spouse is eligible for an employer retirement plan	IRA, if neither spouse is eligible for an employer retirement plan	Roth IRA
Married Filing Joint	$98,000	no phase out	$183,000
Single	$61,000	no phase out	$116,000
Head of Household	$61,000	no phase out	$116,000
Married Filing Separately	$0	no phase out	$0

Non-Deductible IRAs

Some folks may be shaking their head and saying, "I can't contribute to an IRA. I'm in a 401(k) plan."

Or, "I make too much to put money into an IRA."

Not so! You CAN contribute to an IRA, even if you participate in a 401(k) or other retirement plan, and even if you have high income. It's just that you may be unable to take an Income Tax Deduction on your tax return for the IRA. But that's not the end of the game plan for your IRA. After you have funds in an IRA, you can read the next chapter regarding Roth conversion considerations. If you move your traditional IRA to a Roth IRA, it will grow forever tax-free, after you pay any income tax due upon conversion. If you didn't take a deduction for the IRA to begin with, there's no income tax on that pro-rata piece of the conversion of the IRA to the Roth IRA.

Catch Up Contributions ✋

Catch up contributions are a great tool for those over age 50. You can increase your annual IRA contribution by $1K ✈ if you are over age 50. To some, that doesn't sound like a whole lot of money. However, if you consistently make decisions over your lifetime to defer income tax, no matter how small, at the end of your life you will have built more wealth and/or possessed more money for the things you want to buy.

Cash Flow Planning

Cash flow planning is important so you avoid contributions and distributions to IRAs and other retirement plans in the same year, especially for those under age 59½. Times are tough and folks have a rough time climbing out from under their piles of bills at times. The financial responsibilities of family, medical expenses, college tuition, and many other things can be staggering. At the same time, you have the best of intentions to meet your annual retirement plan contribution goal. But then life gets in the way, and the plan gets put on hold.

In my private practice, I've seen a number of good folks who contribute to an IRA or retirement plan and take an Income Tax Deduction 💰 for it, but before year end, they end up pulling out the year's retirement plan contributions, taking a distribution in order to pay for unexpected expenses. This is no good for the client, because when they are under age 59½ there is a 10% penalty for doing this. So, not only did they fail to grow their retirement plan, they also paid a 10% penalty to get that cash back.

To avoid this cash flow problem, you should keep a liquid cash account to cover at least 4 months' expenses. Some experts say the liquid savings should be at least the equivalent of 6 months' expenses. Keeping the liquid savings will eliminate the need to break into retirement funds, and eliminate the related penalty. Having that emergency fund may also reduce financial stress for you, when unexpected expenses pop up.

Timing of IRA Contributions

A person has until April 15 each year to make their IRA or Roth IRA contribution for the previous calendar year. (If you extend your income tax return past April 15, the deadline to purchase an IRA is still April 15, and that deadline is not extended.) This April 15 deadline is helpful because a draft of your income tax return can be completed, and then you can decide on whether to contribute to an IRA or Roth IRA (see the discussion in the next chapter regarding considerations on which is best for you based on your particulars). This is also helpful if you need the additional time to save for your IRA contribution.

Spousal IRAs 👍

A nonworking spouse may contribute to their own IRA (or Roth IRA) if their spouse has earned income. The working spouse will need enough earned income to equal (or exceed) the total IRAs purchased for both spouses. A nonworking spouse who is over age 50 is also eligible for the $1K catchup contribution, assuming the working spouse has adequate earnings that equal or exceed the total IRAs purchased for both spouses.

Chapter Summary

IRAs and Roth IRAs are important pieces of retirement savings, even if you do participate in your employer's retirement plan. If you earn too much to take an Income Tax Deduction 👍 for an IRA, and you earn too much to contribute to a Roth IRA, you may want to consider purchasing an IRA anyway (and not take an Income Tax Deduction for it), and then convert it to a Roth IRA. (More on converting IRAs to Roth IRAs in the next chapter.) This may cost you income tax to convert to a Roth IRA, if you have other IRA accounts. But once converted to the Roth IRA, the funds will grow income tax free indefinitely. If you are over age 50, you are eligible to contribute an extra $1K ✈ to an IRA or Roth IRA. If you have or are a non-working spouse, you still may be eligible for an IRA or Roth IRA, using the spousal IRA rules. Make sure you won't need to pull contributions back out of your retirement accounts so that you may avoid potential penalties. You can purchase IRAs and Roth IRAs through April 15 for the previous tax year. You will need the savings and growth from both the IRAs and an employer retirement plan in order to have a more comfortable retirement. Saving for retirement using tax-efficient tools will help you grow the retirement plan more quickly. You owe it to yourself to save for your retirement, and you can do that more efficiently using the tax efficient retirement and IRA tools.

Chapter 7
Roth IRAs and Roth Conversion Considerations

> **Chapter 7 Trail Route**
> - Decision factors for converting your IRA to a Roth IRA
> - Taxability of conversion

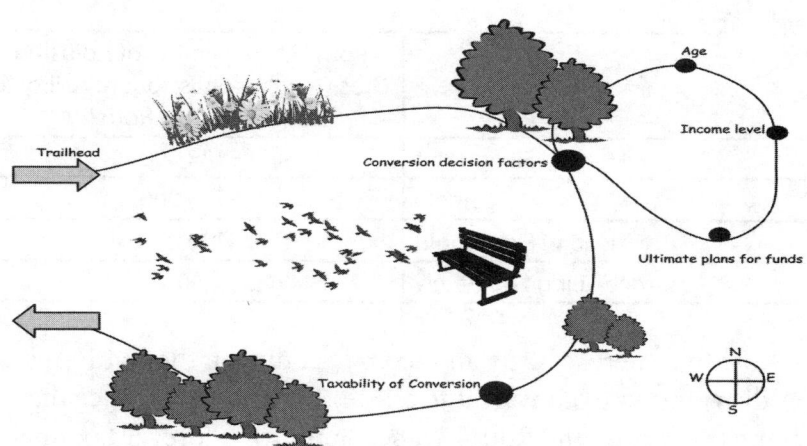

As many of you may already know, a traditional IRA grows tax deferred 👍; it's taxable when the funds are taken out of the account. (There is a small exception if you contributed to a traditional IRA and didn't take a deduction for it; if that's the case, a pro-rata portion of the traditional IRA distributions are income tax free.) Because of the time value of money, deferring income tax makes great sense. Additionally, many folks are in a lower income tax bracket in retirement, lessening the income tax burden.

And as many of you may also already know, a Roth IRA grows income tax free 👍; the original principal and growth are not taxable when the funds are taken out of the account. (Funds must be kept in the account 5 years from the original contribution into a Roth IRA to meet the once-in-a-lifetime satisfaction of the holding period requirement, to qualify the distribution of earnings as income tax free.)

Roth IRAs are popular for younger workers, because the Roth IRA has more time to grow income tax free. The benefit of the tax-free growth interests younger workers more than being able to take a current year Income Tax Deduction for the IRA (as is allowed for traditional IRAs). Additionally, the thresholds to be able to contribute to a Roth IRA are higher than that of the IRA. For 2015, the phase outs to contribute to a Roth IRA are as follows, based on filing status:

	Roth IRA, beginning of Adjusted Gross Income phase out of ability to contribute to a Roth IRA
Married Filing Joint	$183,000
Single	$116,000
Head of Household	$116,000
Married Filing Separately	$0

Note that there is likely an income tax due on the traditional IRA distribution to convert it to a Roth IRA, however, once that income tax is paid, the Roth IRA account grows forever tax free. Income tax free growth is significant, because retirees can have cash distributed as needed without an income tax liability at all. The tax-free growth of the Roth IRA is even better than the tax-deferred growth of the IRA. The concept of converting from an IRA to a Roth IRA is also applicable to 401(k) and 403(b) funds. Beginning in 2006, employers were allowed to amend their 401(k) and 403(b) plans to allow Roth treatment of these funds, and to allow conversions.

Below is a chart that shows the spectrum of tax free, partially taxable and fully taxable distributions from retirement plans:

Tax-free distributions - >>>	Roth IRAs and Roth 401(k) plans
Partially tax-free distributions ->>>	Taxpayers with any IRAs with basis
Fully taxable distributions ->>>	Taxpayers with IRAs without basis, 401(k)s, 403(b)s, 457 plans, SIMPLE IRAs, SEP IRAs

*An IRA is said to have "basis" to the extent you contributed to the RA and didn't take an Income Tax Deduction. This most commonly happens when folks exceed the income limitation to deduct an IRA contribution, but still want tax-deferred growth, so they go ahead and contribute to the IRA.

Considerations for Converting

There are some variables to consider before converting your traditional IRA to a Roth IRA. An analysis from a CPA or financial adviser is needed to see if this is a good move for you.

Age

Your age is a variable to consider before converting a traditional IRA to a Roth IRA. The younger you are, the more time your Roth IRA will have to grow tax free, thus the younger you are, the more attractive the conversion to the Roth IRA will be. And note that for married couples, this decision can be made in unison or separately. The IRA accounts are individual (separate) accounts, and the couple may come up with different decisions for each of them.

Income Level & Tax Bracket

Your income level should also be considered before converting a traditional IRA to a Roth IRA. Perhaps you are at the height of your career, and also earned a huge bonus in the year in which you are considering the conversion from a traditional IRA to a Roth IRA. If you are in an elevated income tax bracket, it will more expensive to do the conversion than if you could convert in a lower income year. Perhaps the following year, you can foresee there will be no bonus and reduced commission income; that might be an opportunity to convert an IRA to a Roth IRA at a cheaper income tax rate.

Many times I have calculated in December what income tax bracket clients are falling in for that year, so final year-end tax moves can be made, similar to an airline pilot completing final flight checklists. After learning what estimated taxable income is, we convert the amount of traditional IRA to a Roth IRA in order to maximize their current income tax bracket. If there is $30K of additional "room" in the 15% bracket, then we convert $30K of traditional IRA money to the Roth IRA before year-end, so as to fully utilize this lower income tax bracket. This is important when a client is about to jump from the 15% to the 25% income tax bracket, as that's a significant jump. At the same time, if a client is already firmly in the 25% bracket, sometimes they don't mind if they maximize the 25% bracket and crack the 28% bracket, since that's only a minimal jump in income tax rate.

Let's look at the 2015 income tax brackets below for a Married Filing Joint couple and focus on the variance between each bracket. The same marginal increases exist for all filing statuses, even though I only displayed them for the Married Filing Joint filing status.

Taxable income level →	Tax bracket	Marginal increase from previous bracket
$0-$18,450	10%	
$18,451-$74,900	15%	5%
$74,901-$151,200	25%	**10%**
$151,201-$230,450	28%	3%
$230,451-$411,500	33%	5%
$411,501-$464,850	35%	2%
$464,851 and above	39.6%	4.6%

If a person moves from the 15% to the 25% income tax bracket, the 10% jump in rate is significant. (I often get telephone calls from clients when they jump in income tax brackets by 10%; they see it and feel the financial pinch.) But when a person moves from the 25% to the 28% income tax bracket, that small 3% increase isn't as painful to folks.

Plans for the Funds

What do you plan to do with these traditional IRA funds that you are considering converting to a Roth IRA? Do you plan to use them in 2 years? 10 years? Leave them to your beneficiaries?

If you plan to use the funds in the relative short term, say if you are retiring in 2 years, then it isn't a good idea to pay the income tax on the conversion when your income tax rate is higher now, while you are still working, than it will be after you retire. After all, only 2 years tax-free growth isn't all that helpful.

Let's assume you are retiring in 10 years. In that case, you will have 10 years of income tax-free growth. Many good thinkers could assume that the income tax brackets overall will increase over the next 10 years, except that often a person's tax bracket decreases upon retirement, so those two changes to your income tax rate likely counterbalance each other. In this case, my suggestion is to go ahead and covert to the Roth IRAs, to the extent of maximizing your current income tax bracket. However, each person's variables and assumptions of future income tax rates will differ, so no one answer will fit all scenarios.

Now let's make the assumption these IRAs are funds that you will never need. You intend to tap other funds to live on in retirement, such as a pension, or other non-retirement account funds. If that's the case, you likely want to leave these funds to your beneficiaries. If you convert the IRAs to Roth IRAs now, the funds will grow income tax free for the rest of your life (after you pay any tax upon conversion). This scenario could allow you to gift a Roth IRA that will not be income taxable to your beneficiary. If you can afford to pay the income tax on the conversion to the Roth IRA and you are in a relatively low income tax bracket, then it's a good tax move to convert to the Roth IRA, if you plan on leaving the Roth

IRAs to your beneficiaries. The inheritance of a Roth IRA is more valuable than the inheritance of a regular IRA because no income tax is due on the Roth IRA.

Paying the Income Tax on the Conversion

A major consideration when converting from a traditional IRA to a Roth IRA is whether you can afford to pay the income tax on the conversion. You will owe Federal--and likely state--income tax on the conversion from a traditional IRA to a Roth IRA, at regular income tax rates. Folks over age 59½ can take out enough funds from the IRA to cover the income tax if they need to, but folks that have not yet attained the age of 59½ don't have this choice, because the portion used to pay the income tax (and not rolled into the Roth IRA) would be considered an early distribution, and would be subject not only to income tax, but to the 10% early distribution penalty.

The following scenarios show the differences in same-sized conversions from a traditional IRA to a Roth IRA for persons over and under age 59½ who must pay the income tax and penalty (applicable to those under age 59½) out of IRA funds:

	Fred, age 60	Susan, age 45
IRA account balance, and there is no basis in the IRA (an Income Tax Deduction ☙ was taken each year as funds were contributed)	$80,000	$80,000
Conversion of IRA to Roth IRA	$60,000	$58,000
IRA distribution to pay the income tax on the conversion, taken out of IRA account	$20,000	$20,000
Penalty on early distribution, participant < 59½ years old	$0	$2,000

One thing minimizes the income tax on the conversion from a traditional IRA to a Roth IRA: cost basis. If you made contributions to your traditional IRA and were unable to take an Income Tax Deduction for the contribution (perhaps due to high income), or chose not to take an Income Tax Deduction for them, then that pro-rata portion of your conversion is not income taxable. Below is a formula to determine the tax-free piece of a conversion from a traditional IRA to a Roth IRA:

$$\frac{\text{Value of IRAs with basis (no Income Tax Deduction taken when IRA money was contributed)}}{\text{Total IRAs (those with and those without basis)}} = \text{Percentage of IRA conversion that is income tax free}$$

You will need to consider all of these variables before you can decide whether you should convert from a traditional IRA to a Roth IRA. Note that the conversion doesn't have to be done all in one year. The above variables can be analyzed annually in order to determine if and how much should be converted before each year end.

The scenarios shown in the chart on the next page display the variables' effect on the decision making process on whether to convert a traditional IRA to a Roth IRA.

A certified financial planner telephoned after I talked to a mutual client about converting his traditional IRA to a Roth IRA.

"Lisa, Tommy is 65 years old. A conversion to a Roth IRA makes no sense."

I said, "Well, let's think about this together. Tommy is asking me where he can invest all of his excess cash. Tommy is no longer self-employed, so he doesn't qualify to contribute to a retirement plan anymore."

"Yeah."

"Tommy can't contribute new money to an IRA or Roth because he has no earned income (such as from a job or self-employment). He has put some money in the stock market but is reluctant to invest more. He has also placed funds in muni bonds. But he still has excess cash."

"Oh."

	Stephanie	Jeff	Sam	Debra	George
Age	25	35	45	55	65
Tax bracket	15% bracket	25% bracket	25% bracket	28% bracket	15% bracket
Amount of funds in traditional IRA	$20K	$50K	$80K	$80K	$200K
Plans for the funds	Hold until retirement age	Hold until retirement age	Hold until retirement age	Hold until age 59½ (when she wants to retire)	Hold until death, and then leaving to beneficiaries
Paying the tax	Has funds set aside	Has funds set aside	No funds available	Has funds set aside	Has funds set aside
Convert?	Convert to the Roth IRA in current year, assuming she stays in 15% Federal income tax bracket.	Convert to the Roth IRA in current year to the extent that the 25% or 28% tax brackets are maximized.	Can't convert b/c he can't afford the tax, but encourage him to save for the tax and convert next year in the amount needed to maximize the 28% bracket.	Don't convert. Not a lot of time for the funds to grow tax free, and she's in a high tax bracket.	Convert enough each year to maximize the 15% bracket.

"He never plans on using this Roth IRA money. He plans to leave it to his nephews. By converting to a Roth IRA, he'll be gifting something better than an IRA; he'll be gifting a Roth that will be tax free to the nephews!"

From there, the financial planner agreed with my thinking relative to this client and Tommy finalized his decision. Tommy converted to the extent of maximizing the 28% income tax bracket.

Chapter Summary

Your age, income tax bracket, and plans for the retirement funds are all important considerations regarding whether you should convert your traditional IRAs to Roth IRAs. You also will want to calculate the income tax that will be due upon a conversion, to make sure you have adequate cash to pay the income tax on the conversion. Those over age 59 ½ can use IRA funds to pay the income tax due upon conversion, without being subject to the 10% early withdrawal penalty. Converting traditional IRAs to Roth IRAs will allow those funds to grow income tax-free 👆, which is even better than the tax-deferred treatment of traditional IRAs. Making this move can save a lot of income tax in the long run, and help you take care of your and your spouse's retirement needs.

> IRS Form 8606 is used to calculate IRA basis and the tax on converting IRAs to Roth IRAs.

Chapter 8
Let Your Retirement Plan Help You During Hard Times

Chapter 8 Trail Route
- Retirement plan loans
- Hardship withdrawals
- IRA withdrawals
- Roth IRA withdrawals
- Exceptions to 10% early withdrawal penalty
- 72(t) election
- IRA rollover "loan"
- Qualified Domestic Relations Order (QDRO)
- Mortgage escrow accounts

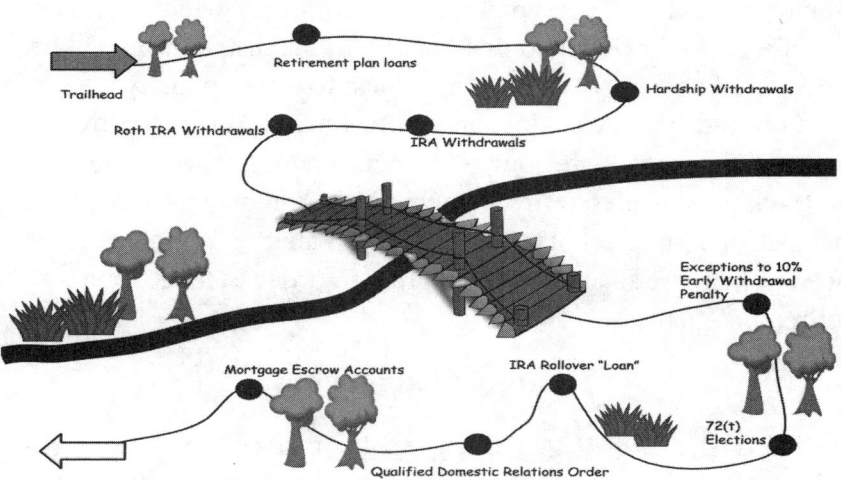

I hope hard times never befall you or your family. But it can happen. Layoffs happen, sometimes to both spouses. Let's explore several ways to help you through, if you are experiencing a financial crunch.

Retirement Plan Loans

Many retirement plans, including 401(k) plans, defined benefit pension plans, profit sharing plans and 403(b) plans, allow participants to borrow from their balance in the retirement plan, and the loan proceeds can be used for any need. The loan must be paid back within 5 years, unless the loan is for a principal residence, in which case it must be paid back within 15 years. The maximum allowable loan from a retirement plan is $50K, but may be less because the loan cannot exceed 50% of the value of your plan. (Certain other retirement plans do not allow loans, such as traditional IRAs, Roth IRAs, SEP IRAs and SIMPLE IRAs.)

Warning: if you stop working for the company with which the plan is affiliated, you will need to immediately repay the loan in full, or the company will be legally forced to treat the unpaid portion of the loan as a retirement plan distribution, which is income taxable. If you have not attained age 59½, the distribution will be considered an early distribution, subject to a 10% penalty.

One additional warning: once your financial crunch is over, make sure you evaluate your retirement savings to see if you are on track to be able to retire at some point. You may need the assistance of a financial planner for such an analysis. And you may need to increase savings in other areas in order to meet your retirement goals.

Hardship Withdrawals

Plans such as 401(k), 403(b), and 457 plans often allow Hardship Withdrawals, also called Hardship Distributions, of the employee's contributions (not any of the employer matching funds) in cases of extreme financial need. Employers can set their plans up to define "hardship," but generally, these include:
- Funeral cost of immediate family;
- Medical expenses of immediate family;
- Purchase of principal residence;
- Post-secondary education expenses of immediate family;
- To prevent eviction or foreclosure of home;
- Repair costs of home related to casualty (such as tornado

or fire); and
- Income taxes and penalty incurred related to the hardship withdrawal.

Make sure you check with your employer to find out how your retirement plan is written, if you are seeking a hardship withdrawal, to see if your circumstance qualifies.

In a recent meeting with a client, I said, "The balance due with your return is $5,400, including the 10% penalty for early withdrawal from your retirement plan."

"Oh, I normally get a refund. Why do I owe? That was a Hardship Distribution, approved by my company. They said it's okay to take the money out, so there shouldn't be a penalty."

"Okay, we're talking about two different issues. Yes, your company must to approve your Hardship Distribution, that's true. But the matter of there being a penalty on a retirement plan withdrawal before age 59 ½ is an IRS rule, and your company has no say in that."

"What?! No one told me about a penalty!"

"I'm sorry your employer didn't tell you about the early withdrawal penalty on the hardship withdrawal. I already checked and you don't qualify for any of the exceptions to avoid the 10% penalty."

IRA Withdrawals

You may take withdrawals from IRAs, SEP IRAs, and SIMPLE IRAs. However, these are also subject to the 10% penalty for early withdrawal if the plan participant has not attained age 59½. As with retirement plan early withdrawals, I worry about those who take these early withdrawals from IRAs and Roth IRAs, and then are caught short on cash at retirement time.

Roth IRA Withdrawals

Your contributions (principal portion) in a Roth IRA may be taken out anytime without any income tax being due, and without any penalty. This is true because you didn't take an Income Tax Deduction when you contributed to the Roth IRA; or, if you converted from a traditional IRA to your Roth IRA, you paid income tax when you converted. Distributions first come from your contributions, and then from earnings. If you take out earnings from the Roth IRA, those will be income tax- and penalty-free if you make a Qualified Distribution.

> *Roth IRA Qualified Distributions defined:*
> *Distribution is after the 5 year holding period that begins on the date the account owner first contributes into the Roth IRA and one of the following applies:*
> - *The account owner is over age 59 ½; or*
> - *Account owner is deceased or disabled; or*
> - *Distribution is for a first time homebuyer, eligible to escape the 10% early withdrawal penalty.*

Exceptions to the 10% Early Withdrawal Penalty

If your IRA withdrawal will be used to pay for qualified medical expenses (medical expenses in excess of 10% of total income or over 7.5% of total income for those over age 65), or to pay for qualifying higher education expenses, then the withdrawal escapes the 10% early withdrawal penalty.

Series of Substantially Equal Annual Withdrawals from an IRA

This is sometimes referred to as a 72(t) election. If you take withdrawals from your IRA scheduled in a series of substantially equal annual payments to you, that last over your life expectancy (or joint life expectancy of you and your beneficiary), you can escape the 10% early withdrawal penalty. Once the IRA owner has reached age 59½, and has taken at least 5 years of the annual payments, the election may be terminated.

IRA Rollover "Loan"

Although not tecÚically a loan, you may use the funds from a rollover for emergency needs by using the rollover rules to your advantage.

- You can roll IRA funds to a different IRA, or return the funds to the original IRA, within 60 days. This is considered an IRA rollover. During this 60-day period, you can use the funds for emergency needs.
- Only one tax-free rollover of this nature is allowed for each 12 month period, beginning with the receipt of the IRA funds.
- Be careful, because if you fail to return the funds to an IRA account within the 60 day period, the transaction will be considered a taxable IRA distribution, and if you are under age 59 1/2, the distribution will be subject to the 10% early withdrawal penalty.
- Additionally, banks and brokerage houses are supposed to withhold 20% Federal income tax for rollovers that are not going directly to another IRA account, even though your intention is to return the money to an IRA. But you will be required to return 100% of the IRA distribution to the account within the 60-day period, and this could cause a shortfall because of the 20% withholding for income tax.

I have seen this scenario play out successfully. In one case, a husband and wife started construction on a new home before the husband received his anticipated large bonus. The couple incurred significant expenses for the home, and their mortgage loan paperwork continued to sit on a banker's desk, still not finalized. The couple took $100K out of their IRA accounts, and were quite nervous over it. The bonus and mortgage both finally came through, and then they replaced the IRA funds before 60 days passed. So in effect, they used the IRA account for a 60-day loan.

Qualified Domestic Relations Order (QDRO)

Some folks' hard times are due to divorce. The QDRO is discussed more in Chapter 28, but if you receive part of your ex-spouse's retirement plan via a QDRO and take the funds out of the retirement account instead of placing them in a retirement account for yourself, the distribution escapes the 10% early withdrawal penalty. Make sure you discuss the particulars with your attorney so that you carry out the transactions in accordance with all guidelines and avoid the 10% early withdrawal penalty of retirement savings.

Mortgage Escrow Accounts

This is obviously not a retirement account, but I want to make a point in this chapter about mortgage escrow accounts. Often mortgage companies will allow you to skip the escrow portion of your mortgage payment for up to 4 months if you have lost your job, or are having a financial crunch from some other emergency. However, the mortgage company will want you to catch up the escrow payments after the 4 month period is over. You will need to seek permission from your mortgage company before short paying your monthly mortgage payment for the amount of the escrow payment.

Chapter Summary

If you are experiencing financial hard times, there are a number of ways your retirement accounts can help you during the crisis, and hopefully you can escape the 10% early withdrawal penalty from retirement plans. A retirement plan loan may be an option for you. A hardship withdrawal from an employer retirement plan or IRA withdrawal are also options, but may be subject to a 10% penalty if you are under age 59½. Roth IRA withdrawals have no early withdrawal penalty if you withdraw your contributions only (and no earnings), and meet certain other requirements. There are exceptions to the 10% early withdrawal penalty (such as for medical expenses and college education, limitations apply, and for a 72(t) election for a series of substantially equal annual distributions scheduled to be received over life expectancy.) IRA rollover "loans" are allowed once every 12 months, but the funds must be returned to the IRA within 60 days, or the funds will become taxable and penalties may apply. Qualified Domestic Relations Orders pursuant to a divorce can allow retirement funds to be distributed to an ex-spouse, penalty free. Plan with care so that you still save adequate amounts for your retirement, after taking cash out of your retirement plans. If you keep your goal set as taking care of your (and your spouse's, if applicable) retirement, then it will help guide your current decisions.

> IRS Form 5329, is used to indicate which early retirement withdrawals are not subject to the 10% early withdrawal penalty.

Chapter 9
Which Filing Status: Married Filing Joint or Married Filing Separate?

> Chapter 9 Trail Route
> - Married filing joint
> - Married filing separate
> - Disadvantages of married filing separate
> - Head of household (continued in next chapter)

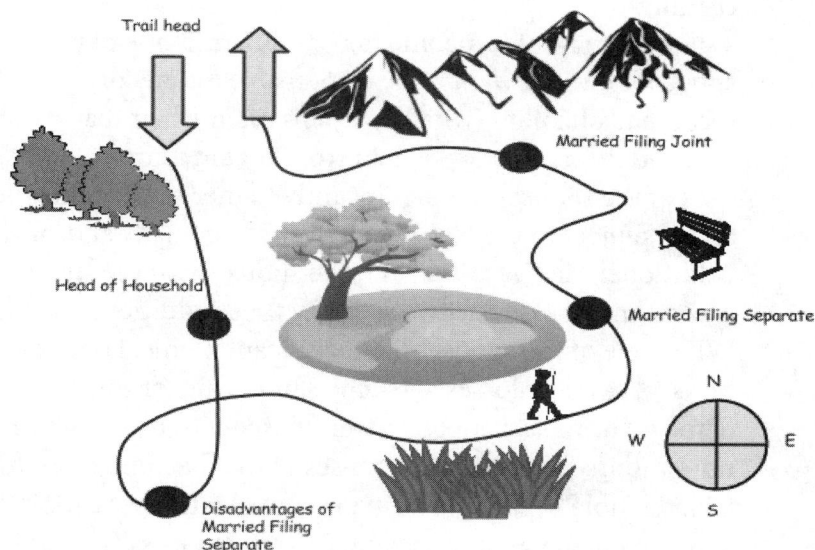

A couple's level of happiness doesn't always indicate their income tax filing status. A happily married couple may choose to File Separately (if they qualify), and an unhappy couple may choose to File Jointly. Filing status discussions are based more on harvesting the best combined income tax refund, or reducing the combined income tax balance due, than on marital harmony. Additionally, engaged couples may decide to put off their wedding until the New Year (because of the infamous "Marriage Penalty," which is less than it used to be), or they may rush and marry before year-end in some situations.

Filing Options

Married Filing Joint

If the couple is still married on the last day of the year, they are eligible to file a Married Filing Joint income tax return.

Married Filing Separate

The question of the filing status of Married Filing Separately most often comes from the following situations:
- Couples that are separated and have begun divorce proceedings;
- When there is joint income tax liability, and one of the spouses does not want to be responsible for any of the income tax liability (which happens often when that spouse received no support or benefit from that income);
- One of the spouses has significantly higher taxable income, and is subject to the Net Investment Income Tax and/or the Additional Medicare Tax, and the spouse with the lesser taxable income doesn't want to pay those additional taxes;
- When one of the spouses has significant medical deductions 👍, casualty losses 👍 (such as hurricane or tornado damage) or miscellaneous itemized deductions 👍 (such as unreimbursed employee expenses👍) that become more fully deductible because these types of deductions are limited as a percentage of total income (Adjusted Gross Income);
- When one of the spouses can claim Head of Household status due to (non-joint) children, and the combined result is more advantageous; and
- When there is less Alternative Minimum Tax if the couple files separately.

Because of the number of variables to consider, it usually isn't possible to determine which filing status should be used simply based on the facts; an actual calculation will provide a more telling, thorough answer. You need good headlights to see through the fog of all of the variables. The necessary calculation will include a mockup of the couple's income tax return as if they are filing jointly, and then each the husband's and the wife's individual income tax return, as if they are filing Single or Head of Household, as allowable. The two individual returns' income tax liabilities are combined and compared to that on the joint tax return to determine which route provides the greater total refund or least total balance due.

> Married Filing Separate Requirements:
> - ~~If married on last day of year, couple must have lived apart for the last 6 months of the year, if they want to file separately.~~
> - If one spouse died during the year, it's allowable to file separately.
>
> However, most of the time, the overall result is better when you file as Married Filing Joint.

Tax software packages used by CPA firms, or some software available at the retail level, have the ability to calculate the most preferable filing status if every income, deduction 👍, exemption 👍 and credit ❖ item is entered as being attributable to either the husband or the wife. Once all tax data are entered, you can view the return for each spouse Filing Separately, and with the couple Filing Jointly. By adding the results of the Married Filing Separate returns, and comparing to the Married Filing Joint return, you can determine the correct answer for you. Some tax software packages have a report just for this purpose that can be generated, called the Filing Status Optimization Report.

Generally, the combined Federal and state income tax is less if couples file jointly, but I've been surprised a few times with a Married Filing Separate result being more advantageous. Because this is something that is so easy to check, instead of guessing which way is best, I go ahead and let the tax software calculate the resulting Federal and state income tax under both filing methods, and review each to make sure all income, exemptions 👍, credits ❖ and deduction 👍 items are properly attributed to the correct spouse. It's only in rare instances where it's advantageous to file as Married

Filing Separate, but it does happen.

Disadvantages of Married Filing Separate

Beware, before you make the decision to file separately, review your results carefully. The lost benefits below will be included in your Filing Status Optimization Report or similar analysis you have prepared. To make sure you understand the lost benefits of Married Filing Separately, I've listed them below:

- Both spouses must use the same method for reporting deductions 👍. If one spouse itemizes their deductions 👍, the other spouse must do the same, which may leave one spouse with few or no itemized deductions. The spouse with few or no itemized deductions is not eligible to take the Standard Deduction, if their spouse already filed, itemizing their deductions 👍. (I've seen, and participated in, races between spouses, so that one of them could take itemized deductions 👍 when the other spouse intended to take the Standard Deduction 👍. The spouse wanting to itemize their deductions 👍 must file first, so that the IRS would not force them to only take the Standard Deduction 👍 if their spouse filed first.)
- Many Income Tax Credits ❖ are lost when filing as Married Filing Separately, such as the Child & Dependent Care Credit ❖, Earned Income Credit ❖, Credit for Elderly or Disabled ❖, and the Adoption Credit ❖.
- Contributions to IRA accounts can be limited, and Spousal IRA rules do not apply.
- Education benefits will be lost, such as Education Credits ❖, Student Loan interest deductions 👍, Tuition and Fees deduction 👍, and Savings Bond interest exclusion 👍.
- Passive loss treatment is modified: rental losses are reduced and one spouse's passive income cannot be offset by the other spouse's passive loss carry-forwards.
- Social Security may be taxable to a greater extent.
- Alternative Minimum Tax may increase.

This isn't a complete list of the lost benefits when filing Married

Filing Separate; you should make this decision with the help of a CPA or qualified tax preparer, who is familiar with your particular situation.

Head of Household

This is a preferable filing status allowed for a single or married-filing-separate individual who contributes more than half the cost of providing a home for more than half the year for their child or qualifying relative. The Head of Household income tax brackets are more advantageous than that of the Married Filing Separate tax brackets (but not quite as advantageous as the Married Filing Joint tax brackets).

To illustrate, below is a comparison of the 25% income tax brackets for 2015 for all filing statuses:

Filing Status	2015 25% tax bracket ✈
Married Filing Separate	$37,451-$75,600
Single	$37,451-$90,750
Head of Household	$50,201-$129,600
Married Filing Joint	$74,901-$151,200

You usually cannot choose which filing status you are able to use, but when you can, you can see above which filing statuses are more advantageous. The Head of Household 25% income tax bracket starts at a much higher income level than that of the Married Filing Separate filing status. See Chapter 10 for a more thorough discussion of the Head of Household filing status.

We accepted a new client, Gloria, during our March rush last year. She was a high-speed train with only one destination in mind: she asked that we prepare her Married Filing Separate income tax return, itemizing the $60K in deductions 👍 before her estranged, unemployed husband filed, taking the Standard Deduction 👍. She wanted the income tax return prepared that very day! The IRS would accept the first tax return filed, and force the second spouse to file to use the same method of filing deductions

👍. The client didn't want to lose the huge Itemized Deductions 👍, which she alone had paid for and she needed to offset her large income.

Gloria faxed, emailed and couriered all documents to us, and we prepared, reviewed, and issued the income tax return by the end of the same day.

"Gloria," I told her at day's end, "you won the race, and filed your income tax return first; you lowered your Federal tax liability by $21K by filing first!"

Chapter Summary

You may be able to lower your income tax balance due or increase your refund by reviewing your filing status. If you are eligible to file as Married Filing Separate or Head of Household, sometimes this provides a better overall result than Married Filing Jointly or Single. (See the next chapter that discusses Head of Household status in more detail.) The biggest hurdle to clear in order to use the Married Filing Separate filing status is that you must have lived apart for the last 6 months of the year. There are quite a few disadvantages to Married Filing Separate, so you will need your income tax preparer to calculate your income tax return using the various filing statuses to see which will give you the best overall combined result. A Filing Status Optimization Report will determine which filing status is best for you, and which status will save you the most income tax dollars. This is something you owe yourself! Reduce your income tax whenever possible, so you will have more cash available for you and your family.

Chapter 10
Head of Household Status

Chapter 10 Trail Route
- Head of Household tax brackets
- Head of Household requirements

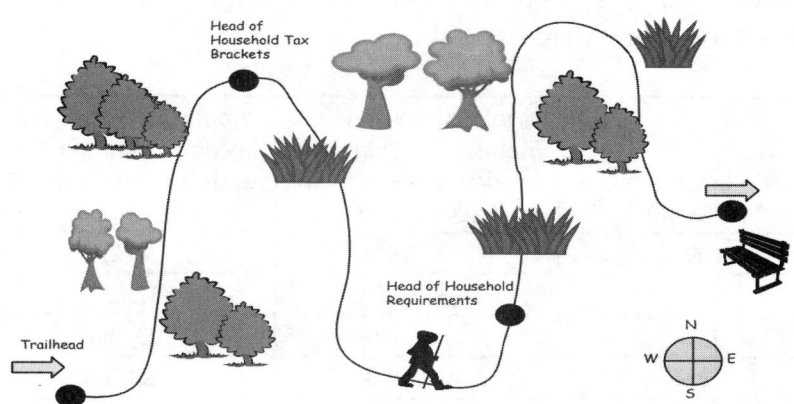

Many middle-income households have only one parent leading the hike. If that's you, you have the pressure of earning a living to support the family, running the house, raising the children, cutting the grass, cooking, and much more. I do know what it's like being a single parent, except I don't cook often. Sure, it's challenging at times, and hectic, but being a parent has its own rewards.

Head of Household and the Single Parent

Whatever circumstance brought you to being a single parent, there is an income tax advantage for you. Head of Household status may be right for you. As soon as I say that to someone, I hear, "So why is it advantageous?"

I explain, "The income tax rates are better for the Head of Household status than for the Single status. And the Standard

Deduction 👍 is higher for the Head of Household status than for the Single status." That's all I ever have to say, and the person is ready to look at the requirements to see if they qualify for Head of Household status.

Head of Household Tax Brackets

Below is a chart of the 2015 income tax rates, where you can compare the Head of Household income tax rates with the Single income tax rates, and at the bottom is the Standard Deduction for each of those filing statuses:

2015 Income Tax Brackets ✈	Head of Household Status, taxable income maximum for each tax bracket listed ✈	Single Status, taxable income maximum for each tax bracket listed ✈
10%	$13,150	$9,225
15%	$50,200	$37,450
25%	$129,600	$90,750
28%	$209,850	$189,300
33%	$411,500	$411,500
35%	$439,000	$413,200
39.6%	Endless	Endless
Standard Deduction 👍	$9,250	$6,300

For each income tax bracket listed, see how much more you can earn as Head of Household without going to the next higher income tax bracket? And see how the Standard Deduction 👍 is 47% higher as Head of Household? These income tax benefits add up to fewer dollars you will have to pay in income tax. That equates to more dollars you keep for your family.

Head of Household Requirements

There are four requirements you must meet in order to claim the Head of Household status:
1. You paid for more than half of the cost of maintaining your own household

2. The home was the principal residence for more than half the year for a Qualifying Child (see Chapter 11) or Qualifying Relative (see Chapter 12)
3. You are not married on the last day of the year (there is an exception to this below)
4. You are a US citizen or resident for the entire year

A note for divorced parents--even if you released the right to claim a child as an exemption on your income tax return, you can still claim Head of Household status with respect to that child. (See Chapter 28 for more discussion related to releasing a dependency exemption.)

If you are married, but are filing a separate income tax return from your spouse, your spouse did not live with you for the last 6 months of the year, and your home was the main home for your child, stepchild, adopted child, or foster child for more than half the year, then you are deemed to have passed test number three above. In this circumstance, you are considered unmarried for purposes of using the Head of Household status.

If the taxpayer or Qualifying Child or Qualifying Relative is born or dies during the year, then instead of the requirement that the home be their residence for half of the year, the requirement is modified. In these cases, the home must be their residence for at least half of the days they were alive during the year. If the taxpayer or Qualifying Child or Qualifying Relative is gone from the home for a short period of time because of illness, work, education, vacation, military service or incarceration, that absence period is still considered to be time that applicable person lived in the home.

Chapter Summary

If you qualify to file as Head of Household, this will be more beneficial than the Single or Married Filing Separate filing statuses because the income tax brackets are much more favorable, and the Standard Deduction👍 is higher (if you don't itemize your deductions👍). Make sure you qualify to use the Head of Household filing status before doing so. The biggest requirement is that you need to maintain a principal residence for more than half the year for a Qualifying Child. Selection of the most advantageous filing status can reduce your income tax burden to a great extent. Remember, you deserve to pay the least amount of income tax that is legally possible.

Chapter 11

Maximize the Value of Kids' Exemptions

Chapter 11 Trail Route
- Dependency tests
- AMT consideration
- Strategy for the Exemption

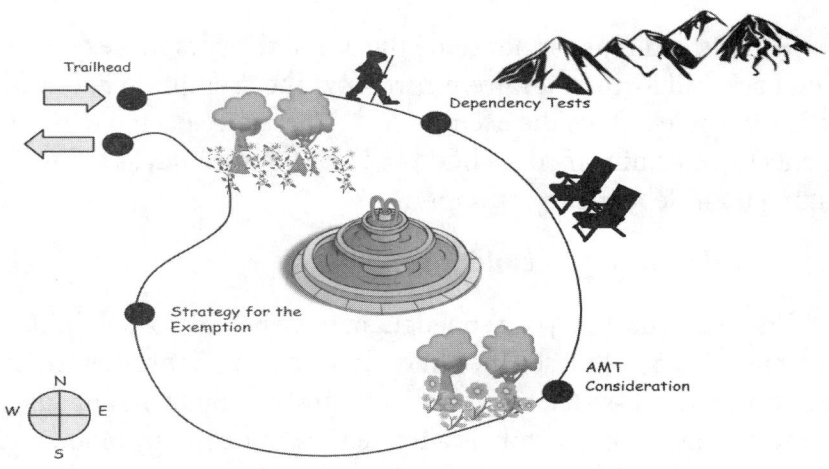

I hear this comment several times each year: "My child wants to take her own income tax exemption, but I want to take the exemption myself." The child in this case is working part time while also attending high school or college, and they feel they are laboring hard, and want their own exemption to reduce their income tax on the money earned at their part-time job.

But Mom and Dad feel the financial crunch because they are or will be paying for the college tuition and room & board costs, and pay so much more than their child in income tax. And Mom and Dad feel they should take the exemption for the child on their own income tax return because they are in a higher income tax bracket, and feel they need the child's exemption more. Each exemption is worth $4K ✈ for 2015, and that is a reduction to taxable income.

Qualifying Child

Who is providing at least 50% of the support for that child? The IRS has a support test, discussed below, and to take an exemption, you must be providing more than half of the support for that person. A high school or college student is probably not providing more than half of his/her own support, if you consider all expenses, in addition to the housing and college costs, if applicable.

Dependency Tests

Parents and kids cannot trade the use of the personal exemption back and forth as if it were currency. The exemption goes with who is eligible to take the exemption 👍. There are specific requirements to determine if your child is a Qualifying Child, as far as taking their dependency exemption.

1. **Relationship of child**

The child must be your son, daughter, stepchild, foster child, or a child of any of these. The child can also be your brother, sister, half-brother, half-sister, step brother, step sister, or a child of any of these. Your adopted child is a treated as your child by blood and they or their children could be a Qualifying Child for purposes of the dependency exemption.

2. **Age of child**

The child must be under age 19, or under age 24 if a full time student. And the child must be younger than the person wanting to take their dependency exemption.

3. **Residency**

The child must have lived with you for more than half of the year, except short term absences for illness, school, business, vacation or military services are ignored.

4. **Support**

As mentioned above, the child cannot have provided more

than half of his/her own support.

5.   **Joint return**

The child, if married, cannot file a joint return with anyone else.

6.   **Tie-breaker test**

If the child qualifies as the Qualifying Child of more than one person for the dependency exemption, then the tie-breaker rules must be applied. The tie-breaker test is beyond the scope of the subject area of this book, but if you need tecÚical advice in this area, you should seek out a CPA.

In limited cases, a college student may indeed be providing half of his/her own support. Harold, a deceased client, set up his estate planning so that several annuities in his retirement account would be left, upon his death, to his grandchildren, Megan and Jack. Harold's widow and adult children were already secure in their financial situations so the plan made good sense. At Harold's death, Megan and Jack began receiving the annuity distributions. Because these grandkids are receiving more than half of their support from the annuity distributions, they are able to claim their own dependency exemptions, despite being young college students.

> *Parents and kids cannot trade the use of the personal exemption back and forth as if it were currency.*

Qualifying Relative

See Chapter 12, in which the Dependency of a Qualifying Relative (other than a child) is discussed.

Exemption

See Chapter 16, where I explain how parents can make the decision to forego the child's exemption, so that the child can take an Education Credit ❖. In that case, the child still can't take their own exemption, unless they are eligible to do so based on the support test (which is usually the test that makes them ineligible to take their own exemption) and other dependency tests that are detailed above.

Alternative Minimum Tax (AMT)

If the parents are subject to AMT, then the personal exemptions (for themselves and their children) aren't helping them anyway. If you look at the AMT calculation schedule, it starts with the regular taxable income BEFORE the exemptions are deducted. If both the child and parents provided 50% of the support for the child, and if the parents are subject to AMT, then they should forego the child's exemption, because it's not helpful to them anyway.

Strategy For The Exemption

Perhaps you determine that the parents and the child both provided 50% of the support for the child, and the parents are not subject to AMT. Then you may want your CPA to do an analysis to see who will benefit more by taking the exemption.

The following chart is an example analysis of who should take the exemption for a child, if both parent(s) and child seem to be eligible for the exemption:

	Parent(s)	Child
Total Income (Adjusted Gross Income)	$220,000	$14,500
Federal Income Tax Bracket	28%	15%
Tax savings effect of including child's exemption, including estimated state rate of 6%	$1,343	$830

You will also need to determine the effect of any education credits ❖ in this calculation, so you will need to read Chapter 16 about College Education Credits ❖ before making a final decision on the exemption for your child.

Chapter Summary

Filing income tax returns that allow for the lowest tax burden for the entire family unit should be the goal. This may mean the parents taking their child's exemption, or this may mean the parents foregoing their child's exemption, so that their child can take an Education Income Tax Credit ❖. If the parents are subject to AMT, the children's exemptions are not helpful anyway, so foregoing the children's exemption may not be an issue for the parents. The taxpayer taking the child's exemption must be eligible to do so, and the largest requirement is that the taxpayer taking the exemption must have provided more than half of the support for that child. Dependency exemptions cannot be traded like currency between parents and children, but in some cases, both the parent's and the child provided half of the support for the child. Parents' and children's income tax returns may need to be prepared by the same income tax preparer and at the same time, so strategic decisions can be made, to obtain the best overall result (and save the most income tax) for the family as a whole.

Chapter 12
Do You Qualify for Grandma's Dependency Exemption?

> **Chapter 12 Trail Route**
> - Qualifying relative
> - Dependency tests

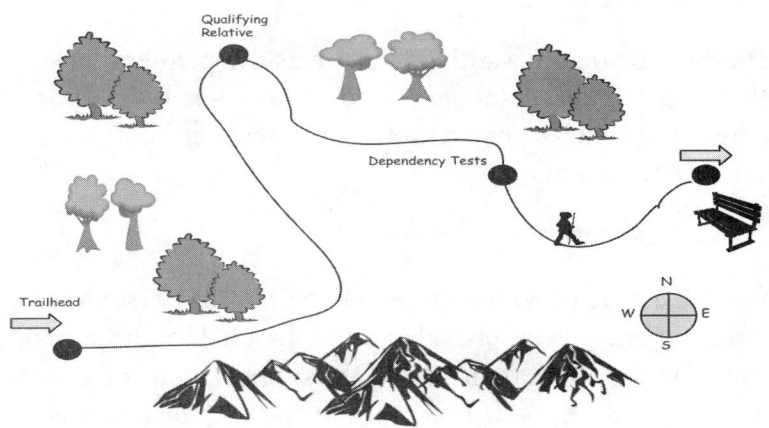

Your elderly parent is living with you, as well as your children, and their babies. The house is cramped and bursting, and is more hectic than Grand Central Station at rush hour. Cash is tight in the family. You could use all the help you can get with income tax savings ideas. With such a large household, you have many challenges.

Qualifying Relative

You should consider whether you are eligible to take the income tax exemption for those family members that are living with you. In the last chapter, the rules to be a Qualifying Child for purposes of the dependency exemption were discussed. This chapter is different because now the discussion is about the rules related to a Qualifying Relative, who can be any age and doesn't have to be related to you. Keep in mind, if you are subject to Alternative Minimum Tax, additional dependency exemptions will not be helpful.

Dependency Tests

There are some tests that you will need to consider in order to determine which of the household members are appropriate to include on your income tax return.

1. Gross income test

The person you are wanting to claim as a dependent must have less than $4K →in gross income for 2015 (and for this purpose, gross income excludes tax-exempt interest and certain nontaxable social security benefits).

2. Support test

You must have provided more than half of the person's support, or if no one person provided more than half of the support, but you provided more than 10% of the support, you still may be able to take the dependency exemption. You will need to seek the advice of a CPA to discuss your specific situation.

3. Member of household or relationship test

This person must have lived with you for the entire year if they are not a relative, or qualify as your relative in one of these ways, but not necessarily in your household: (1) your child, (2) your stepchild, (3) your foster child, (4) your grandchild, (5) your great-grandchild, (6) your sibling or their children, (7) your step-siblings, (8) your half-siblings or their children, (9) your parents, (10) your grandparents, (11) your step-parents, (12) your uncle or aunt, (13) your in-laws.

My Mom worked as a state social worker before she retired, and she remembers a family who at the same time, included five living generations, all in one household. Mom said they needed financial help, but nothing specific. This family consisted of a mother as head of the household, her daughter (age 16) and newborn baby, and the mother's mother and grandmother.

In this situation, the mother likely takes her own 16-year old daughter and the baby as exemptions, and well as her mother. Her grandmother likely has taxable social security, and likely makes more than $4K per year (2015 limit), so no one else can take her dependency exemption, if that's the case.

Chapter Summary

You want to evaluate each member of your household (in addition to the children) to determine if they are eligible to be claimed on your income tax return as an exemption. You may be eligible to take the exemption of a Qualifying Relative if these tests are met: Gross Income Test, Support Test, and Member of Household Test. The more exemptions you have on your income tax return, the lower your income tax liability will be, but unfortunately, if you are subject to Alternative Minimum Tax, additional exemptions are not helpful. You will need to strategically examine this situation, in order to obtain the lowest possible income tax liability and keep the income tax savings for use for your household.

Chapter 13
The Kiddie Tax is More Advantageous Than You Think

> **Chapter 13 Trail Route**
> - Income shifting
> - Gifting to children
> - Limits on gifts
> - Working children
> - Unearned income
> - Effect of young adult marrying

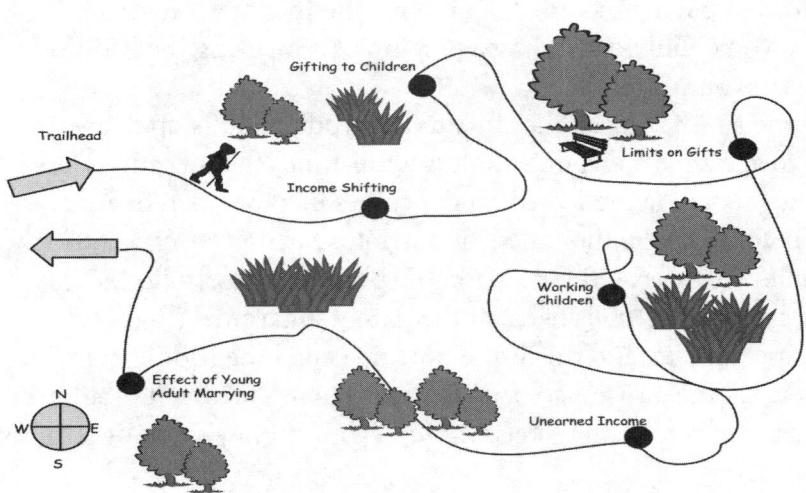

M ost folks (me included) grumble about additional income taxes and new types of taxes. But, the Kiddie Tax isn't quite as bad as you might think because, if your family is subject to the Kiddie Tax, that means you capitalized on paying income taxes on some of your portfolio income at your child's low 0% and 10% income tax brackets before being taxed at your marginal (highest) rate. You may still be moaning and fussing if you weren't even aware a Kiddie Tax existed before reading this, but if you avail yourself to these rules, they can benefit your family by lowering overall family income tax.

Kiddie Tax Rules

Income Shifting

Here's how to maneuver so the Kiddie Tax rules can benefit your family: parents can gift the children money, and then invest it for the children. For 2015, the children are taxed at 0% ✈ for Federal income tax purposes for the first $1,050 ✈ of portfolio (interest, dividends, and Capital Gain) earnings, and then 10% ✈ for Federal purposes for the next $1,050 ✈ of portfolio earnings. This is preferable 👍 to the parents, rather than doling out cash for income tax on these portfolio earnings at their higher income tax rates, which may be at 25%, 28%, 33%, or more. Visualizing how instead of paying income tax on portfolio income at these high rates, you could be avoiding a portion of it by using the Kiddie Tax rules to your advantage.

The Kiddie Tax applies to kids and young adults up to age 18 (up to age 24 if the young adult is a full-time student) and refers to the income tax reflected on the child's income tax return, for the income tax on the excess of portfolio earnings over $2,100 (the Kiddie Tax threshold for 2015). The portion of portfolio income that exceeds $2,100 is taxed at the parent's marginal (highest) income tax rate, and this is the portion called the Kiddie Tax. So why is Kiddie Tax not so bad? Because paying income tax at lower rates is a way for you to keep more of your money for your family's other needs.

See below how it benefited this family to shift income to the child:

	Parents, Tom & Jane	Child, Trisha
Portfolio earnings that were shifted to Child, Trisha	$2,100	$2,100
Tax on the portfolio earnings	Marginal rate = 33%, tax =$693	First $1,050 is tax-free, next $1,050 is taxed at 10%, rest (if any) is taxed at parents' marginal rate of 33%. Tax = $105

* (interest and short term dividends)

The tax savings in this example is $588. Now ponder doing this year after year, and for more than one child. This planning point is helpful for up to $2,100 ✈ in portfolio earnings in 2015 for each child, subject to increase annually.

You may have noticed in the above example that I included only interest and short-term dividends. This is so the income tax calculation would be straightforward. But, if part of the earnings had included long-term Capital Gains and/or qualified dividends, a similar type of outcome would be the result using the Capital Gain tax rates.

Gifting to Children

Gifting to children can start small, but should start early in their lives in order to maximize income tax savings. If your investments earn 5%, and if you (and others) gift your child a lifetime total of $40K, then you will achieve maximum benefit of the Kiddie Tax Rules. Annual earnings on $40K at 5% equals approximately $2,100, which is the 2015 Kiddie Tax ceiling.

You are probably sighing and thinking, "How can my kids possibly acquire that much in investments?"

This doesn't all have to be done at once! I have made the personal decision of only gifting my kids the amount needed to earn $2,100 annually in portfolio income, and no more at this point. It took me years, and help from their father, to climb up to the goal.

I recommend fully funding your retirement plans annually before making gifts to children. You should discuss with your financial planner if this type of gifting is appropriate for your level of savings, goals, and needs.

> *I recommend fully funding your retirement plans annually before making gifts to children.*

Be aware that some parents may need to think twice about putting money into their kids' names, if they are uncomfortable with those children having control of those funds at age 18 or 21 (depending on the laws in your state). I have not been worried about this with my children, but you know your own kids best. You do not have to disclose the gifts to your children while they are minors.

If you are wanting to gift significant amounts of assets to your children, common investments to shift to a child are tax-exempt investments, so as not to surpass the Kiddie Tax threshold, $2,100 ✈ for 2015, are as follows:
- Growth stocks that pay low or no dividends, but that will appreciate;
- Rental real estate (due to the large depreciation deductions 👍, and no tax on the appreciation until sold);
- Municipal bonds; and
- U.S. savings bonds (you can elect to pay tax annually, to use up the tax free bracket of $1,050 ✈ for 2015, or to pay income tax in a later year, when the bond is cashed).

One other thought on building your child's investment portfolio: perhaps grandparents can only spend half of what they normally spend on toys, electronics, and clothes for your children on holidays and birthdays, and then deposit the remaining half into the child's savings account.

To calculate and report the Kiddie Tax, use Federal Form 8615, Tax for Certain Children Who Have Unearned Income. You will need to include the parent(s)' taxable income, Capital Gains, and other information on the child's Form 8615, in order to calculate the Kiddie Tax. A draft of the parent(s)' income tax return must be completed first in order to have the information needed to complete the child's Form 8615. It is an option to include the Form 8615 on the parent(s)' income tax return, instead of the child's, to avoid the child even having to file a Federal income tax return. But, I never opt for this choice, because the child must still file a state income tax return in most states and thus a Federal tax return is needed in order to file a state tax return.

Limits on Gifts

Each person can gift up to $14K ✈ annually to another person, without filing a Gift Tax Return (this is the 2014 and 2015 limit). A married couple can each give another person $14K annually, for a total of $28K. For purposes of shifting assets to your children to capitalize on their lower income tax rates, I don't recommend gifting more than the annual gift limitation.

Effect of a Working Child and Unearned Income on Kiddie Tax

My son, Troy, loves athletic shoes, the ones designed or endorsed by famous basketball players. Troy owns more than a dozen pair of these expensive athletic shoes, and I refuse to let him buy anymore until he needs a larger size. Troy is considering starting a business where he buys and sells used high-cost tennis shoes to kids at school and on the internet. He's shown me where there is a market for these used designer athletic shoes. Since both I and Troy's father have our own businesses, Troy has learned a lot about running a business, even though he's just twelve years old.

If a child is working, it does change the Kiddie Tax calculation a bit. No matter if the child is self-employed, or is an employee, the child's Standard Deduction ✒ increases to be equal to his or her earned income plus an additional $350 ✈, but not to exceed $6,300 ✈ in total for 2015.

The calculation for the Kiddie Tax starts with the child's unearned income, but does include a line for total taxable income. You just want to make sure you understand the definitions Unearned Income and Earned Income, so that you get the best result on your Kiddie Tax calculation.

Unearned income is earnings from interest, dividends, Capital Gains, rental income, royalties, or anything that is not due to an active participation in the activity.

Earned income is earnings from self-employment or a job, or from active participation in a partnership or corporation. A child's earned income above the designated level does not get taxed at the parents' higher income tax rates; only the unearned, portfolio income is subjected to the Kiddie Tax rules.

Marriage of Young Adult

If a young adult who is otherwise subject to the Kiddie Tax marries, and files a joint return with their spouse, then the Kiddie Tax is no longer applicable. (Encouraging your children to marry at a young age is NOT a tax planning move! I mention this for the one person that will email me and ask.)

Chapter Summary

Use the Kiddie Tax rules to your family's advantage, by protecting portfolio income up to $2,100 for 2015 ✈ per child per year from the parents' higher income tax rates. Learn about Income Shifting and Gifting to set your plan in place to save income tax on portfolio income, and use the Kiddie Tax rules to help you pay minimal income tax on the portfolio income. There are limits to the amount of gifts one can give per recipient, before an annual gift tax return must be filed. Kiddie Tax may still apply to working children, if they are under age 18 (or under age 24 for full time students), but the Kiddie Tax is no longer applicable once they marry. The Kiddie Tax rules can help a family reduce income tax on portfolio (unearned) income. I hope you use the resulting income tax savings for important family needs.

IRS Form 8615, Tax for Certain Children Who Have Unearned Income, is used to calculate the Kiddie Tax.

Chapter 14
Which Will Net You the Better Tax Advantage: Dependent Care Benefit or Dependent Care Credit?

> ### Chapter 14 Trail Route
> - Dependent Care Benefit 👍
> - Dependent Care Credit ❖
> - Strategy on which to use, or a combination of both

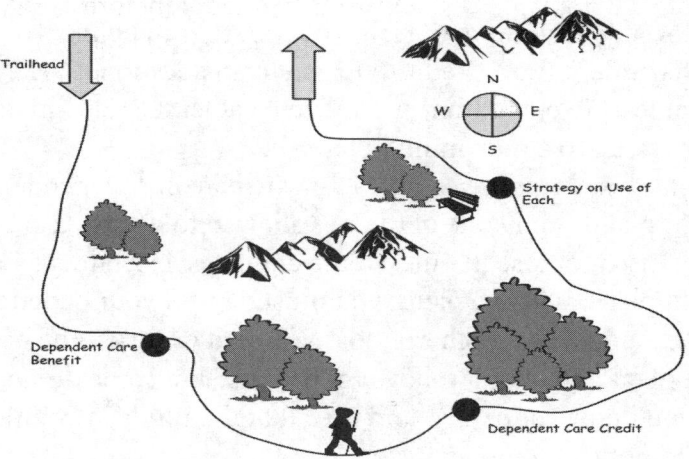

Daycare expenses can be excessive, a huge part of a family's budget. Daycare dollars flow out of parents' pockets like water drains from a bucket with holes in it. Because of the excessive cost, parents want to make the most of the income tax laws so daycare dollars go further. My four kids were born (and adopted at birth) within a span of six years, so daycare dollars rolled out of our account in very large amounts for many years; for several years in a row, our annual daycare expense exceeded $22K!

Daycare-Related Benefits

The two tax benefits related to daycare are so similar in name, it's important to make a distinction:

Dependent Care Benefits 👍

Funds deducted from an employee's pay on a pretax basis, up to a maximum of $5K ✈ per year, are set aside in an employer account to reimburse for or pay dependent care costs. This benefit is in effect a Tax Deduction 👍 because the funds reduce taxable income that is shown on an employee's Form W-2 issued after each year-end. The benefit is calculated on the lesser of each spouse's earned income, the amount placed into the plan, or the amount actually incurred for daycare costs.

If you maximize use of a Dependent Care Benefit 👍 for the total allowable amount of $5K ✈, you are still be eligible to calculate the Dependent Care Credit ❖ for up to an additional $1K, if you have at least two children, and incurred at least $5,001 in daycare expenses, up to a maximum of $6K ✈.

If both spouses are eligible to participate in a Dependent Care Benefit plan 👍, only one of them is allowed to do so. Also beware of any "use it or lose it" rules of the employer Dependent Care Benefit plans. In some plans, you must deplete your dependent care account before each calendar year end or forfeit the balance. Some plans allow for a rollover of benefits, but some do not. Make sure you know your rules, and use all of the funds in your account, so as to not waste money.

Dependent Care Credit ❖

There is an Income Tax Credit for dependent care (daycare) costs paid, also called the Daycare Credit ❖ or Childcare Credit ❖. The credit is 20% ✈ (for middle-income households) of the daycare costs paid on up to $6K of daycare expenses for two children (only $3K if you have just one child), and is not applicable for a quantity of children in excess of two. If the parents make less than $6K per year (or $3K for just one child), the Daycare Credit ❖ is calculated on the lesser-earning parent's earned income from a job or self-employment. Since this is an Income Tax Credit, this is a dollar-for-dollar offset of Federal income tax.

The Dependent Care Credit ❖ is based on the percentage applicable to each income level, but since this book is directed to middle-income families, and the applicable percentage is 20% for those with income over $43K ✈, we'll only mention that percentage, and assume the percentages for incomes lower than $43K are not applicable for readers of this book. There is no income phase-out for the Dependent Care Credit.

What Strategy Should You Use?

Before parents can make a decision on whether to take the Dependent Care Benefit ☙ or the Dependent Care Credit ❖, they need to know their marginal income tax rate, which will help determine which of the benefits will give them a larger tax break.

So what is a marginal tax rate? Every new dollar of income is taxed at your marginal income tax rate (also referred to as marginal income tax bracket). The Wikipedia definition at the side is good, but to state it in a more concise way, Marginal Tax Rate refers to the tax rate that is applied to every new dollar of income.

> *Marginal tax rate as defined by Wikipedia is: the tax rate that applies to the last (or next) unit of the tax base (taxable income). In plain English, the marginal tax rate is the tax percentage on the highest dollar earned. For example, in the United States, the top marginal tax rate is 39.6%, but that rate applies only to earnings over (approximately) $400K per year; earnings under (approximately)$400K have a lower tax rate of 35% or less.*

Example 1

For purposes of determining your personal solution to this issue, let's assume you have one child, your marginal income tax rate is 28% for Federal purposes and 6% for state purposes, and both spouses work and earn at least $3K per year.

Dependent Care Benefit ☙ (through employer)
$5K maximum benefit x (28% Federal marginal rate + 6% state marginal rate) = tax benefit of $1,700.

Dependent Care Credit ❖
20% credit x $3K (for 1 child) = tax benefit of $600.

In this circumstance, it's more beneficial to use the Dependent Care Benefit ☙ through the employer. The reasoning for this result is that the Dependent Care Credit is limited to 20% of only $3K (since there is only one child), while the Dependent Care Benefit ☙ is based on the combined marginal tax rate, which is higher than the 20% credit, and is based on the total benefit of $5K, not just based on the $3K maximum of Daycare Credit ❖.

Example 2

Now let's assume there are two children, the parents' marginal tax rate is 15% for Federal and 6% for state, and the parents both earn greater than $6K per year.

Dependent Care Benefit ☙ (through employer)
$5K maximum benefit x (15% Federal marginal rate + 6% state marginal rate) = $1,050.

Dependent Care Credit ❖
20% credit x $6K (for 2 children) = tax benefit of $1,200.

So in this second example, it is more beneficial to take the Dependent Care Credit ❖. The difference between these two examples is that when there is only one child, the Dependent Care Credit ❖ can only based on a maximum of $3K, not the $6K for two children. Also, when the marginal tax rate differs from the 20% Dependent Care Credit ❖ rate, it changes the final answer. Every family's answer is dependent (pun unintended!) on their circumstances related to the number of eligible children, income level, and whether both parents are working.

Look at the chart on the following page, and if you can find a column that is similar to your family situation, you won't have to do your own calculations on which child care tax benefit is more advantageous for you:

Are both parents (or a single parent not filing jointly) making >$3K for 1 child or >$6K for 2+ children	Yes	Yes	Yes	Yes	Yes	Yes
# of children	1	2	1	2	1	2
Total income >$43K	Yes	Yes	Yes	Yes	Yes	Yes
Marginal tax rate (Federal + state combined)	21%	21%	30%	30%	34%	34%
Amount of Dependent Care (DC) Benefit♦ available through employer	$5K	$5K	$5K	$5K	$5K	$5K
Tax benefit of DC Credit•	20% x $3K = $600	20% x $6K = $1,200	20% x $3K = $600	20% x $6K = $1,200	20% x $3K = $600	20% x $6K = $1,200
Tax benefit of DC Benefit♦ thru Employer	21% x $5K = $1,050	21% x $5K = $1,050 plus you can still take the Dependent Care Credit• on the last $1,000 for an add'l $200 benefit, for a total of $1,250	30% x $5K = $1,500	30% x $5K = $1,500 plus you can still take the Dependent Care Credit• on the last $1,000 for an add'l $200 benefit, for a total of $1,700	34% x $5K = $1,700	34% x $5K = $1,700 plus you can still take the Dependent Care Credit• on the last $1,000 for an add'l $200 benefit, for a total of $1,900
Which provides better tax savings?	DC Benefit♦	DC Benefit♦ and DC Credit• for the last $1,000	DC Benefit♦	DC Benefit♦ and DC Credit• for the last $1,000	DC Benefit♦	DC Benefit♦ and DC Credit• for the last $1,000

So, why bother doing all of these calculations? Because you want the best personal income tax advantage as possible, so you can save your dollars for your precious family! The largest savings in the above table is $1,900 annually, and that's a huge savings that a family can use for a family vacation, retirement savings, or to fund college savings accounts.

Chapter Summary

Consider whether you should be taking the Dependent Care Benefits 👆 (through your employer) or use the Dependent Care Credit ❖ (on your income tax return), based on the number of children you have and your combined Federal and state marginal income tax rates. Dependent Care Benefits 👆 are for an unlimited number of children, but for only up to $5K ✈ in annual daycare costs. The Dependent Care Credit ❖ is for either 1 or 2 children only, up to $6K ✈ in annual daycare costs. For both of these income tax benefits, both spouses listed on the income tax return (or a single or Head of Household filer) must have earned income that equals or exceeds $3K for 1 child or $6K for 2 children. You can prepare a calculation like that shown in this chapter in order to determine which of these Dependent Care income tax savings, or a combination of both, are best for you and your family.

IRS Form 2441 is used to calculate the Dependent Care Credit and to report Dependent Care Benefits.

Chapter 15
Adoption Credit: Make the Difference in the Life of a Child, and Earn a Tax Credit Along the Way

> ### Chapter 15 Trail Route
> - Adoption Credit ❖
> - Employer-Provided Adoption Benefits 👆

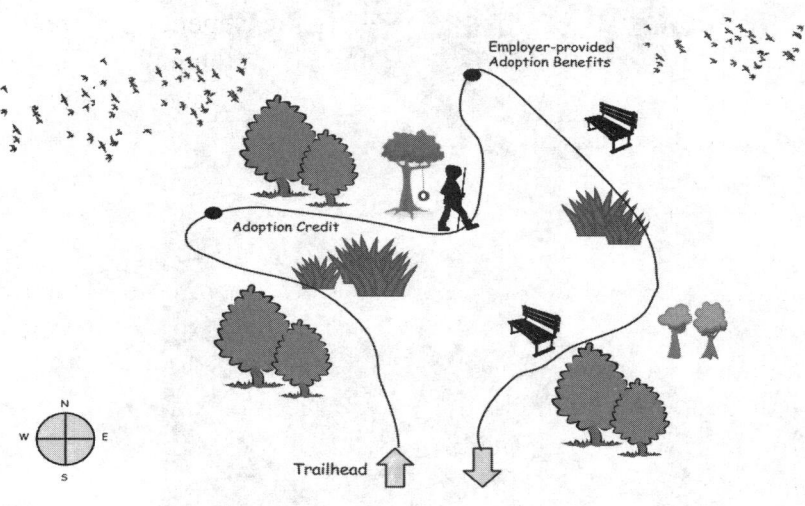

I couldn't wait to write this chapter. My four children are adopted and the subject is of primary importance to me and my family. This book isn't about the adoption process; regardless, I can never pass up an opportunity to thank the brave birth moms that carried these children for 9 months, knowing someone else would be parenting them. My kids all came to us as newborns and are aged twelve through nineteen as this book goes to print, and the joy they bring to life is immense. The stress can be intense, but thank goodness, usually short-lived. They are four fabulous young people, just at the beginning of finding their way in this world, and I'm delighted I am able to parent them through it.

There's an Adoption Credit ❖ (dollar-for-dollar reduction of

Federal income tax), as this chapter is titled, and some employers provide Employer-Provided Adoption Benefits ☙that are income tax-free. I'll go through each of these adoption tax benefits.

Adoption Tax Benefits

Adoption Credit ❖

For a foreign adoption, the Adoption Credit ❖ is taken in the year the adoption is final, or the year costs are incurred, if after. Note that for a foreign adoption to be finalized outside of the United States, the foreign country must file a final decree of adoption or the Secretary of State will issue a Hague Adoption Certificate; you will need to seek the advice of an attorney familiar with foreign adoption. If a foreign adoption is finalized within the borders of the United States, then similar to a domestic adoption, the adoption is final when a court issues a final adoption decree.

Adoption Credit ❖ specifics ✈
- The amount of the Adoption Credit applies to up to $13,400 in adoption expenses per child for 2015;
- The adoption costs incurred may span over more than one year;
- Qualified Adoption Expenses include agency fees, legal fees, court costs, travel, meals away from home, etc.;
- Qualified Adoption Expenses specifically exclude surrogate parenting arrangements, cost of adopting a spouse's child, expenses paid or reimbursed by an employer, expenses that violate state or Federal law, and costs otherwise allowed as a Tax Credit or Tax Deduction;
- To be able to take the Adoption Credit ❖ for a special needs child, you need not have actually incurred Qualified Adoption Expenses; you take a Credit ❖ for the maximum allowable, $13,400 for 2015, even if your actual costs are less or none;
- The Adoption Credit phases out beginning at $201,010 of total income (Adjusted Gross Income) for 2015 and is completely phased out at $241,010 of total income, and this applies to the year that the Adoption Credit ❖ is earned;
- The Credit ❖ can be carried forward for a total of 5 years, if not used in the year it is earned;
- The Adoption Credit may offset AMT & regular tax;
- For a domestic adoption, you take the Adoption Credit in the year the adoption is final (when a court issues a final adoption decree), even if some of the costs were incurred in a previous year;
- Costs of an unsuccessful adoption are added to the cost of the subsequent successful adoption, and taken in the year the successful adoption is final; and
- If you incur Qualified Adoption Costs in the year following when your adoption is final, and have not exceeded the per child limit, you can claim those costs in the year they are incurred.

Employer-Provided Adoption Benefits 👍
(also called Adoption Benefit Exclusion)

Employers may pay for adoption expenses incurred by their employees, or they may reimburse the employee. The income phase-out for these benefits is the same as for the Adoption Credit ❖; tax-free status of these benefits phases out beginning at $201,010 of total income (Adjusted Gross Income) for 2015 and is completely phased out at $241,010 of total income. These benefits are excludable 👍 from income if you qualify.

Both the Adoption Credit ❖ and
the Employer-Provided Adoption Benefits 👍

Both of these benefits can be claimed for the same adoption (but not for the same expenses), and both are limited to $13,400 ✈ for 2015. (For example, if you incurred $26,800 in Qualified Adoption Expenses, and your employer reimbursed the maximum allowable of $13,400 ✈, you would still be eligible to take the Adoption Credit ❖ on the remaining $13,400.)

An eligible child, for purposes of these two adoption tax benefits, must be under age 18 when the expenses were incurred, or is physically or mentally unable to care for herself.

Jim and Allison are clients in my private practice. They adopted four special needs children, and at the same time Allison stopped working, so taxable income decreased. On the next page, you will find a table that shows the income tax effect of the adoptions that the court finalized at the end of 2013 and the related Adoption Credit ❖.

	2013	2014
Jim & Allison's taxable income (Allison not working in 2014)	$170,000	$105,000
Federal Tax	$34,000	$16,000
Adoption Credit ❖ (non- refundable, but carries forward for up to 5 years if not completely used in the year the credit is earned)	($34,000)	($16,000)
Resulting Federal Tax	$0	$0
Adoption Credit ❖ remaining at the end of 2013 ($12,970 x 4), less $34K credit used	$17,880	
Adoption Credit ❖ remaining at the end of 2014 ($17,880 from the end of 2013, less $16,000 used in 2014)		$1,880

As you can see, Jim and Allison didn't use all of the Adoption Credit ❖ in 2013, and have a carry forward of Adoption Credit ❖ for use in 2014 and 2015.

Now let's look at an example and assume Jim and Allison made use of both the Employer-Provided Adoption Benefits 👍 and the Adoption Credit ❖. If we assume the employer benefit is $5K per adopted child, their revised table would look like this:

	2013	2014
Jim & Allison's taxable income before employer-provided adoption benefit 👍 (Allison not working in 2014)	$170,000	$105,000
Employer-provided adoption benefit 👍 (employer paid adoption expenses directly to adoption agency, 4 children x $5,000 per child)	($20,000)	-
Jim & Allison's taxable income	$150,000	$105,000
Federal Tax	$29,000	$16,000
Adoption Credit (non-refundable, but carries forward for up to 5 years if not completely used in year the credit is earned)	($29,000)	($16,000)
Resulting Federal Tax	$0	$0
Adoption Credit remaining at the end of each year	$22,880	$6,880

Chapter Summary

If you are adopting, you will want to see if you qualify for the Adoption Credit ❖ ($13,400 ✈ maximum for 2015) or Employer-Provided Adoption Benefits ☙ (also $13,400 ✈ maximum for 2015), to help offset your adoption expenses. If you adopt a special needs child, you are eligible to receive the Adoption Credit ❖, regardless of whether or not you incurred adoption costs. The unused portion of an Adoption Credit ❖ carries forward for up to 5 future years, and foreign adoptions are also eligible for the Adoption Credit ❖. There is an income phase out relative to the Adoption Credit ❖ and Employer-Provided Adoption Benefits ☙ based on filing status, and costs of an unsuccessful adoption can be added to the cost of a subsequent successful adoption, for use in calculating the adoption tax benefits. If you are growing your family by adoption, you should take advantage of the adoption income tax savings benefits; you'll need the extra money until they're grown, believe me!

> IRS Form 8839 is used to calculate The Adoption Credit and to report Employer-Provided Adoption Benefits.

If you haven't been able to adopt a child yet, I wish you the patience of a saint, and hope your family plans work out beautifully, as mine have.

Chapter 16
Force Uncle Sam to Help Pay for College

> ### Chapter 16 Trail Route
> - Savings bond interest exclusion 👍
> - 529 college savings plans 👍
> - Education savings accounts 👍
> - American Opportunity Credit ❖
> - Lifetime Learning Credit ❖
> - IRA withdrawals to pay for college expenses
> - Tuition & Fees Deduction 👍
> - Scholarships & grants 👍
> - Discounted tuition 👍
> - Employer education assistance 👍
> - Student loan interest deduction 👍

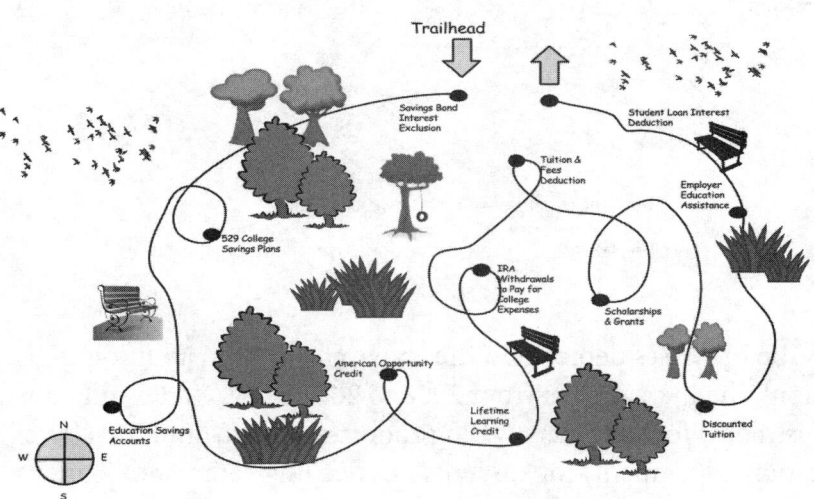

When my four kids were toddlers and preschoolers, I would often open the back of the minivan, dump four or five baskets of clean laundry into it, and then have the kids drive their tricycles and "vehicles" on the driveway, so I could fold the laundry without "help." As intimidating as the mountain of laundry was, I was even more intimidated by the cost of educating all of these little people. I thought of their future often, when I saw them driving around in their little vehicles with so much life and confidence.

You may have, or will have, a college-bound child, and while you may want to help with the financial aspects of their college venture, you want to do that as cost effectively as possible. College costs are rising at alarming rates; news stories about this may make you cringe. According to The College Board, the inflation-adjusted cost of a public four-year college has increased as follows from the 1973-1974 school year to the 2013-2014 school year:

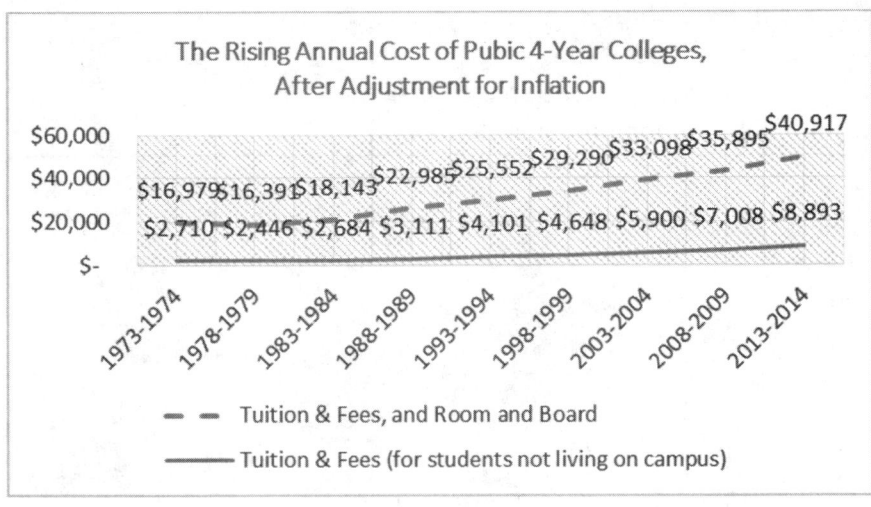

The increases depicted in the above chart are in addition to inflation! The increase just from 2008 to 2013 is 14% (after inflation adjustment) for students needing room and board, and 27% (after inflation adjustment) for students not needing room and board. This information is hopefully convincing enough that you need all the help you can get, to assist with paying for your child's college education.

Because our economy has been tight over the past few years, more students are staying in college because they haven't been able to land a position in their chosen career field. That means more students are competing for grants and scholarships than ever. On top of that, college-aged kids are having a harder time finding part-time jobs to help with college expenses, causing these young adults frustration. Paying for college is a big issue for almost every student and their family.

Saving for college expenses should begin early, even during your future student's infancy. Folks who wait until the year before college begins to save for their child or loved one are stressed and can be financially strapped. Removing the financial stress of college allows the student and family to focus on making a good college selection. Putting funds away monthly over the years will become routine, and not be as large of a financial drain, as compared to funding college semester by semester. Lastly, investing funds early gives the funds time to grow and compound. So start that college savings account early for a better overall result. If you establish a habit of saving, it will become routine and less painful.

Every Halloween, my kids were so trained about the "Mom Tax" I initiated, where they would hand over their Hershey chocolate bars (no almonds) to me after they went trick-or-treating, that they would bring them to me as soon as they got home, without me even asking. Too bad, this year all of my kids will be too old to trick-or-treat! You can make saving for college as automatic as the "Mom Tax" proved to be for my kids. If it's included in your monthly cash budget, it will become routine and automatic.

If your children are older, it's still not too late to start saving for their college. Sure, we all wish we could change our actions (or inaction) from the past, but you can start now, and that will be much better than taking no action at all.

The interest-compounding concept is best seen in pictures; see graph on next page. After saving $200 per month for 10 years, your contributions will total $24K, but with 6% interest and compounding, the account will be worth $32,940. After saving $200 per month for 18 years, your contributions will total $43,200, but with 6% interest and compounding, the account will be worth $77,858. Interest compounding will help you increase the college savings exponentially.

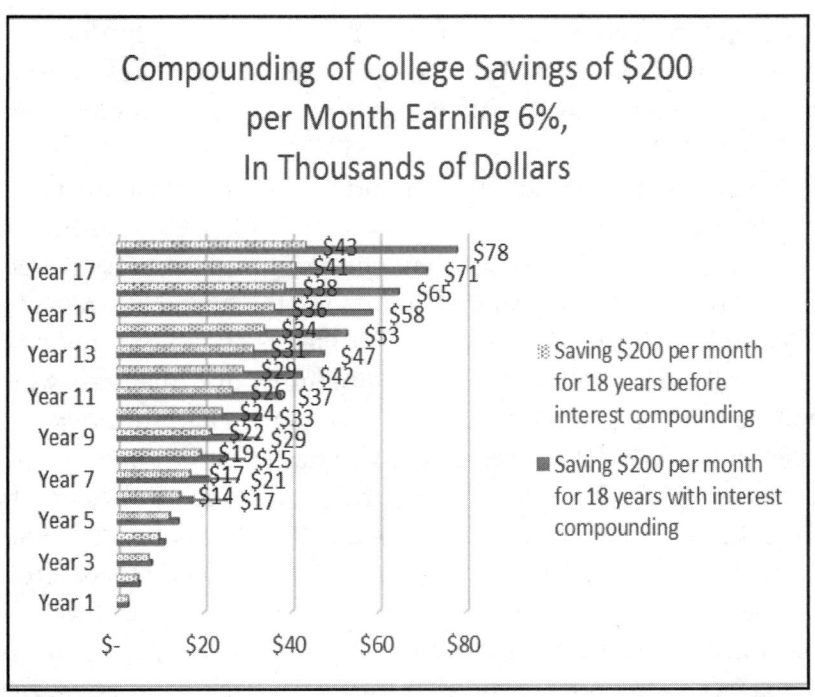

To help organize the various college education income tax benefits, this chapter is organized into categories based on when they need to be considered: Before College, During College, and After College. This will allow you to focus on the category that fits your needs at the present time and then you can refer back to this chapter as your student progresses.

As the various college income tax benefits are discussed, keep in mind the income phase-out levels that are shown. A phase-out refers to the reduced eligibility of use of an Income Tax Deduction 👍 or Income Tax Credit ❖ as income rises. Each Tax Deduction 👍 and Tax Credit ❖ has its own phase out thresholds.

Before College

Savings Bond Interest Exclusion 👍

A savings bond is a debt security issued by the U.S. government that pays interest at maturity to the purchaser. When you think of savings bonds, you may be thinking of your grandparents' stash of paper savings bonds, they likely kept hidden behind the laundry detergent, in the cupboard, in a coffee can, or likely even in a mattress. Family members who knew about these hidden spots likely begged your grandparents to use a safety deposit box, but your grandparents likely held strong to their principles. But electronic savings bonds can now be purchased at banks, and they can be a huge help with college savings.

If a person bought a savings bond every time they got paid, that could build up quite a savings over time. The sooner you begin saving with savings bonds, the more time the bonds will have to grow and compound. See the box on page 125 for specifics on the Savings Bond Interest Exclusion.

Qualified Tuition Program 👍
(widely known as a 529 College Savings Plan)

A well-intentioned father in my private practice said to me, "I cashed in $8K of my IRA and bought a 529 for my daughter, Sara." He obviously felt good about making this contribution to his daughter's future.

"But Dave," I said, "you're under age 59½. You will owe a 10% penalty on pulling money out of a retirement plan."

"What? But I invested in a college savings plan."

I explained, "OK, but you will end up paying income tax plus the 10% early withdrawal penalty on that money. That will only be partially offset by the Missouri Income Tax Deduction 👍 of 6% for contributing to a 529 plan." Not all states allow an Income Tax Deduction 👍 for college savings plan contributions.

Dave should have checked with me before making such a big move. I do like Qualified Tuition Programs, but they should not be funded out of a retirement plan where income tax and penalty will be due upon withdrawal.

Many taxpayers limit their contribution to a 529 college savings plan to (a) the amount of the annual allowable state Income Tax Deduction 👍 or (b) the amount of the annual Federal Gift Tax Exclusion ($14K ✈ for 2014 and 2015). See the box on page 126 for specifics on Qualified Tuition Programs.

Education Savings Account (ESA) 👍

This education savings account is less popular than the Qualified Tuition Plan discussed above, because the annual contribution is limited to $2K ✈ and you cannot change the beneficiary.

There are a couple small niche uses for this plan. It is the only education plan that is eligible not only for college expenses, but also for use in paying for private school for kindergarten through twelfth grade. Additionally, this plan allows contributions for a special needs person of any age. See the box on page 127 for specifics on Education Savings Accounts.

Clients often ask, "Should I save for my kids' college education OR my retirement?" Parents want to do the right thing, and are often torn on this issue, because they cannot afford to fund both of these needs. However, because retirement funds can be tapped without penalty for use for a dependent's college education, and because (non-Roth) retirement plan contributions have a much larger Income Tax Deduction 👍 associated with them, I suggest not funding the college savings accounts each year until your annual retirement contributions have been fully funded.

Get the Kids Involved!

Can you imagine third graders comparing their portfolio strategies for their college savings accounts? "Billy, do you think my college savings accounts will be adequate?"

"I don't know, but I think you're a little ahead of me."

"Grandpa keeps telling my parents to move me into the market, that I have a long way to go before I need to tap the funds."

"I'm only 50% in the market, hoping to be all in next time there's a dip."

Perhaps high school students could get more involved in their college savings. How about a project for an accounting class demonstrating the compounding of interest? How about a psychology project on investment styles in comparison to personality types. How about a fundraiser for college?

While I don't foresee these things happening in the short term,

I ask, "Why not?" The kids are tomorrow's leaders. Perhaps they should be more involved in the financing of their futures.

During College

In a recent tax strategy meeting with new clients, they explained that all three of their kids are in college now, and so we explored how we can use the maximum amount of college education tax benefits.

Tom, the father, asked, "If we use the College Education Credit ❖ for our oldest, Tom Jr., can we still use a Tax Credit for Katy and for Kendra? His expenses are the highest."

I explained, "Yes, I believe we can work it out. We just can't use the same education expenses more than once for the same child or for the same credit."

My wheels started turning. Tom and Sandra, who file Married Filing Joint, expect to have total income of $105K for 2015, very similar to 2014, and they are not subject to Alternative Minimum Tax. They are expected to be in the 25% Federal income tax bracket and the 6% state income tax bracket.

Tom Jr., the oldest child, is in law school, so I'm certain he can no longer use the American Opportunity Credit ❖, having already completed his undergraduate degree. The Lifetime Learning Credit ❖ is an option, as well as the Tuition and Fees Deduction ☝. The Lifetime Learning Credit ❖ limit is per taxpayer (limit of one for the whole family), but this isn't a barrier for this family, because only Tom Jr. will be interested in that credit (the girls still qualify for the more favorable American Opportunity Credit ❖ because they are still in their first four years of college). Tom Jr.'s Qualified Education Expenses for 2015 are expected to be $28K.

Katy and Kendra are both in the first four years of college, both still working on their bachelor's degrees. For them, the American Opportunity Credit ❖ and the Tuition and Fees Deductions ☝ are both options. The American Opportunity Credit ❖ is on a per-student basis, so both girls' college expenses would be eligible for this credit. Katy and Kendra's Qualified Education Expenses for 2015 are expected to be $12K and $5,500, respectively.

"Let's talk about Tom Jr.'s college tax benefits first. He's eligible for either the Lifetime Learning Credit ❖ or the Tuition and Fees Deduction ♠, however, taking the Lifetime Learning Credit ❖ is to your advantage because the tax benefit would be $2K (maximum eligible expenses of $10K x 20%). If we instead take the Tuition and Fees Deduction♠, the tax benefit would only be $1,240 (maximum of $4K in eligible expenses x 31% combined Federal and state marginal income tax rates)."

Tom and Sandra nodded, "OK, how about the girls?"

"Those smart girls are eligible for the American Opportunity Credit ❖ or the Tuition and Fees Deduction ♠," I said, "but the Tuition and Fees Deduction ♠ is limited to $4K per tax return, so only one of them could take it. Under the American Opportunity Credit ❖, the combined tax benefit is a total of $5K, and if one of the girls takes the American Opportunity Credit ❖, and the other takes the Tuition and Fees Deduction ♠, then the total benefit is only $3,740 ($2,500 for the American Opportunity Credit ❖ for one of the girls plus $4K x 31% combined Federal and state income tax rate). So, we should stick with the American Opportunity Credit ❖ for both girls."

Sandra was very happy with the analysis. "OK, um, well we didn't include the sorority fees. Will we get more refund back if we include those?"

I said, "No, I'm sorry, we took advantage of the maximum allowable Qualified Education Expenses already, so more expenses wouldn't be helpful. And the sorority fees aren't Qualified Education Expenses."

"OK, I thought I'd try. I want to go back to school too. Are we pushing it if we take Education Credits ❖ for me too?"

I said, "No, I really don't think that's pushing it. It's completely allowable, and you would have the supporting documentation. OK, so the grand total of the education tax benefits we expect for 2015 is $7K. $2K for Tom Jr. and $2,500 for each of the girls."

All I saw from Tom and Sandra was relief and smiles when they heard they would be getting $7K in college Tax Credits ❖. In the end, we amended the previous two years' income tax return, because their family-friend-preparer failed to include college Tax Credits on their previous income tax returns, and this brought them additional refunds totaling over $8K.

American Opportunity Credit ❖

This education tax benefit is among the most common and it's a partially refundable Tax Credit, which means it is a dollar-for-dollar reduction of income tax, that is at least partially eligible to be refunded to the taxpayer when the Tax Credit exceeds the income tax liability. Most Tax Credits are not refundable.

Also, you can only take one of the education Tax Credits for the same student, either the American Opportunity Credit, or the Lifetime Learning Credit, as discussed later, but not both.

If the student has earned income, and can use this American Opportunity Education Credit ❖ on his or her own income tax return, the credit can be moved over to the student's tax return if the parents' forego claiming the student as an exemption on their tax return (but that doesn't mean the student may take his own exemption if he/she doesn't otherwise qualify). See Chapter 11 for discussion of the Support Test, and who is eligible to take a child's exemption.

Christy and her parents are clients of mine in my private practice, and Christy is in college, working toward a bachelor's degree in business. She's a bundle of energy, and works full time during summers, at a fireworks stand, and as a waitress at a local restaurant. Christy works part-time during the school year. Christy's parents, Nedra and Ted, provide more than half of Christy's support, and Nedra and Ted are subject to Alternative Minimum Tax (AMT) and their income is too high to take an Education Income Tax Credit ❖. As discussed in Chapter 23, if you are subject to Alternative Minimum Tax, your personal exemptions do not lower your total Federal income tax liability, and thus are not helpful to reduce Federal income tax.

Nedra and Ted do not claim Christy on their income tax return, so that Christy is allowed to take her own American Opportunity Credit ❖. On the following page is an excerpt of the projection I prepared for Christy and her parents for this year:

	Nedra and Ted	Christy
Adjusted gross income	$180,000	$15,300
Itemized deductions ☙	($26,500)	N/A
Standard Deduction ☙	N/A	($6,300)
Exemptions (helpful portion only)	N/A (Nedra and Ted are subject to AMT, so the exemptions are not helpful	N/A (Christy does not provide more than half of her own support, so does not receive her own exemption)
Taxable income	$153,500	$9,000
Tax liability, including AMT	$33,900	$900
Nonrefundable portion of American Opportunity Credit ❖	N/A	($900) (Limited to the income tax liability)
Refundable portion of American Opportunity Credit ❖ (up to 40% of total credit)	N.A	($1,000)

By allowing Christy to take her own American Opportunity Credit ❖, it not only saved her $900 in income tax that she would have otherwise owed, but also allowed her a $1K income tax refund, for a total benefit of $1,900. The cost to the parents totaled zero for Federal income tax purposes, but they did lose her state Income Tax Deduction, which cost them $72 (in Missouri), which they agreed to forego, so that Christy could receive the $1,900 benefit.

Christy said, "Mom, I'll write you a check for $72 when I get my refund."

Nedra just patted her hand, "That's not necessary." Nedra and Ted are so proud of their hard-working and considerate daughter. See the box on page 128 for specifics on the American Opportunity Credit.

Lifetime Learning Credit ❖

This education tax benefit is also one of the most common and is a credit ❖ (meaning a dollar-for-dollar offset of Federal income tax), not just a Tax Deduction 👍 (which reduces the taxable income that is subject to income tax).

If the student has earned income, and can use this Lifetime Learning Education Credit ❖ on his or her own income tax return, the credit can be moved over to the student's tax return, if the parents' forego claiming the student as an exemption on their income tax return (but that doesn't mean the student may take his own exemption if he/she doesn't otherwise qualify). See Chapter 11 for discussion of the Support Test, and who is eligible to take a child's exemption. See the box on page 129 for specifics on the Lifetime Learning Credit.

IRA Withdrawals to Pay For College Expenses

Think back to my client, Dave, and his young daughter, Sara, that I discussed in the Qualified Tuition Program area of this chapter. Dave pulled out retirement funds to contribute to a Qualified Tuition Program for Sara, and I broke the news to Dave that he would be subject to a 10% early withdrawal penalty because he was under age 59½. Well, this is how I would have preferred that whole conversation to have gone:

Dave could have said, "Lisa, I'm considering withdrawing $8K from my retirement plan to contribute to a college savings plan for Sara."

I would then say, "Oh, let's think about that for a minute...did you know you can withdraw from an IRA for college education expenses and be exempt from the 10% early withdrawal penalty?"

Dave would have nodded, wanting more information.

I would continue, "Dave, if you pull money out of your retirement plan, you'll pay income tax and the 10% penalty on those funds now. Why don't you keep the funds in the retirement plan. Then when you need them for Sara's college expenses, then take the funds out. That way, you postpone paying the income tax and you completely escape the 10% penalty. This will save you $3,520 in income tax and penalty this year."

If only Dave had given me a call, he would have saved $3,520. See the box on page 130 for specifics on IRA withdrawals to pay for college expenses.

Tuition & Fees Deduction 👍

This education tax benefit is an Income Tax Deduction 👍 (which reduces the taxable income that is subject to income tax). If you take the Tuition & Fees Deduction 👍, you may not take an Education Tax Credit ❖, discussed earlier.

The Tuition and Fees Deduction is part of legislation that so far has been renewed annually by Congress since its inception (instead of being a permanent deduction). This Income Tax Deduction was most recently renewed on December 19, 2014 for the year ended December 31, 2014. If you are interested in taking this deduction, check my website, www.LisaBcpa.com or check www.irs.gov to make sure it has been renewed for the tax year in which you want to take it. See the box on page 131 for specifics on the Tuition & Fees Deduction.

Scholarships and Grants 👍

I was the typical busy teen. I worked at a Burger King, and then later as a grocery store checker. I played volleyball, was moderately social, and frustrated my parents at times. I have two older brothers, and all three of us attended college at the same time. That would frighten any parent. I applied for college scholarships and received only a couple very small ones. I remember thinking about working full time and going to college part time after high school, but then the envelope came. As I mentioned in the beginning of this book, Wal*Mart awarded me a full ride academic scholarship to the state college of my choice! See the box on page 132 for specifics on scholarships and grants.

Discounted Tuition 👍

It is common for parents of college students, and soon-to-be-college students, hold onto their jobs at universities in St. Louis, where my private tax practice is, so their children can complete their degrees in the discounted (free) tuition programs. See the box on page 132 for specifics on discounted tuition programs.

Employer Education Assistance 👍

Some folks looking for jobs seek employers that offer the education assistance program. This is of particular interest to those who cannot attend college full time after high school, but instead attend night school so they can work full time to support themselves. See the box on page 132 for specifics on Employer Education Assistance.

After College

Student Loan Interest Deduction 👍

A young physician client in my private practice has over $200K in student loan debt, and his annual income is $260K. His wife doesn't work and they have two small children. When he looked at his completed income tax return last year, he looked frustrated.

Derek said, "Why didn't you deduct my student loan interest? I really need a refund."

I responded sympathetically, "I'm sorry, but for a married person, if your income exceeds $160K for 2014, then no Student Loan Interest Deduction 👍 is allowed."

Derek took the news well enough. See the box on page 133 for specifics on the Student Loan Interest Deduction.

It's a good move for the student (and not the parents) to take out a loan (where the student is responsible for the repayment) when the repayments are not due until after graduation, at which time the parents are likely no longer taking the student as an exemption. This way, the student would be able to take the

Student Loan Interest Deduction 👍 because he/she is personally liable and his or her parents are no longer taking his dependency exemption.

If the student's parents pay the student loan interest, and the loan is in the student's name, then the payments are considered a gift to the student, so the student is still eligible to take the Student Loan Interest Deduction 👍.

Because of the income phase-outs of the Student Loan Interest Deduction 👍, a person should attempt to pay off their student loans early in their career, before their income rises above the phase-out thresholds. After a person's income is above these thresholds, the student loan interest is no longer income tax-deductible.

Savings Bond Interest Exclusion 👍 Specifics
- *Interest from Series EE bonds issued after 1989 and Series I bonds is income tax free if used for Qualified Education Expenses*
- *The Qualified Education Expenses being paid must be for the taxpayer, spouse or their dependent*
- *This benefit can be used for undergraduate or graduate programs*
- *At time of issuance, the bond owner must be at least 24 years old*
- *Qualified Education Expenses relative to Savings Bond Interest Exclusion are:*
  - *Tuition and fees,*
  - *Contributions to Qualified Tuition Programs,*
  - *Contributions to Education Savings Accounts*
- *Qualified Education Expenses relative to the Savings Bond Interest exclusion specifically exclude:*
  - *Supplies*
  - *Equipment*
  - *Room and board*
- *Income phase outs for 2015 for this benefit are*
  - *Married Filing Joint and Qualifying Widower, phase out begins at $115,750 of Adjusted Gross Income and is fully phased out at $145,750 of Adjusted Gross Income*
  - *Single and Head of Household, phase out begins at $77,200 of Adjusted Gross Income and is fully phased out at $92,200 of Adjusted Gross Income*
  - *Married Filing Separate filers are not eligible for this benefit*

Qualified Tuition Program (529 College Savings Plan) Specifics
- *Funds must be spent for the Qualified Education Expenses of the account beneficiary*
- *The beneficiary can be anyone the account owner selects and can be changed by the account owner (if the originally selected student wins scholarships, for example, and doesn't need these funds, or if they decide not to complete their college degree)*
- *Funds can be used to purchase prepaid college fees*
- *Funds can be used for undergraduate or graduate programs*
- *Contributions are non-deductible for Federal income tax purposes, but interest grows income tax free*
- *Many states allow a state Income Tax Deduction for contributions to a 529 college savings plan*
- *Contribution limit is the total amount needed to cover the beneficiary's Qualified Education Expenses*
- *Qualified Education Expenses for purposes of this program include:*
    - *Room and board, if the student attends at least half time*
    - *Tuition and fees*
    - *Books, supplies and equipment (including a laptop if required for course study)*
- *There are no income phase-outs for this benefit; anyone can qualify for this benefit, no matter how high their income*

Education Savings Account 👍 Specifics ✈
- *Contributions are non-deductible for Federal income tax purposes but interest from Education Savings Accounts grows income tax free*
- *The contribution is a maximum of $2K per year per child under age 18 and there is no age limit for a special needs child*
- *Funds can be used for kindergarten through high school, undergraduate or graduate programs*
- *Funds must be used only by the account beneficiary (who can be anyone), and there is no provision for changing the beneficiary*
- *Qualified Education Expenses for purposes of this program include:*
  - *Room and board, if the student attends at least half time*
  - *Tuition & fees*
  - *Books, supplies and equipment, if required for coursework*
  - *Contributions to a Qualified Tuition Program (described above)*
- *Income phase outs for 2014 for this benefit are:*
  - *Married Filing Joint, phase out begins at $190K of Adjusted Gross Income and is fully phased out at $220K of Adjusted Gross Income*
  - *Single, Head of Household, Qualified Widower and Married Filing Separate filers phase out begins at $95K of Adjusted Gross Income and is fully phased out at $110K of Adjusted Gross Income*
- *Plan requires mandatory distributions beginning at age 30*

American Opportunity Credit ❖ *Specifics*
- The maximum allowable credit is $2,500 per student (100% of the first $2K of Qualified Education Expenses plus 25% of the next $2K of Qualified Education Expenses)
- The credit can be taken for the taxpayer, spouse or dependent
- The credit can be used only for the first four years of undergraduate studies
- The student must be attending college at least half time, in a degree program, for this credit to be taken
- This credit is up to 40% refundable (if credit exceeds tax liability)
- Qualified Education Expenses for purposes of this program include:
  - Tuition & fees
  - Books, supplies and equipment, if required for coursework
- Income phase outs for 2015 for this benefit are:
  - Married Filing Joint, phase out begins at $160K of Adjusted Gross Income and is fully phased out at $180K of Adjusted Gross Income
  - Single, Head of Household and Qualified Widower filers, phase out begins at $80K of Adjusted Gross Income and is fully phased out at $90K of Adjusted Gross Income
  - Married Filing Separate filers are not eligible for this benefit

Lifetime Learning Credit ❖ Specifics
- *The maximum allowable credit is $2K per tax return (20% of the first $10K of Qualified Education Expenses)*
- *The credit can be taken for the taxpayer, spouse or dependent*
- *The credit can be used for undergraduate or graduate studies*
- *The credit can be taken for an unlimited number of years;*
- *This credit is not refundable, thus is not helpful unless the taxpayer has an income tax liability*
- *Qualified Education Expenses for purposes of this program include:*
  - *Tuition & fees*
  - *Books, supplies and equipment, if required for coursework and must be paid directly to the educational institution*
- *Income phase outs for 2015 for this benefit are:*
  - *Married Filing Joint, phase out begins at $110K of Adjusted Gross Income and is fully phased out at $130K of Adjusted Gross Income*
  - *Single, Head of Household and Qualified Widower filers, phase out begins at $55K of Adjusted Gross Income and is fully phased out at $65K of Adjusted Gross Income*
  - *Married Filing Separate filers are not eligible for this benefit.*

IRA Withdrawals for College Expenses Specifics
- *Withdrawals from an IRA by a taxpayer that has not attained age 59½ escape the 10% early withdrawal penalty if the funds are used to pay Qualified Education Expenses for the year in which the withdrawal occurs*
- *Funds can be used for undergraduate or graduate programs*
- *Qualified Education Expenses for purposes of this program include:*
    - *Tuition & fees*
    - *Books, supplies and equipment, if required for coursework*
    - *Room and board for a student who attends at least half time*
- *Funds can be used for the taxpayer, their spouse, their child or their grandchild*
- *There are no income phase outs for this benefit*

Tuition & Fees Deduction 👍 Specifics
- *The maximum allowable deduction is $4K of Qualified Education Expenses*
- *Deduction can be taken for the taxpayer, spouse or dependent*
- *Taxpayer can't use the same Qualified Education Expenses for the Tuition & Fees Deduction, if the expenses are already used in calculating other education credits• or benefits*
- *Qualified Education Expenses for purposes of this program include:*
    - *Tuition & fees*
    - *Books, supplies and equipment, if required for coursework and must be paid directly to the educational institution*
- *Funds can be used for undergraduate or graduate programs*
- *Benefit is not allowed for 2014 if Adjusted Gross Income before this deduction exceeds:*
    - *Married Filing Joint, $160K*
    - *Single, Head of Household and Qualified Widower filers, $80K*
    - *Married Filing Separate filers are not eligible for this benefit*

Scholarships and Grants 👍 Specifics
- *Funds received for tuition, books, supplies and/or equipment are income tax free*
- *The award can be based on academics, athletics, financial need, or other reasonable basis as determined by the donor foundation*
- *Funds for room and board ARE income taxable; and*
- *Funds received by a college student who is not seeking a college degree, no matter the use, are income taxable*

Discounted Tuition Specifics
- *If the student or their parent is an employee of the educational institution, and the student receives discounted tuition, and is an undergraduate student, then the discounted tuition is income tax free*
- *The discount tuition program must not be just for highly compensated college employees*
- *Sometimes the discounts are 100% of the tuition, and the student only has to pay for books, supplies and equipment*

Employer Education Assistance
- *Employers can provide up to $5,250 in annual assistance to an employee, and this is income tax free to the employee*
- *Coursework can be for undergraduate or graduate level classes*

Student Loan Interest Deduction Specifics
- *Up to $2,500 annually of student loan interest is income tax deductible*
- *The student loan interest must be incurred for the tax-payer, spouse or dependent*
- *Student must have attended college at least half time;*
- *Person claiming the student loan interest deduction must be legally obligated to repay the loan*
- *Interest on loans from a retirement plan, from relatives, or from other non-bank sources do not qualify for the Student Loan Interest Deduction*
- *You may not be claimed as a dependent on someone else's income tax return and still be eligible for the Student Loan Interested Deduction*
- *Income phase outs for 2014 for this benefit are:*
  - *Married Filing Joint, phase out begins at $130K of Adjusted Gross Income and is fully phased out at $160K of Adjusted Gross Income*
  - *Single, Head of Household and Qualified Widower filers, phase out begins at $65K of Adjusted Gross Income and is fully phased out at $80K of Adjusted Gross Income*
  - *Married Filing Separate filers are not eligible for this benefit*

Chapter Summary

There are numerous income tax benefits for college that can be considered during these timeframes:
- Before College: savings bond interest exclusion 👍, 529 college savings plans 👍, education savings accounts 👍;
- During College: American Opportunity Credit ❖, Lifetime Learning Credit ❖, IRA withdrawals to pay for college expenses, Tuition & Fees Deduction 👍, scholarships & grants 👍, discounted tuition 👍, and employer education assistance 👍; and
- After College: Student Loan Interest Deduction 👍.

You will need to consider each of these benefits relative to your income level and other specifics to see which benefits are advantageous to you. Your college dollars will go farther if you take advantage of the college income tax savings benefits.

> IRS Form 8863 is used to calculate Education Credits.

> IRS Form 8917 is used to calculate the Tuition and Fees Deduction.

Chapter 17
Additional Medicare Tax

> **Chapter 17 Trail Route**
> - Income thresholds for the Add'l Medicare Tax
> - Withholding to cover the Add'l Medicare Tax
> - Estimated tax payments to cover the Add'l Medicare Tax
> - Defensive moves

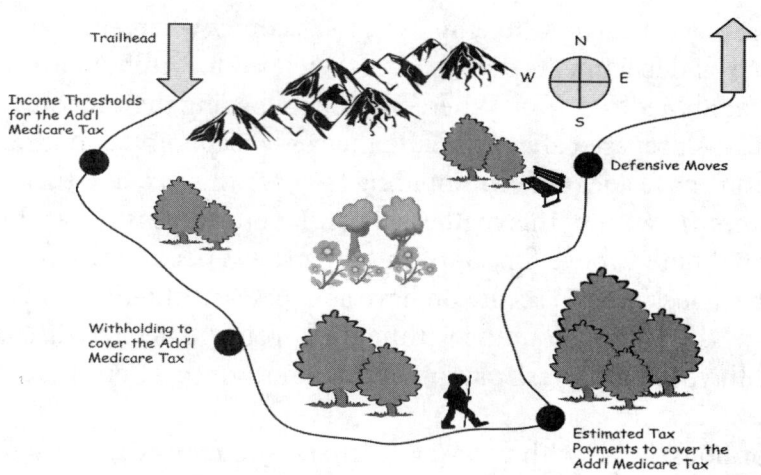

Income Thesholds for the Additional Medicare Tax

Employees earning higher wages are being hit--clobbered, actually--with an additional 0.9% Medicare Tax beginning in 2013. This additional Medicare tax also applies to self-employment income. Below is a chart of the income levels where this Additional Medicare Tax phases in and will affect you:

Filing status >>>	Married Filing Joint	Single	Head of Household	Married Filing Separate
Total income (Adjusted Gross Income)	$250,000	$200,000	$200,000	$125,000

Wages and self-employment income above the thresholds listed in this chart are subject to the Additional Medicare Tax of 0.9%.

Payroll Withholding for the Additional Medicare Tax

The biggest surprise to employed folks comes when employers' payroll departments don't realize they need to withhold for the Additional Medicare Tax. When folks begin having their income tax returns prepared after year end, they are disappointed to find they don't have adequate withholding to cover this tax, and that they weren't aware of this matter sooner. If your wage is above the threshold noted above for your filing status, you need to review your paycheck stub to see if you have adequate withholding. If you have any questions about the withholding, you will need to discuss this with your employer's payroll or human resources department, or your CPA.

For households with two wage earners, you may be at particular risk of not having enough Additional Medicare Tax withheld, if each of the wage earners on their own is not near the threshold. Employers are supposed to withhold the Additional Medicare Tax once wages exceed $200K, but if both spouses have less than $200K in earnings, they can still have over $250K of total wage income on a combined basis. In cases such as these, once the couple has their income tax return prepared, the combined income may be above the threshold, and there may not have been any withholding to cover the liability. This same situation can also surprise a person who has worked at more than one job during the year.

I received telephone calls this year, and last year, as payroll providers began withholding the Additional Medicare Tax on the applicable employees who earned incomes over $200K. Of course, the employees felt frustrated with the news of this new Additional Medicare Tax. From my communications with those affected, the fact that the Medicare system is in need of a financial boost is of no consolation.

> Employers are supposed to withhold the Additional Medicare Tax once wages exceed $200K, but if both spouses have less than $200K in earnings, they can still have over $250K of total wage income on a combined basis, and be subject to the Additional Medicare Tax.

Estimated Tax Payments to Cover the Additional Medicare Tax

For those of you that are self-employed and make quarterly estimated tax payments, you should review the amounts being paid in to see if they are adequate to cover the Additional Medicare Tax. You may need the help of your CPA in order to make this determination.

I have a single client, Tamra, who is managing her income to reduce the Additional Medicare Tax. Tamra sells computer systems and can often steer when a transaction will close, and when she will receive the related commission. At the end of last year she postponed commissions that pushed her income over $200K. She thinks this year may be a down year, and will not have earnings greater than $200K for the current year, so moving the income to the New Year made a good plan for her. Tamra saved almost $1K in Additional Medicare Tax by postponing her commissions.

Additional Medicare Tax Defensive Moves
- *Moving income from high-income years to low-income years, called Income Smoothing (which is discussed in detail in Chapter 30), so that income is less than the Additional Medicare Tax threshold for your filing status*
- *Participating in a Deferred Compensation Plan, if your employer offers such a plan*

Chapter Summary

Both employees and self-employed workers are subject to the Additional Medicare Tax of 0.9% for the amount of earned income over applicable thresholds based on filing status. You need to check your withholding or quarterly estimated tax payments to ensure you are paying in enough to cover this tax. To avoid the Additional Medicare Tax, you can use income smoothing, moving income to a lower income year, if possible. The Additional Medicare Tax is new for 2013, and hits many working families. If you manage your income to reduce or eliminate the Additional Medicare Tax, those income tax savings can be put to great use for other household needs, I'm sure.

IRS Form 8959 is used to calculate the Additional Medicare Tax.

Chapter 18
The IRS Raised The Bar, and So Must You
(Itemized Deductions 👍, Medical Expenses 👍, & Personal Exemptions 👍)

> Chapter 18 Trail Route
> - Phase out of itemized deductions 👍
> - Thresholds to deduct medical expenses 👍
> - Personal exemptions 👍 phase out

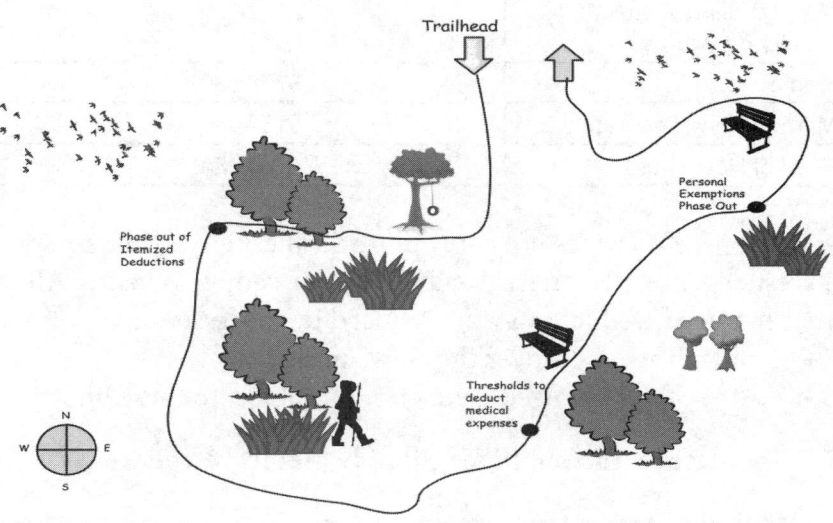

For many families, income tax time is pretty tense in their homes. Mom is running around the house, digging to find charity receipts, and Dad is adding up the medical expenses. Both are stressed, and the kids are clambering for supper. The telemarketers seem to have collaborated, because they keep calling to sell insurance and windows, and their interruptions are unwelcome. The teenage son begs to have the car for Friday night to attend some event he won't identify, and the daughter wants her school field trip permission slip signed. There's never a good time for income tax time.

The couple described above, and countless families like them, learn of three disheartening changes to income tax law that took effect for 2013, and this discourages them further.

Itemized Deductions 👍 Phase-Out

If your total income (AGI) exceeds certain levels, the total allowable Itemized Deductions 👍 are reduced. Let's look first at the 2015 income levels where the phase-out begins:

✈	Total income (Adjusted Gross Income) where phase-out begins
Married Filing Jointly or Qualifying Widower	$309,900
Single	$258,250
Married Filing Separately	$154,950
Head of Household	$284,050

The phase-out does not apply to medical expenses, investment interest expense, personal casualty losses, or gambling losses. All other Itemized Deductions👍 are reduced by the lesser of:
- 3% of the excess over the above limits, or
- 80% of the Itemized Deductions👍 subject to these limits.

Increase to Threshold for Eligible Medical Expenses 👍

Medical expenses must exceed 10% ✈ of total income (AGI) before dollar one can be deducted, for those under age 65. Since this threshold has increased from 7.5% to 10% of total income beginning in 2013, it's not a very common Itemized Deduction 👍. For folks over age 65, the threshold remains 7.5% for now. If you are nowhere near the threshold to be able to deduct Medical Expenses, you may not want to incur the time to gather that information. If you do have enough medical expenses to deduct them, you are eligible to also take auto mileage related to medical transportation at $0.23 ✈ per mile for 2015.

A couple in my private practice had a terminally ill child. The mother stayed at home and the father reduced his work schedule leading up to the passing of their daughter. Because of the father's reduced income, and the significant medical expenses, they itemized their deductions 👆 for 2013 without any phase-out, and the medical expenses exceeded 10% of the total income. Below is a snapshot of how this worked out income tax-wise for the year before and the year of their family tragedy, as well as for 2013 if the Husband had not reduced is work schedule and there had been no medical crises or medical expenses:

	2012-Actual	2013-Actual	2013*
Total income (AGI)	$355,000	$82,000	$355,000
Medical Expenses that exceed 7.5% of total income for 2012 and 10% of total income for 2013	$0	$102,000	$0
Itemized Deductions 👆 before phase-out**	$47,000	$130,000	$47,000
Itemized Deductions 👆 after phase-out	$47,000 (no phase-out was in effect for 2012)	$130,000 (no phase out due to income being below applicable level)	$45,350
Personal exemptions (Father, Mother, Child)	$11,400	$11,700	$6,552
Taxable Income	$296,600	$0	$303,098

* With no decrease in income and no medical expenses
** Not applicable for 2012, includes medical where applicable

Besides the catastrophic effect of the medical issue on the family, take note of another thing in the above table: see how the assumptions are the same for the first column and third columns. Then, see the increased taxable income for the latter of $6,498. That equates to an increase of more than $2K in income tax, had there been no medical issue, due to the phase-out of exemptions and Itemized Deductions 👆. That's a big increase for a family.

Personal Exemptions ✌ Phase-Out

If your total income (AGI) exceeds certain levels, the personal exemptions (which are worth $4K ✈ each for 2015) are reduced or eliminated. Below are the income levels where the phase-out begins and where the Personal Exemptions are completely phased out for 2015:

✈	Total income (AGI) where phase-out of Personal Exemptions begins	Total income (AGI) where Personal Exemptions are completely phased out
Married Filing Jointly or Qualifying Widower	$309,900	$432,400
Single	$258,250	$380,750
Married Filing Separately	$154,950	$216,200
Head of Household	$284,050	$406,550

See Chapter 23 about Alternative Minimum Tax (AMT), which discusses the fact that if you are subject to AMT, you are not gaining any income tax benefit from your exemptions at all. Perhaps that fact will lessen any disappointment related to the Personal Exemption phase-out.

While this book is mostly about how to take proactive steps to keep more of your money and give away less to Uncle Sam, this chapter is more in line with what to watch out for, so you are aware of how it affects your income tax return. The above three losses of deductions ✌ and exemptions ✌ are frustrating, and the best that can be done with them is to understand them, so as to not depend on these deductions ✌ more than is realistic.

Folks who don't have enough Itemized Deductions ✌ can take the Standard Deduction✌ as follows:

Filing Status	2015 Standard Deduction 👍 ✈
Married Filing Joint or Qualifying Widower	$12,600
Single	$6,300
Head of Household	$9,250
Married Filing Separately	$6,300
Dependent	$1,050

It is often a goal of taxpayers to be able to itemize their deductions 👍, because that means Uncle Sam is subsidizing their expenses, such as home ownership or charity. If you are not to the point of having enough eligible itemized deductions, consider this list. Knowing these items are deductible 👍 (within the limits discussed in this chapter) may guide you to spend your money differently:

- Medical expenses, as discussed above;
- State and City income taxes (see AMT chapter for a limitation) or Sales Tax (generally renewed annually by Congress✈);
- Real estate tax;
- Personal property tax;
- Mortgage interest (for main residence and one vacation home, and there are upper limits, see Chapter 20);
- Mortgage points;
- Mortgage insurance premiums (limitations apply);
- Investment interest expense;
- Charity (see Chapter 19);
- Casualty Losses, such as a fire or tornado (limitations apply); and
- Miscellaneous Itemized Deductions (see Chapter 21).

My client, Ruth, who is over age 65, waits each year until December to make any charitable gifts. Each even-numbered year in December, I get a call like this:

"Lisa, can you tell me if I'm itemizing this year?"

"Yes," I reply, "tell me about how much medical expense you've had for the year."

"Hardly any medical. I've been feeling really good. Oh, and I paid off that mortgage. I know you suggested I not do that, but I worry about missing a payment."

"Okay, then looks to me like you don't have enough to itemize your deductions this year, before any charity, that is."

"Okay, that's what I needed to know. Since I can't itemize, I'll push the charity into next year."

Ruth is a smart, deliberate lady. She's the wise old owl, sitting in the tree, watching and waiting. Ruth's rationale is that if she can't itemize her deductions in an even-numbered year, considering all deductions except charity, then she lumps her charity into the odd numbered years, and itemizes in the odd years only.

With the increased challenge of being able to itemize deductions, deduct medical expenses, and with the personal exemption phase-out, income tax refunds are going to be smaller, and for those who usually owe with their income tax return, the balances due are going to be larger. These three changes, beginning in 2013, have hurt a lot of pocketbooks.

Chapter Summary

There are three relatively new ways the IRS is raising your income tax burden. Itemized Deductions 👍 are subject to phase-out, based on income; medical expenses 👍 now must exceed 10% of total income for most taxpayers in order to be deductible; and Personal Exemptions 👍 are subject to phase-out based on income. You likely need to be aware of which of these higher thresholds are applicable to you and avoid them when possible, so you can save your dollars for your own needs, and not Uncle Sam's.

> IRS Schedule A is used to report Itemized Deductions.

Chapter 19
Charitable Donations Help You More Than You Think

Chapter 19 Trail Route
- Cash donations
- Noncash donations
- Charitable deduction limitation

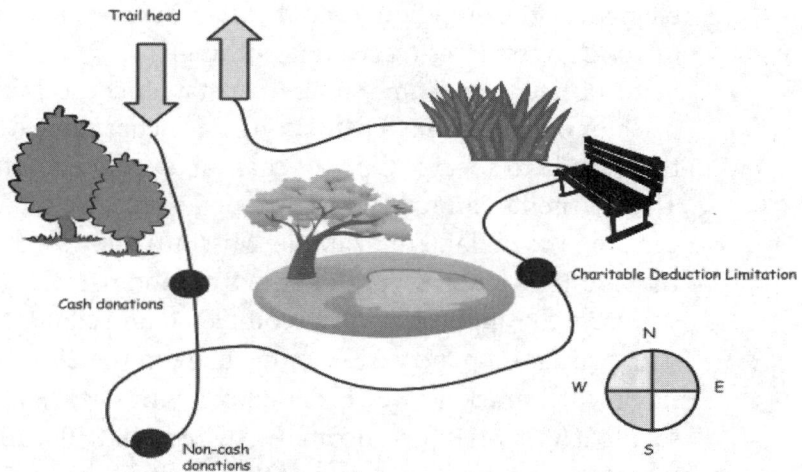

Charitable donations 👍 just may be your answer, or at least part of your answer, to save income tax. You are paying too much in income tax, and you have an urgency to be saving for other family priorities, including retirement. Charitable giving is the humanitarian act of giving to someone in need. Much has been written about the incidental benefit of charity to the donor, in addition to the income tax benefit. Intangible benefits can include feelings of happiness, cohesiveness, and personal fulfillment. If you want a charitable Income Tax Deduction 👍 too (as I always do), you need to make sure you are following IRS guidelines.

Cash Donations 👍

The most common type of deductible charitable donation is a cash donation 👍 (includes donations made by check or credit card). Specific items to note about cash charitable donations follow:

- Receipt. If you donate more than $250 to an organization in one single day, you must have a receipt to substantiate that donation. The donation acknowledgement must state the fair market value of any goods or services received in exchange for the donation, even if the amount of goods or services received is nothing.
- State Tax Benefits. Some states offer state Income Tax Credits ❖ or enhanced Tax Deductions 👍 for charitable donations made to specific types of charitable organizations. These benefits can reduce the cost of a charitable gift to 22 cents on the dollar. For example, Missouri allows a 50% Income Tax Credit ❖ for donations to food pantries (once you have the applicable forms completed and signed). If you give a food pantry $1K, and you are in the 28% Federal income tax bracket, your Federal tax savings is $280. Add that to a 50% Missouri Income Tax Credit of $500, and your total income tax benefit of the charitable gift is $780, making your actual cost of this donation only $220.

Qualified charities
- *Public parks and recreation areas*
- *Churches and other organized, registered places of worship*
- *Public charities, a/k/a 501(c)(3)'s, such as the Salvation Army, MERS Goodwill, and the Red Cross*
- *Private charities*
- *Nonprofit schools*
- *Nonprofit hospitals*
- *Volunteer fire districts*
- *Governments, including state and local governments, if used for the public good*

Noncash donations 👍

Noncash donations are also a key way charitable organizations raise funds. The following are some details you should know:

- Receipt. Same as for cash donations, if you donate more than $250 in goods to an organization in one single day, you must have a receipt to substantiate that donation. The donation acknowledgement must state the fair market value of any goods or services received in exchange for the donation, even if the amount of goods or services received is nothing.
- List. Prepare a very thorough list of the items that are being donated.
- Pictures. Take pictures of the items you are donating.
- Value. Value the goods at thrift shop value for clothing, household goods and other non-collectibles. (The Salvation Army has a valuation guide on their website.)
- Appraisal. Generally, if you donate property with a value in excess of $5K, you must get an appraisal to support your Income Tax Deduction 👍. However, this rule does not apply to publicly traded securities.
- Donation of appreciated collectible property. You will receive a charitable deduction 👍 for the fair market value of the goods, even if your cost of the goods is much less. Say you have a valuable painting that you bought for $100, and at the time of your donation, the value is $2,000. You will receive the $2,000 as the charitable donation deduction 👍.
- Automobile, boat or airplane. If you donate an automobile, boat or plan, make sure you receive the applicable tax form from the charity to affix to your income tax return.

IRS Form 1098-C is used to report donations for autos, boats and planes and is issued by the charitable organization to the donor.

- Donation of appreciated Capital Gain property 👍. Of special interest to some, gifts of appreciated mutual funds or securities of publicly traded companies are deductible 👍 at Fair Market Value as of the date of the gift. At the same time, the taxpayer escapes paying the regular or Capital Gain Tax on the sale of the security, depending on whether the asset is held for over 1 year. Each year in my private practice, we have a number of clients that gift publicly traded stock to their church or to other charities. See the inset on next page for an example.
- Donation of biological parts. Donation of body parts, such as a kidney, blood, plasma, or long hair are not income tax-deductible items.
- Charitable Mileage 👍. If you incur mileage costs in performing charitable acts, keep a detailed log. You can deduct your charitable miles at $0.14 ✈ per mile for 2015.

This year a client, Katie, asked, "How much can I deduct for my late husband's vintage record collection?"

"What's the approximate fair market value?" I asked.

"I already read on www.irs.gov about Form 8283. You want to know if it's over $5K, and the museum I'm donating the collection to said it is worth more than $5K."

"Awesome," I said. "Then did you read where you need an appraisal?"

"Yes, I have an appraisal ordered," she said.

She is always so with it! She's a very informed client!

Charitable Deduction 👍 Limitation

There is a limit to the amount of charity you can deduct on your income tax return. Cash or property excluding Capital Gain property may be deducted up to 50% of your Adjusted Gross Income. For rules governing Capital Gain Property, see the chart on page 150.

In 2014, Conoco Phillips stock was gifted.	
Cost basis of the Conoco Phillips stock, the owner purchased the stock in the early 1980s @ $32 per share, and he purchased 2,500 shares	$80,000
Fair market value at date of gift, owner gifted the stock to a qualified 501(c)(3) charitable organization in mid 2014, when the fair market value of the stock was $62 per share	$155,000
Charitable donation	$155,000
Capital Gain that escaped taxation ($155,000 fair market value less $80,000 cost basis)	$75,000
Positive tax effect: tax savings on the donation is the FMV of $155,000 x combined Federal and state tax rate of 31%, and the saved taxes not paid on the Capital Gain is $75,000 x combined Federal and state Capital Gain rate of 21%=	$63,800

This client saved $63,800 in income taxes by gifting this stock, and his original cost amounted to only $80K! In the end, he only paid 20 cents on the dollar for donating to his favorite charity.

Capital Gain Property*	Allowable Amount
If donor elects to deduct the Fair Market Value of the Capital Gain property	Charitable donation cannot exceed 30% of your Adjusted Gross Income.
If donor elects to deduct their Cost Basis of the Capital Gain property	Charitable donation cannot exceed 50% of your Adjusted Gross Income.
If recipient is a certain charitable organization** and donor elects to deduct the Fair Market Value of the Capital Gain property	Charitable donation cannot exceed 20% of your Adjusted Gross Income.

*Property that if sold at a gain would qualify for Capital Gain treatment
** Such as veterans organizations, fraternal societies, non-profit cemeteries

For donations of cash or a non Capital Gain property, the charitable donation cannot exceed 50% of your Adjusted Gross Income.

If you are unable to deduct all of the charity in the year given, you are allowed to carry the charitable deduction 🍂 forward and use it in the next year, for a total carry-forward of 5 years.

For a recent year, two couples in my practice "won" IRS audits for their charitable donations 🍂 (and only their charitable deduction; the IRS did not request documentation for any other deductions). The couples possessed total income ranging from $130K - $180K, and deducted charitable donations ranging from $22K - $26K. Clearly, the large amount of charitable deductions 🍂 relative to the income level raised suspicion at the IRS. Because they received the notices within days of each other, I felt confident in my thinking that the trigger responsible for the audits was the high level of charitable giving.

One family, the JoUsons, had an easy time gathering their proof. They maintained detailed receipts for every donation over $250, and for their noncash donation charity, they kept not only the receipts, but also lists detailing the items given, and pictures. They submitted all of the documentation to the IRS by the requested deadline. Several weeks later, the JoUsons received a letter from the IRS stating the IRS proposed no changes to their charitable deductions 🍂. The "no change letter" is the best possible response that could have been received. They were as pleased as straight-A students getting their report card. Their $26K in charitable deductions 👍 remained intact.

The other family, the Garcias, learned they had significant work to do. They chased down a couple of missionaries in South America for receipts, created the required mileage logs from their calendar, and neatened up and organized the lists of supplies they purchased and donated to the local food pantry. In the end, they were allowed only 92% of the charity originally claimed. They learned a lot about how to keep better records in case of a future audit, despite feeling like chastised children getting caught not doing all of their chores.

The IRS can challenge your Income Tax Deduction 👍 on any charitable donation to an unqualified organization. You may want to familiarize yourself with the following list, which details organizations that do not qualify as charities.

> *Organizations to which charitable giving is not income tax deductible (list may not be all inclusive):*
> - *Organizations that have not yet received their non-profit 501(c)(3) status from the IRS (but if and when the organization is approved by the IRS, then all prior donations are deductible👍)*
> - *Civil groups*
> - *Sports clubs*
> - *For profit groups*
> - *Homeowners' associations*
> - *Political contributions, lobbyists*
> - *Social clubs*
> - *Labor unions*
> - *Chambers of Commerce*

Chapter Summary

For your charitable donations 👍, you should likely make sure you are donating to qualified charities, and that you receive the proper receipts so that you will receive all of the charitable deductions 👍 you deserve, with no issues with the IRS. Contributions can be made in cash, with property, and donated property with a value over $5K must be appraised, except for publicly traded securities. There are charitable donation limits, depending on the type of charitable organization to which you are giving, and unused charitable deductions 💧 can be carried to up to 5 future years. Donating with full knowledge of the rules will help you save income tax, and use those moneys elsewhere; you likely prefer to choose where your money will do the most good!

Chapter 20
Pay Off Your Mortgage or Build More Savings?

> Chapter 20 Trail Route
> - Mortgage interest Tax Deduction 👍
> - Savings/investment benefits
> - Self-employed individuals and mortgages
> - Home equity debt 👍
> - Vacation home debt 👍

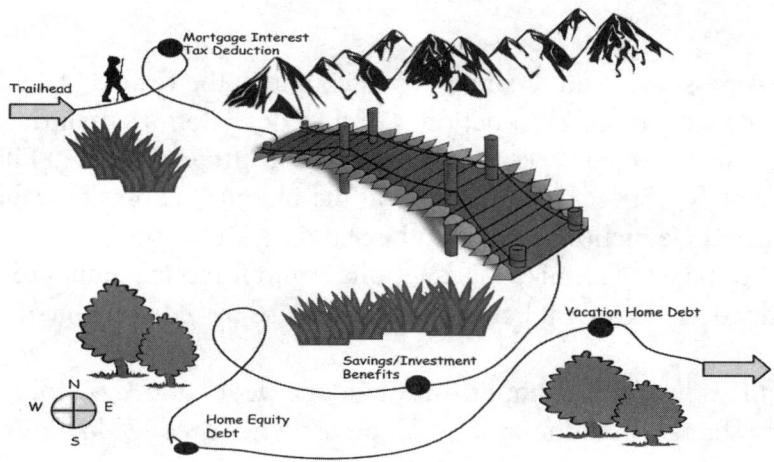

Everyone's life-long dream is to pay off their mortgage, right? It's been an uphill journey with terrible weather at times, an emotional decision, and it equates to a feeling of financial security. There is only one goal for some folks: home ownership without debt. You work very hard and sacrifice so much for your family, and paying off that mortgage will be a large heavy burden lifted from your shoulders.

I understand this sentiment, coming from a conservative background myself. We all want to retire, and relax on the back porch sipping cold sweet tea, and not have to worry about a mortgage payment after we're done working.

Almost every adult and married couple in the United States is awarded a Standard Deduction 👍, if they don't itemize their deductions 👍 (except in certain cases of those filing as Married Filing Separately). But for many in the middle-income tax brackets, their Itemized Deductions 👍 exceed the Standard Deduction, so they elect to take the Itemized Deductions 👍 and forgo the Standard Deduction, because it benefits them to do so by reducing income tax.

(This figure does not list the Standard Deduction 👍 ✈ for all filing statuses and does not list all possible Itemized Deductions 👍.)

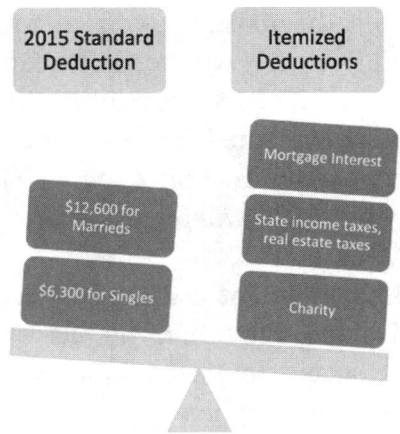

Mortgage Interest Tax Deduction 👍

Those in the middle-income tax brackets rarely reap any kind of government rebate, incentive, or assistance, other than using Itemized Deductions 👍, to reduce their income tax burden. So, if Uncle Sam is going to grant you the deduction 👍 for the mortgage interest, why not let him? Let the government subsidize your home ownership, and enjoy the income tax break! (I'm not condoning purchasing more house than you can afford, and note that houses with mortgage debt of over $1 million have limits to the amount of deductible mortgage interest, but that is outside the middle-income scope of this book.)

Benefit From the Savings

What if you didn't use excess cash to pay down your mortgage? What if you instead invested that excess cash at an interest rate that is higher than your mortgage rate? I've asked this question many times. So, let me ask you, would you ever purchase a 30 year investment, that at most would only ever pay 4%?

You likely would say, "No, interest rates will hopefully increase in the future."

If that's the case, then you should consider investing excess cash instead of paying down a mortgage, if your average annual rate of return on the investment will exceed the mortgage interest rate you are paying. This line of thinking is more suitable for younger investors, whose risk tolerance for investments finds them investing in products with a level of return greater than the rate of a mortgage; it is less suitable for more mature investors, who are likely to be investing in bonds or bond mutual funds that produce rates of return similar to that of the rate they are paying on a mortgage.

If the idea of investing excess cash instead of paying off your mortgage makes you nervous, open a brokerage account and call it your "House" account. Strive to build and then keep the account at an amount equal in value to your unpaid mortgage balance. That way if you are ever disabled, or some other emergency befalls you, you can purpose the "House" account to pay off the mortgage. Investments can decline in value, as we saw in 2008 and 1987, so this idea may not be within your risk tolerance, but it's definitely something to ponder. You will need to locate the intersection where your risk tolerance meets a return higher than your mortgage rate.

Self Employed Individuals and Mortgages

Because self-employed persons have a tougher time procuring mortgage loans in the current banking environment, they may be more likely to pay off a mortgage at a higher rate than refinance at current low mortgage rates, just because the low interest rate mortgages are less available to them.

When I was newly divorced, I failed to qualify for a 30-year fixed rate mortgage. The bank required two years of income tax returns showing my self-employment income, which I did not yet have. I didn't want to burden anyone to cosign, and I couldn't get a nine-to-five job, and still take care of my children the way I wanted. My heart belonged in the arena of being a self-employed CPA. Three reputable banks refused my loan application. Finally, a local bank loaned me the money for my house, but it was only a 3-year loan at a rate significantly higher than that of a 30-year fixed rate mortgage. I muddled through, and eventually refinanced, once I could show a two-year history of being profitably self-employed. So, while I see the benefits of keeping the mortgage for the Income Tax Deduction ♦, I don't think that's a good idea if the rate on the mortgage is above the market rate, such as mine used to be.

The best example of maximizing the mortgage interest deduction 👍 was played out by my clients, Bill & Kathy. They accumulated enough cash (thanks to an inheritance) to pay off their $255K mortgage; however, without the mortgage interest deduction 👍, they wouldn't be able to itemize their deductions 👍 anymore. Bill & Kathy invested their inheritance in an index mutual fund and it earned approximately 10% during 2013. Here is a picture of their situation:

	Without mortgage	With mortgage
Mortgage interest deduction 👍	$0	$11,475
Total Itemized Deductions 👍, including the mortgage interest	$7,000	$18,475
Standard Deduction 👍	$12,200*	$12,200*
Itemized Deductions 👍 or Standard Deduction 👍, whichever is higher (more helpful)	$12,200	$18,475
Taxable Income	$105,000	$98,525
Tax	$18,108	$16,489
Investment Savings	$0	$255,000

The Standard Deduction 👍 for a Married Filing Joint couple for 2015 is $12,600, and I'll update this on my website annually, www.LisaBcpa.com.

Bill & Kathy earned approximately 10% on their investments, and only paid 4.5% in mortgage interest. Because the rate on the investment exceeds the rate on the mortgage, and because they deducted the larger Itemized Deductions 👍, keeping the mortgage makes sense for them. Keep in mind, the market does not consistently perform, and that some borrowers are not eligible for an extremely low mortgage interest rate.

I talked a client into buying their first home. JoÚ and Diane owned a siding business and were profitable year after year. They kept their extra money in certificates of deposit, earning pitiful interest rates. They used a portion of their rental home for the business--for office work and billing needs. They had three kids, and their tiny rental home was bursting at the seams. They parked business vehicles in their driveway, and up and down their street.

"Lisa," JoÚ asked, "I think we can afford to buy a house, don't you?"

"Yes, I think you can. You will need to keep a safety fund of liquid cash for personal use and for the business, but yes, I think you can pull it off."

"Diane is worried . . . if the business has a downturn, then we won't be able to make the payments."

I said, "Have you ever missed a rent payment in the past 10 years?"

"No."

Diane liked having $250K in certificates of deposit; it represented security to her, and I can understand that, to a point.

The next time I met with this couple, I put it in pictures for them; I gave them a graph my staff prepared that showed their income from the siding business for the past 10 years. Each year the company made more money than in the previous year, except for two years, in which income remained consistent.

After numerous discussions with the couple, they reached a compromise: they divided the Certificate of Deposit money into three parts. The first $50K was earmarked for personal emergencies. The next $100K was earmarked for business emergencies. The final $100K was used as a down payment on a $400K home. All parties ended happy with the arrangement: JoÚ got his larger home and they were no longer renting. Diane kept most of the excess cash in certificates of deposit. The mortgage company was satisfied because the couple possessed a more than adequate amount of liquid cash, in case they were in danger of failing to make their mortgage payments. Finally, I felt happy, because they would now have a mortgage (at a very low rate) that would give them a much-needed Income Tax Deduction 👍.

Home Equity Debt 👍

Be careful acquiring home equity debt because the interest from this debt is only deductible 👍 on the lesser of $100K or the equity you have in the home (Fair Market Value of the home, less any first mortgage on the home). Another warning: as noted in the chapter on Alternative Minimum Tax (AMT), interest incurred on mortgage loans where the proceeds were not used to buy or improve your home is not deductible for AMT purposes.

Vacation Home 👍

A taxpayer is allowed to deduct mortgage interest on a second home, if the total between their main residence and the vacation home does not exceed $1,000,000 ✈. When you consider the $100K ✈ home equity debt limit, a household can have a total of $1,100,000 in mortgage debt. But do I suggest this? NO, that's a lot of responsibility, and you need a very large and stable income to support that.

Chapter Summary

Mortgage debt is a way for Uncle Sam to subsidize your home ownership 👍, and allows you to invest excess cash, if you can earn suitable returns for your risk tolerance level that exceed your mortgage interest rate. For some, this may not be possible, if they are self-employed and pay higher interest rates than others, or their risk tolerance does not allow for high-yield investments. You will need to decide if you are able to earn more in portfolio income on excess cash, or if you should pay excess cash towards your mortgage. If you can earn more investing in your portfolio, than in your mortgage, you may determine not to prepay your mortgage, and invest those extra dollars instead. Mortgage interest from home equity debt 👍 and from a vacation home 👍 may be deductible 👍, but there are limitations. In the end, using the income tax savings and building the portfolio may help you build more wealth for you and your family.

Chapter 21

Miscellaneous Itemized Deductions 👍 - Gather Enough to Deduct

> ### Chapter 21 Trail Route
> - Potential Miscellaneous Itemized Deductions 👍
> - Home Office Deduction 👍
> - Simplified Home Office Method 👍
> - Job hunting 👍
> - Potential solutions
> - AMT's effect on Miscellaneous Itemized Deductions

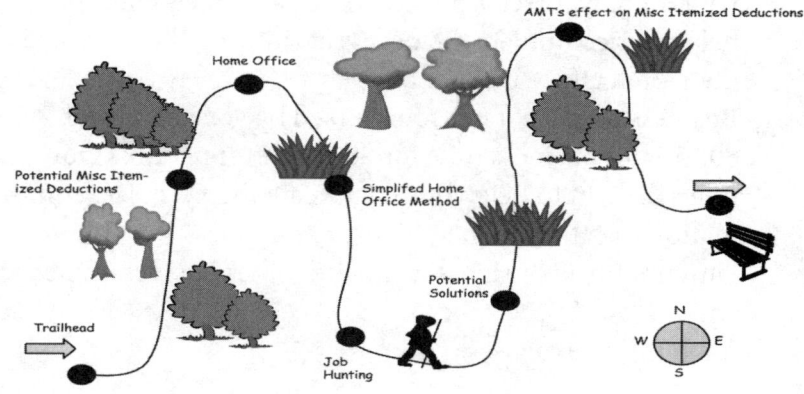

Miscellaneous Itemized Deductions 👍 are only deductible once they exceed 2% of your total income (Adjusted Gross Income). Let's say your Miscellaneous Itemized Deductions are below the 2% threshold, which is a very common issue. Well then, you may want to examine what other Miscellaneous Itemized Deductions 👍 will help you push above the 2% threshold.

Potential Miscellaneous Itemized Deductions

Other Miscellaneous Itemized Deductions 👍 that you may consider (not an all-inclusive list) are:
- Tax preparation fees;
- Investment adviser fees;
- Estate planning fees (for the portion related to tax planning and asset protection);
- Safe deposit box fees;
- Professional association dues;
- Job related subscriptions;
- Course fee for job related classes (if you won't be reimbursed from your employer);
- Home Office Deduction 👍 if the home office is required by your employer (see Appendix B for a Home Office form, to help you accumulate the necessary information to calculate the Home Office Deduction 👍);
- Business mileage if not reimbursed by your employer – $0.575 per business mile for 2015 (see Appendix C for a mileage form to help you accumulate the necessary information to calculate the mileage deduction 👍);
- Unreimbursed business meals and other business expenses; and
- Job hunting expenses.

You might feel self-assured that you're getting every possible deduction 👍, even giving your CPA your unreimbursed employee expenses, such as those listed above, to deduct. You feel smug taking the Home Office Deduction 👍 because your employer insists you work out of your home. But if these Miscellaneous Itemized Deductions 👍 did not exceed 2% of Adjusted Gross Income, they were not deducted on your income tax return.

Your goal should be to increase these deductions 👍 to the point of being able to deduct them, if you can't get reimbursed for them. I hope you can see and smell these Miscellaneous Itemized Deductions 👍, like my kids scout candy, so you can gather as many as possible. And note that even if you exceed the 2% threshold, it's only the amount that exceeds 2% of total income that is deductible.

Home Office 👍

If your employer requires you to work regularly out of your home, and you have an office in your home that is used exclusively for your job, you can add the Home Office Deduction 👍 to your unreimbursed employee expenses. In the past, many accountants feared taking the Home Office Deduction 👍 for clients, due to concern of an IRS audit. But these days, this is not a risk and Home Office isn't on the IRS's audit initiative list, per my discussion with an IRS auditor in 2013. Many people work from home these days.

Simplified Home Office Method 👍

Although not my personal preference, there is a Simplified Home Office calculation where you simply deduct $5 ✈ per square foot of the home office, up to a maximum of 300 square feet. You still must meet the requirement of using the office regularly and exclusively for work. Using the Simplified Method, you are not allowed to take depreciation on the home office, hence my dislike for the method. However, if you don't have the information to calculate the depreciation, then this would be a straightforward way to proceed. This method may also be preferable if you have a quite inexpensive home.

Job Hunting Expenses 👍

A new client came to us last year because of an IRS audit notice he received related to his job-hunting expenses. He prepared his own income tax return, but didn't know how to proceed through an IRS audit.

I said, "How do you know that it is the job hunting expenses that caused your IRS audit?"

"Well," Steve replied, "the Feds asked for the supporting papers for my job hunting expenses, and I sent them in. Now I have this paper from them saying my full return will be audited."

"Steve, can I see what you sent to the IRS?" Steve is an architect, and thus very detail-oriented. I knew he would have a copy of the support he submitted to the IRS. I looked the papers over, and identified the issue within one minute, when I saw all of the tuition statements.

"Steve, education expenses don't go on Schedule A, as job hunting expense. You could have included the education expenses as a Lifetime Learning Credit ❖."

Steve said, "Yeah, but it made my refund bigger when I went the other way, and recorded the MBA as job hunting. I spent $26K and got my MBA to help me find a new job."

"That was likely a good move, since architecture jobs are hard to find. But education expenses are not allowed as part of your job-hunting expenses. Education expense as a Miscellaneous Itemized Deduction 👍 is only deductible if the coursework was required by your employer, and education expenses to qualify you for a new industry aren't allowed. Architecture and a business degree are not closely related."

"Oh" was all Steve could choke out. He lost his IRS audit, and paid $9K in additional income tax, penalties, and interest.

Being able to deduct job-related expenses can often be the difference between the employee making an adequate living or not. For one client in my private practice, I calculated his mileage cost, despite it not being deductible in his case. I then showed the client his real earnings from this job, after considering the mileage cost, and it fell short of acceptable, at only about $6.50 per hour. The decision came easily for him at this point. He resigned the position that same day.

Potential Solutions for Job-Related Expenses

Ask your employer to set up an Accountable Expense Reimbursement Plan (adheres to IRS requirements) to reimburse you for your business expenses, and then lower your regular W-2 pay by the amount of the expenses. The employer may be willing to do this for you, in order to keep you as an employee.

Another potential solution would be to become self-employed in the same line of work (become an independent contractor), so that the expenses will be deductible 👍 as a business expense for you and offset any income from the business. This would not be a solution for mileage, because that is very identifiable with specific business trips. However, it is applicable to things like professional licenses or dues. If you are considering this, be mindful of any non-compete agreement you have signed with your employer. See Chapter 24 for the Pros and Cons of being an independent contractor.

> Potential solutions to be able to deduct job related expenses
> - Request employer set up an Accountable Expense Reimbursement Plan
> - Become self-employed
> - Lump expenses into even numbered years, to get above the 2% threshold

Lastly, a person could pay Miscellaneous Itemized Deductions 👍 in even-numbered years only, for expenses that have some flexibility in when they are paid. You could prepay business tax preparation fees and professional dues, for example. By lumping more Miscellaneous Itemized Deductions 👍 into even years, perhaps you will be able to deduct the amount that exceeds 2% of your income, at least every other year.

Alternative Minimum Tax and Miscellaneous Itemized Deductions

See Chapter 23 for a discussion of the effect of AMT on Miscellaneous Itemized Deductions 👍. In short, if you are subject to AMT, you do not receive a benefit for deducting Miscellaneous Itemized Deductions.

Chapter Summary

Miscellaneous Itemized Deductions 👍 are only deductible for the portion that exceeds 2% of Adjusted Gross Income, so you likely want to gather as many Miscellaneous Itemized Deductions 👍 as possible that are applicable to you (see list in chapter) to be able to receive the deduction. The Home Office Deduction 👍 (or perhaps the Simplified Home Office Deduction 👆) and job-hunting expenses 👆 should also be considered for inclusion in your Miscellaneous Itemized Deductions 👆 (if you qualify). Potential solutions to being unable to deduct Miscellaneous Itemized Deductions 👆 include requesting your employer set up an Accountable Expense Reimbursement Plan, becoming self employed and/or lumping Miscellaneous Itemized Deductions 👆 into even-numbered years. Increasing your Miscellaneous Itemized Deductions 👆 will lower your income tax burden, so that you can keep more of your money. You likely will be the best person to decide on a better use of your money, and not the government.

> IRS Form 2106 can be used to calculate Unreimbursed Employee Expenses.

Chapter 22
Escape Tax on the Sale of a Personal Residence

> **Chapter 22 Trail Route**
> - Residential sale gain exclusion 👍
> - Contractor opportunity
> - Step up in cost basis 👍
> - Surviving spouse residential sale gain exclusion 👍

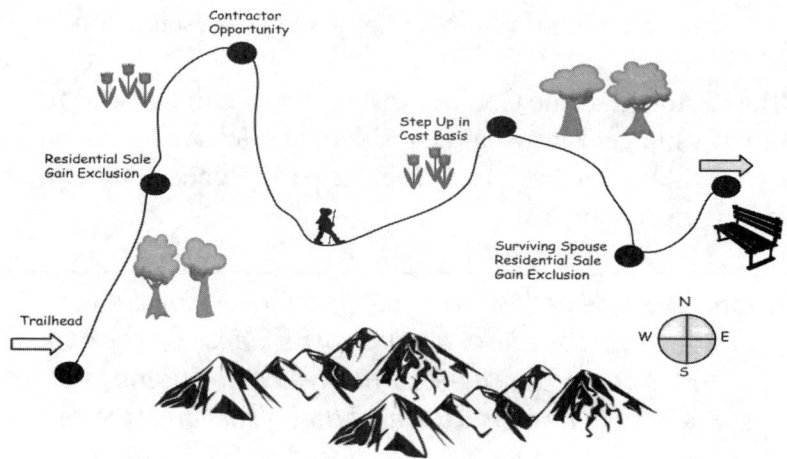

Your home is a substantial part of your net worth, and whether you're downsizing, or needing a larger home, you don't want to pay income tax on any gain on the sale of your home. You likely want to take the gain, and roll it all into a new home, or perhaps build your investment portfolio. This chapter will help you time the sale of your home so that there is no income tax on the sale--or, in the unusual case that there is an income tax on the sale, it can be minimized.

Residential Sale Gain Exclusion 👍

You must have lived at your principal residence for 2 of the past 5 years prior to the sale date to qualify for the residential sale gain exclusion. A principal residence, for purposes of this rule, is where you live most of the time, and is the home that is close to these locations:
- where you work;
- where you provide an abode for your spouse and children;
- the address shown on your income tax returns, driver's license, and voter registration;
- nearest to where you do your banking; and
- nearest to where you attend any religious establishment.

The Residential Sale Gain Exclusion is a rule that can be used to your advantage! Knowing the residential sale gain exclusion rule, you will be able to time your principal residence sale so that there is no tax on any gain.

Principal residence exclusion of gain upon sale 👍 specifics
- *Gain from the sale of a principal residence can be excluded 👍 from income if the owner lived in the home in 2 (not required to be consecutive) of the 5 years prior to the sale*
- *The excluded gain is limited based on Filing Status:*
  - *Single, $250K*
  - *Married and Qualifying Surviving Spouses, $500K*
- *This exclusion rule can only be used every 2 years*
- *For married couples, only one of them must have owned the house, but both will need to have lived in the home in 2 of the 5 years prior to the sale*
- *Proration of the gain exclusion is allowed if the home was occupied for only part of the 2 year required period in the 5 years prior to the sale*

Contractor Opportunity

The residential sale gain exclusion rules 👍 are of particular interest to a contractor who is willing to move every 2 years. (Admittedly, this may be of more interest to a young contractor, before marriage and children, or someone who has grown children.)

Here's how this works: a contractor could buy a home that needs a lot of fix-up work, and move into the home, using the home as his principal residence. The contractor could do the necessary repairs and betterments, increasing the value of the home, as the work is completed. Then after 2 years, the contractor can sell the home, and pocket the gain, without paying any income tax on the gain. Under current law, the contractor could do this every 2 years, and end up making quite a bit of tax-free income from these moves. Without paying income tax on the gains from the sale of the homes, the contractor would have more funds available for future projects, or for accumulating in his or her investment portfolio.

Step-Up in Cost Basis 👍

This residential sale gain exclusion rule can also assist the elderly. The one example that comes to mind is an elderly couple in my private practice. The couple lived in their home for over 30 years, and it sat nestled in a quiet area that experienced dramatic appreciation over the years. The husband and the wife each owned half of the home, and were each other's beneficiary. At the time of the husband's death, the home appraised at a fair market value of $825K, and possessed a cost basis of $400K. The widow decided she better move to a condominium that would require little upkeep and included onsite medical assistance if she ever needed it.

This very smart lady asked me almost immediately whether she would owe income tax upon the sale of the house. Although the $825K final selling price exceeded the original cost basis of $400K by $425K, and the widow remained single for more than two years after her husband's death, still no income tax resulted.

Here's what happened: when her husband died, she received a step-up in cost basis to fair market value for her husband's half of the home. Her revised cost basis of $612,500, is calculated as follows:

Cost basis of husband's half of home that was left to his wife is stepped up to fair market value as of the date of his death ($825K divided by 2)	$412,500
Cost basis of wife's half of the home (original $400K cost basis divided by 2)	$200,000
Revised cost basis	$612,500

Because the sales price of $825K less the revised cost basis of $612,500 is less than $250K, there is no resulting income tax on the sale of the home. This nice lady giggled and squealed like a schoolgirl when she learned there would be no income tax on the sale, and I got a hug out of that one!

Surviving Spouse Residential Sale Gain Exclusion ✤

If one spouse dies, the survivor can still use the married exclusion of $500K ✈ if (a) the home is sold within 2 years of the spouse's death, (b) at least one of them owned the home, (c) both of them used the home as a principal residence for the 2 years preceding the death, and (d) neither spouse used this exclusion rule within the past 2 years.

In the example above regarding the elderly couple, if the widow sold the home prior to the second anniversary of her husband's death, they would have been eligible for the married exclusion of $500K. Regardless, no income tax on the gain upon the sale of their home resulted either way.

Another case from a client: JoÛ, an elderly father in a nursing home, hoped to recover from his broken hip and shoulder. Mentally, JoÛ stayed sharp as ever, and he wanted to go home. JoÛ's five children did not believe their father would recover physically, with JoÛ having recently celebrated his ninety-fifth birthday. Yet they couldn't bring themselves to sell their childhood home while their father still lived. The real estate market sat depressed, and they felt unsure if they would be able to sell the home.

I asked, "Why don't you consider renting the home out?"

The oldest son said they were considering it.

"If you rent the house out no more than three years," I said, "you can still sell the home, and not pay tax on the gain, if the gain is less than $250K." We did expect the gain to be less than $250K.

"What if we want to rent the home longer, if Dad isn't ready for us to sell?"

"You will still get a partial exclusion of the gain. If your Dad lives in the home only 12 of the required 24 months, in the 5 years before the sale, then he would still get a 50% of the $250K exclusion of the gain."

So the children rented the home out, which is helping with the cost of the nursing home. They know they need to sell them home within three years of their Dad moving out, for the complete exclusion of the gain.

Chapter Summary

Timing the sale of a principal residence is important. You need to have lived in a principle residence in 2 of the 5 years prior to a sale, so that you can use the residential sale gain exclusion. The gain exclusion is $250K ✈ for Singles and $500K ✈ for Married taxpayers and Qualifying Surviving Spouses. A contractor could potentially use the residential sale gain exclusion every 2 years, while using the time to improve the residence and increase the value. Then the contractor could sell the home at the end of the 2 years, and pocket the gain, escaping income tax. A person who inherits a home receives a step up in cost basis to fair market value as of the date of death of their loved one (or step up in half of the home if the decedent only owned half the home, such as may be the case for a married couple). Reducing gain on the sale of a principal residence will reduce the income tax burden; reducing the income tax burden means you will have money to spend in a better place of your choosing.

> IRS Form 8949 is used to report any TAXABLE portion from the sale of a principal residence.

Chapter 23
Can You Minimize Alternative Minimum Tax?

> Chapter 23 Trail Route
> - State & local income taxes paid
> - Mortgage interest
> - Miscellaneous Itemized Deductions
> - Incentive stock options
> - Depreciation of fixed assets
> - Disposal of fixed assets
> - Personal exemptions

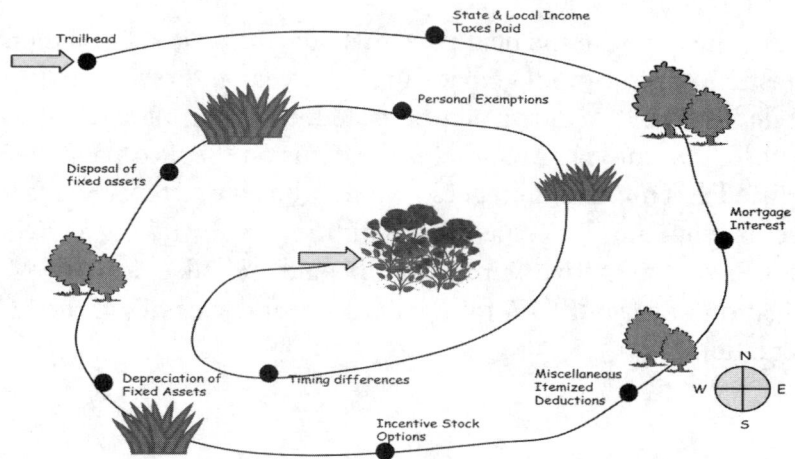

Alternative Minimum Tax (AMT) hits upper middle class taxpayers most heavily. What is this "disease" that so many fear? In the USA, there are two taxing systems, and a person's Federal income tax must be calculated under the regular tax and Alternative Minimum Tax methods. A person then must pay the higher of these two taxes; the excess of AMT over regular tax is referred to as the AMT tax. AMT isn't applicable to the low-income taxpayers, or for high-income tax payers. AMT hits the middle class. Just like the child who is sandwiched between the older sibling superstar, and the baby of the family that's coddled, those hit by AMT feel like the mistreated middle child.

✈ The AMT calculation is a modified flat tax rate of 26% to 28% of AMT Income and many expenses aren't deductible, as they are for regular income tax purposes. In this chapter, my goal is to point out the more common adjustments that trigger AMT, so that you can understand them and control their effect on your AMT calculation and resulting income tax liability.

A client once said, "I'm not paying any AMT. Do my return without that."

"It's not an optional tax," I explained. "If you don't put it on your return, the IRS will bill you for it."

"OK, well at least leave it off my state return!"

"OK," I agreed. This client lives in Missouri, and Missouri doesn't have an AMT.

For the items on the next page that are labeled as a Permanent Adjustment, you cannot go back in a later year and reverse that lost deduction. It's a permanent non-deductible item for AMT purposes. On the other hand, for the items on the next page that are listed as Timing Differences, you may be able to reverse this effect on your AMT calculation in a future year, by taking a Credit ❖ for Prior Alternative Minimum Tax paid and offset future AMT obligations. See your CPA for applicability and specifics of the calculation.

State & local income taxes paid…	are an add back to obtain Alternative Minimum Taxable Income.	A permanent adjustment (described on next page)
Mortgage interest not used to purchase or improve your home…	is an add back to obtain Alternative Minimum Taxable Income.	A permanent adjustment
Miscellaneous Itemized Deductions…	are an add back to obtain Alternative Minimum Taxable Income.	A permanent adjustment
Most Incentive Stock Options that are exercised but not sold…	generate additional income added to Alternative Minimum Taxable Income. (If sold in year exercised, there is not an adjustment to the AMT calculation.)	A timing difference (described on next page)
Depreciation of fixed assets, such as rental property or business assets, where the regular depreciation method differs from the AMT depreciation method…	excess of regular depreciation over AMT depreciation is added back to Alternative Minimum Taxable Income.	A timing difference
Disposal of fixed assets, where the regular depreciation method differed from the AMT depreciation method…	gain or loss is recalculated using AMT depreciation, and Alternative minimum Taxable Income is adjusted.	A permanent adjustment
Personal exemptions for you, your spouse and your children…	are not an allowable deduction for the Alternative Minimum Taxable Income calculation.	A permanent adjustment

State & Local Income Taxes Paid

On your Schedule A, Itemized Deductions 👆, have you noticed that the line for State and Local Taxes allows you to select State & Local Income Tax Deduction 👆 or the Sales Tax Deduction 👆? This is super helpful to our friends who live in states where there is no state income tax; those folks, of course, need to take the Sales Tax Deduction 👍. But this is also helpful for those of us that are subject to Alternative Minimum Tax.

If you are subject to Alternative Minimum Tax, you may want to think twice about taking the State & Local Income Tax Deduction 👍, even though it's higher in amount than the Sales Tax Deduction 👍. All State & Local Income and Sales Taxes are an add-back on the AMT calculation (line 3 of the 2014 Form 6251), and sometimes you get a better result by taking the Sales Tax Deduction 👍 instead of the State & Local Income Tax Deduction 👍. (With the Sales Tax Deduction 👍 almost always being lower than the State and Local Income Tax Deduction 👍, that's a smaller amount added back to the AMT calculation.)

The Sales Tax Deduction is part of legislation that so far has been renewed annually by Congress (instead of being a permanent deduction). This Income Tax Deduction was most recently renewed on December 19, 2014 for the year ended December 31, 2014. If you are interested in taking this deduction, check my website, www.LisaBcpa.com or check www.irs.gov to make sure it has been renewed for the tax year in which you want to take it.

Once I see a client is subject to AMT, I calculate the return taking the State & Local Income Tax Deduction 👍 and then by taking the Sales Tax Deduction 👍. I then document the final result under both methods for both Federal and state income tax purposes. Sometimes the Federal result stays the same, but the state result is better with the Sales Tax Deduction 👍. When I combine the Federal and state results, the overall result can sometimes be better using the Sales Tax Deduction 👍.

Clients Mike & Terri are subject to AMT each year. On the next page is the analysis I did for them in order to determine if we should take the State & Local Income Tax Deduction 👍 or the Sales Tax Deduction 👍:

	Federal tax liability	State tax liability	Total Tax liability
Result using State & Local Income Tax Deduction 👍	$138,387 (made up of $5,238 of AMT)	$29,028	$167,415
Result using Sales Tax Deduction 👍	$138,387 (made up of $1,488 of AMT)	$28,903	$167,290

In looking at the above analysis, you may wonder why the Federal total tax liability remained unchanged under both methods.

Under the State & Local Income Tax Deduction 👍, the Schedule A deduction 👍 was greater, but additional AMT was generated to the extent that the State & Local Income Tax Deduction 👍 exceeded the Sales Tax deduction 👍. Under the Sales Tax Deduction 👍, the Schedule A deduction 👍 was smaller (which created more regular tax), and less AMT was triggered. This trade off happens often, but not always. In this example, it's better to take the Sales Tax Deduction 👍 because it produced a lower overall income tax liability when including the state tax liability. You may want to prepare an analysis for yourself similar to that above.

Mortgage Interest Not Used to Purchase or Improve Your Home

Interest on the portion of your mortgage and/or your home equity loan not used to buy or improve your home is not deductible for AMT purposes. So, if you tap your home equity loan for a family vacation, to pay college tuition, or to invest, that interest is not deductible for AMT purposes.

Dan used his line of credit to take him and his family, including the adult children and their families, on a cruise. He wanted to be able to give his family the memory of a lifetime. The cost proved high, because not only did everyone need a cruise ticket, but most of them needed a plane ticket to get to Miami. He also purchased unlimited food and drink for everyone on the ship. Dan planned on paying off the line of credit over 5 years. When I told him the interest expense from the vacation wasn't deductible for AMT purposes, I think it ruined his good memories of the trip. Sorry, Dan!

Miscellaneous Itemized Deductions 👍

Chapter 21 lists most of the allowable Miscellaneous Itemized Deductions 👍. All Miscellaneous Itemized Deductions 👍 must be added back to the AMT calculation, and so if you are subject to AMT, in effect you are not allowed a deduction for your Miscellaneous Itemized Deductions. This rubs many folks like ill-fitting shoes. For example, outside sales people often are responsible for paying for travel and entertainment with clients, and would like to earn an Income Tax Deduction 👍 from those necessary expenses. And folks should be able to fully deduct tax preparation and planning fees for AMT purposes too.

Incentive Stock Options

This isn't a complete discussion of stock options, because that's beyond the middle-income scope of this book. But for most Qualified Stock Options, when you exercise options is when they are taxable for AMT purposes, and when you sell the options is when they are taxable for regular income tax purposes. So if you exercise in a year, but don't sell the stock, you have created AMT income. Note that in the year in which you sell the shares, you will have a reversal of the effect of the original AMT adjustment, and hopefully will be eligible for the Credit ❖ for Prior Alternative Minimum Tax paid. (See Chapter 30 for more discussion on Incentive Stock Options, and consult your CPA, as these vary greatly between specific plans and employers.)

Brett exercised Qualified Incentive Stock options, and held them before selling, trying to get the highest price possible for the shares in the stock market. He ended up holding the shares into the New Year before finally selling them. I adjusted Brett's AMT calculation for the shares that finally sold, and he proved eligible for the Credit ❖ for Prior Alternative Minimum Tax paid. However, because Brett's income decreased (for reasons unrelated to the Stock Options), it will take him several years to earn back the complete AMT Credit ❖ available to him, but he will eventually receive back all $9K of the AMT he paid.

It would prove easy for a person's Credit ❖ for Prior Alternative Minimum Tax Paid to be lost and accidentally omitted from an income tax return. If a taxpayer changes tax preparation software packages or income tax preparers, this information from prior years could be lost. If you have carry-forward credit related to AMT, you likely need to keep track of that information in your records, so you don't lose the credit. This carry-forward AMT Credit ❖ information will need to be entered in your new tax software, so it can be used or carried forward to subsequent year(s).

Depreciation of Fixed Assets

There are differing depreciation methods for regular tax and AMT tax, and the regular tax depreciation methods have a larger amount of depreciation than AMT depreciation in the early years of an asset. The opposite is true for the later years of a fixed asset--AMT depreciation will result in higher depreciation amounts than regular tax depreciation. For the AMT calculation, the difference between the two depreciation methods is an adjustment; if regular tax depreciation is higher, then it is an add-back to the AMT calculation. If AMT depreciation is higher, then it's a deduction to the AMT calculation.

This is another example of an AMT item that may reverse in a future year, and which may generate a Credit ❖ for Prior Alternative Minimum Tax paid.

Disposal of Fixed Assets

As explained in the previous paragraph, there are differing depreciation methods for regular tax and AMT. The gain or loss on the sale of a fixed asset must be calculated under both methods, and the difference is an adjustment on the AMT schedule.

Personal Exemptions

No personal exemptions are allowed on the AMT schedule. If you believe you are reaping the benefits of the exemptions for yourself, your spouse and your children, you are not, if you are subject to AMT. This is detrimental to families with a lot of children.

A common discussion with clients goes like this:

"Your personal exemptions are not allowable this year because of your AMT."

"Why not?" they ask.

"Personal exemptions are not taken into account for the AMT calculation. I wanted to make sure you knew that."

"OK, if my income stays at this level, then I guess I shouldn't bother claiming the grandkids that I'm supporting either."

Chapter Summary

Numerous adjustments must be made to regular taxable income to obtain Alternative Minimum Taxable income. The most common AMT adjustments are the State & Local Income Tax Deduction, the Mortgage Interest Deduction (for interest on debt not used to buy or improve your home), and the loss of personal exemptions. Being aware of the adjustment items is important so that for the ones you can control, you can manage the amount of AMT you will owe, and keep more of your cash.

> IRS Form 6251 is used to calculate Alternative Minimum Tax.

> IRS Form 8801 is used to calculate The Credit for Prior Year Alternative Minimum Tax.

Chapter 24
Choose Between a W-2 Employee or Independent Contractor

> **Chapter 24 Trail Route**
> - Pros and cons of employees & independent contractors
> - Quantifying your decision process
> - IRS classification of workers

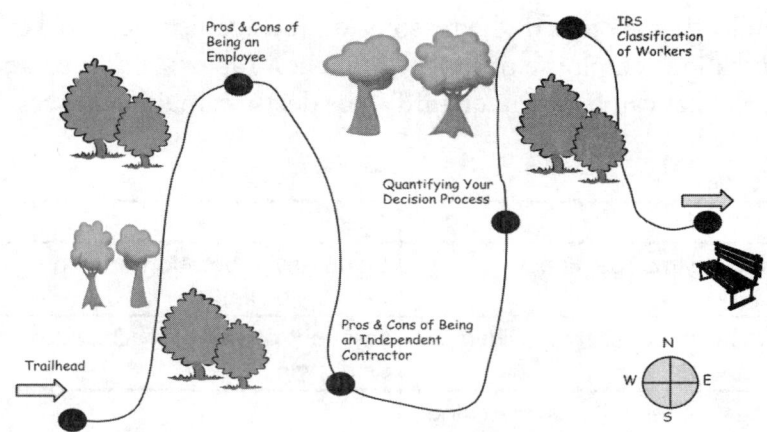

Frequently this question, or some variation of it, pops up from clients in my private practice.

"I have a choice between two jobs. But one wants me to be an independent contractor instead of an employee. Which job should I take?"

I always say, "We have a lot of variables to evaluate to make this decision." And then we go over the charts that follow in this chapter.

Pros and Cons of Employees and Independent Contractors

The choice between being an employee and being self-employed hangs as a big decision on the minds of folks in this situation. The responsibilities resting on the worker's shoulders most commonly include worries of:

- Adequate income for the household;
- Job security;
- Health benefits;
- Retirement savings;
- Life insurance coverage;
- Disability coverage; and
- Unemployment benefits (if ever needed).

Following are lists of the reasons for and against each worker classification (employee or independent contractor), and then an example that can help you quantify this decision making process.

Employee

For	Against
Job security may be higher	Chances of promotion and higher pay may be limited
Health insurance likely provided	Less control over your schedule and work style
Potential retirement plan matching by employer	
Group Life Insurance of up to $50K is often provided by employers at no cost and tax free to the employee	
Disability is often offered by employers, and they often subsidize the cost	

Independent Contractor

For	Against
Pay is generally higher	Less job security, including seasonality to the work
Retirement plan can be set up with the type of plan that is your preference	You will need to fund your own retirement plan
Add'l opportunities may arise when you are self-employed, and you would have the freedom to pursue them	Risk of loss of customers rests on you
Opportunity to deduct expenses that are otherwise not deductible (mileage, home office, business meals, for example 👍)	Health insurance would be your own responsibility, and may be more expensive if you are not in a large group
Larger of chance of being able to work from home, saving commuting time and cost	You won't be covered under an employer's group life insurance policy
More control over your schedule and work style	The employer side of FICA and Medicare would be your responsibility to pay
	You have the responsibility of making quarterly estimated tax payments to the IRS and state
	You won't be covered under an employer's worker's compensation plan
	You won't be covered under the disability policy, unless you obtain that on your own, and pay for it yourself
	No paid time off for vacation, sick days, etc.
	You may not be eligible for unemployment compensation, if the need arises

Quantifying Your Decision Process

Your considerations between being an employee or independent contractor will look similar to this example, but you will need to modify this analysis to suit your situation:

	Employee, for one year	Independent Contractor, for one year
Rate of pay for 1 year, working full time	$80,000	$150,000
Health insurance not paid for by employer		(10,000)
Retirement plan match paid by employer for employee would have to be paid by you as an independent contractor		(3,000)
Life insurance cost not paid for by employer		(1,000)
Disability insurance not paid for by employer		(800)
Employer side of FICA and Medicare to be paid for by independent contractor (on net profit)		(8,415)
Business expenses paid by independent contractor		(40,000)
Recalculated net pay	$80,000	$86,785

In the above situation, the choice leans in favor of the worker being an independent contractor, but some of the decision points are harder to quantify such as:
- Job security;
- Additional opportunities;
- Responsibility for quarterly estimated tax payments;
- Control over your schedule and work style;
- Larger chance of being able to work from home;

- Limited eligibility to unemployment compensation; and
- Limited eligibility to workers compensation and unemployment compensation.

IRS Classification of Workers

The IRS does not necessarily consider the worker classification to which the employer and employee have agreed. The IRS looks to Revenue Ruling 87-41, which contains the common law rules that need to be applied in order to determine if the worker is a contractor or employee. By looking at the 20 points on the next page, you can determine if you should be an employee or contractor based on the preponderance of the answers. This point is important, because in some cases, the worker wants to be an employee, and the law is on their side, and it's just a matter of pointing out the law to the employer. Additionally, an employee can file Form SS-8 with the IRS to allow the IRS to determine the correct worker classification. However, these actions may turn your employer into Frosty, who may give you a cool reception and a blank stare.

In addition to the 20 factors summarized on the following pages, the IRS also looks at 3 additional areas from IRS Publication 1779, also summarized on the following pages.

The last two times the employee versus independent contractor issue came up with clients, the clients both ended up being an independent contractor. In the first case, the worker received a choice of either to become an employee or independent contractor, and after we put a pencil to it, considering all of the factors above, he would be making $12K more annually in the end as an independent contractor, even though he would have to arrange for his own health insurance and retirement plan.

In the second case, the worker possessed no choice; he must either take the position as an independent contractor, or not at all. The employer placed a corporate freeze on hiring employees, and so it proved easier to bring on additional help if they could

20 Factors Based on Common Law, Used to Determine if a Worker is a Contractor or an Employee

1. Instructions. Employees are required to follow directions about when, where and how the work is to be performed, and independent contractors are likely supervised less than employees in these areas.
2. Training. Employees are more likely to receive training from the employer, more so than an independent contractor.
3. Integration. If the work performed is a key piece of the business operations, the worker is more likely to be an employee.
4. Services. An employee must perform his own work, whereas an independent contractor may delegate tasks to others.
5. Hiring, supervising and paying. An employee does not hire others to work for him to complete his work.
6. Continuing relationship. An employee is more likely to have an ongoing working relationship, and an independent contractor is more likely to leave after a project is finished.
7. Set hours of work. Workers that must work during set times, and for certain minimum hours are more likely employees.
8. Full-time requirement. If the worker is required to work full-time, and cannot work for other employers, the worker is more likely to be an employee.
9. Employer's premises. If the worker must perform his/her tasks on the employer premises, the worker is more likely to be an employee.

10. *Order of sequence set.* An employee is more likely to have a required order in which tasks are completed, and an independent contractor is more likely to be able to create his/her own system of working.
11. *Oral or written reports.* An employee is more likely to be supervised to the extent of needing to submit progress reports to the employer. The independent contractor is more likely to be responsible for the end result.
12. *Timing of payment.* An employee is more likely to be paid by the hour or by the payroll time period. An independent contractor is more likely to be paid by the task.
13. *Business and/or travel expenses.* An employee is more likely to have business and travel expenses paid or reimbursed by the employer.
14. *Tools and materials.* An independent contractor is more likely to be required to supply his/her own tools, equipment and work materials.
15. *Significant investment.* An independent contractor is more likely to have made a significant financial investment in his work.
16. *Realization of profit or loss.* An independent contractor has a risk of loss, and can realize a profit.
17. *Working for more than one firm.* An independent contractor is more likely to perform work for more than one firm.
18. *Services available to the public.* An independent contractor is more likely to provide services to the general public.
19. *Right to discharge.* An employee can be terminated at the employer's option.
20. *Right to terminate.* An employee can discontinue providing services to an employer without legal liability.

Excerpts from IRS Publication 1779

The courts have considered many facts in deciding whether a worker is an independent contractor or an employee. These relevant facts fall into 3 main categories (below). In each case, it is very important to consider all of the facts-no single fact provides the answer.

- Behavioral Control
    - Instructions: if you receive extensive instructions on how work is to be done, this suggests that you are an employee.
    - Training: if the business provides you with training about required procedures and methods, this indicates that the business wants the work done in a certain way, and this suggests that you may be an employee.
- Financial Control
    - Significant investment: if you have a significant investment in your work, you may be an independent contractor.
    - Expenses: if you are not reimbursed for some or all business expenses, then you may be an independent contractor.
    - Opportunity for profit or loss: if you can realize a profit or incur a loss, this suggests that you are in business for yourself and you may be an independent contractor.
- Relationship of the Parties
    - Employee benefits-if you receive benefits, such as insurance, pension, or paid leave, this is an indication that you may be an employee.
    - Written contracts-a written contract may show what both you and the business intend. This may be very significant if it is difficult, if not impossible, to determine status based on other facts.

be classified as independent contractors. He accepted the position, and also arranged for his own health insurance. His supervisor explained that at some point, they would try to reclassify him as an employee.

Chapter Summary

If your worker classification appears unclear, you may want to make sure your employer classifies you appropriately. If you are classified as an independent contractor, make sure you arrange for all of the benefits not being provided (listed in the tables in this chapter). If you want to be an employee, and are instead classified as an independent contractor, you can try to persuade your employer, or file Form SS-8 to let the IRS determine your correct worker classification.

The most popular advantages of being an employee are the benefits and job security. The most popular advantages of being an independent contractor are higher pay, more control over your work life, and the opportunity to deduct more business expenses. Make sure you understand the true net pay of being a contractor; you should prepare a comparison of the pay under both worker classifications and adjust for all items you will be paying for yourself, if you are an independent contractor (such as retirement plan contributions, health benefits, etc.) Selecting the correct worker classification for you can have a significant cash and income tax impact for you.

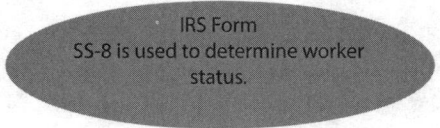
IRS Form SS-8 is used to determine worker status.

Chapter 25
Can You Deduct Moving Expenses?

> **Chapter 25 Trail Route**
> - Distance Test
> - Time Test
> - Qualified Moving Expenses
> - Nonqualified Moving Expenses
> - Moving You and Your Family Members
> - Military Moving Rules

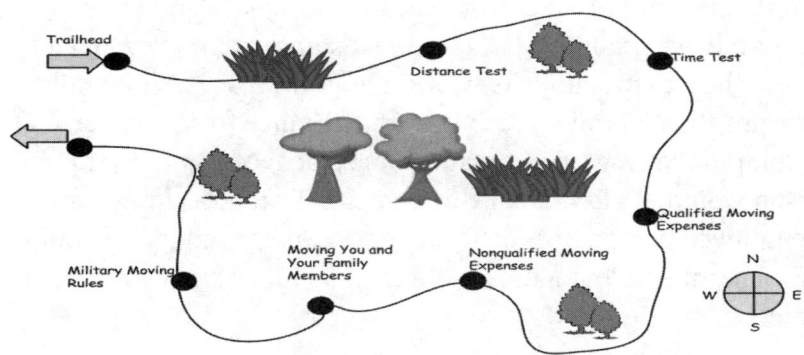

There's a husband and wife we serve in our office, Steve and Candice, and they both serve in the military. Just in the ten years they have been clients, they have moved from Missouri to Tennessee, then to Virginia, then to D.C., then to Ohio, and then to North Dakota…and I probably left at least one move out! What troopers they are to have suffered through all of those moves!

Moving is an expensive activity. Let's see if you qualify for deducting your moving expenses. If you qualify to deduct your moving expenses on your income tax return, you should take advantage of it, in order to save income tax and keep more of your money for you and your family. I'm going to first discuss the Moving Expense Deduction 👆 rules for non-military folks, because that's the majority of the affected folks, and then I'll discuss military moves at the end of this chapter.

The rules are very straightforward. You can deduct the cost of moving you and your family members, and your household goods, less any employer reimbursements of these costs. And you will need to meet the Distance Test and the Time Test in order to qualify to take the Moving Expense Deduction 👆. To elaborate:

Distance Test

To qualify for the Distance Test, the distance between your new workplace and former home must be at least 50 miles more than the distance between your former workplace and your former home. For example, because the distance from Denver, CO (former home) to Kansas City, KS (new workplace) of 600 miles is greater than 50 miles more than the distance from Denver, CO to Colorado Springs, CO (former workplace) of 68 miles, this person would qualify under the Distance Test. For a long-time unemployed person, this distance test is considered met if your new place of employment is more than 50 miles from your former home.

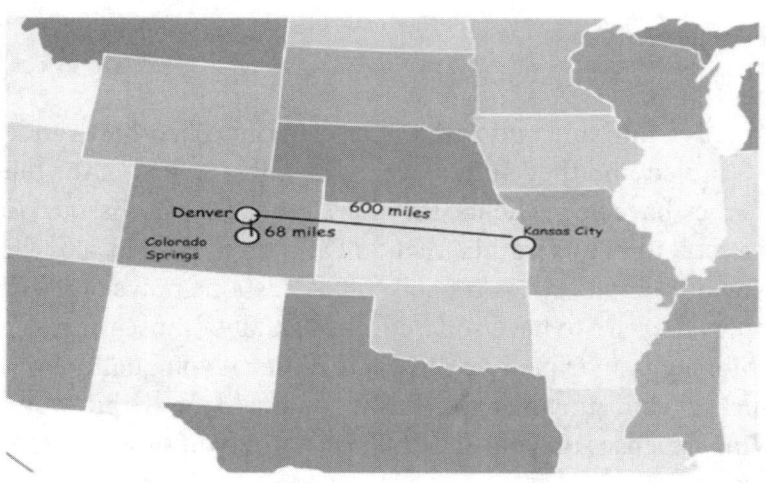

Time Test

To qualify for the Time Test, you need to work at least 39 weeks at your new workplace, in the year immediately following the move. If you are self-employed, then you must meet the 39 week work requirement above, and you also must work at least 78 weeks during the 24 months immediately following your move. The IRS waives the Time Test requirement if the employee becomes disabled, is transferred by the employer and employer initiated the transfer, is terminated due to no fault of his or her own, or passes away.

You can proceed with taking the Moving Expense Deduction 👍 if you have not yet met the Time Test, but if you later fail to meet the Time Test, you will need to either amend your prior income tax return to remove the Moving Expense Deduction 👍, or you will need to include the previously deducted Moving Expense as Other Income on your income tax return for the following year.

If you move and change jobs, but stay in the area of where you just moved to, you can combine the time spent at the two jobs to meet the 39-week work requirement.

Before we go on, it would be helpful to see which expenses are Qualified Moving Expenses and which are not.

Qualified Moving Expenses
- *Transportation to move you*
- *Transportation to move your family*
- *Transportation to move your and your family's belongings*
- *Up to 30 days of storage fees of your belongings*

> *Common Nonqualified Moving Expenses*
> - *House hunting trips*
> - *House closing fees*
> - *Meals*
> - *Temporary living accommodations*
> - *A "Tax Package" from your employer that includes additional compensation and is all withheld as Federal and state income tax to cover the income tax on the rest of the Nonqualified Moving Expenses*

When you deduct Moving Expenses on your income tax return, that is recorded on page 1 of your Form 1040; it is not an Itemized Deduction. So, for those subject to a phase-out of Itemized Deductions and for those who don't itemize their deductions, they won't lose any of their Moving Expense Deduction 👍.

Moving You and Your Family Members

When moving, meals are excluded, and the deduction 👍 is only allowable for one trip for each family member. The family can travel at different times (if one spouse stays behind while the children finish the school year, for example). The mileage rate for 2015 is 23 cents ✈ per mile, and I'll update my website (www.LisaBcpa.com) annually as the moving mileage rate is adjusted by the IRS.

If you are lucky, your employer will pay for additional moving expenses, such as house hunting trips, house closing fees, meals, or temporary living expenses (to name a few), but these costs will be added to your W-2 at year end. They are not deductible on your income tax return. If the employer pays for these nonqualified expenses, they are income to you. If you personally pay for house hunting trips, closing fees, meals, and temporary living expense (or any other expense than moving your persons and your personal possessions and goods), then those nonqualified expenses are not deductible by you.

If you do incur costs to move you and your family, and your possessions that exceeds the amount reimbursed by the employer, then that is deductible 👍 on your income tax return as Moving

Expense, if you meet the Distance Test and Time Test.

Military Moving Rules

Active duty members of the U.S. Armed forces required to move do not have to meet the Time Test or the Distance Test in order to deduct Moving Expenses. Additionally, for applicable military moves, there are some nontaxable benefits for temporary living expenses.

So that I could quantify for you how much the Moving Expense Deduction could be worth, I looked to my client files. The Moving Expense Deduction 👍 for five families for whom we recently prepared income tax returns ranged from $2K to $11K. However, several other times during the year, I informed clients they didn't qualify for the Moving Expense Deduction 👍 (usually because the expenses fell into the nonqualified category), and so their moving expense deduction totaled zero.

Chapter Summary

If you hope to deduct Moving Expenses, you will need to qualify, using the Time Test and Distance Test, relative to your new job. Employer-reimbursed moving expenses are not eligible for the Moving Expense Deduction 👍 and only Qualified Moving Expenses qualify for the deduction 👍. In short, Qualified Moving Expenses include the cost to move your bodies and your stuff. Advanced knowledge of the Moving Expense Deduction 👍 rules may help you determine if you can afford to make the move, and can help you save income tax.

IRS Form 3903 is used to document the Moving Expense Deduction.

Chapter 26
How to Manage Hobby Losses to Avoid IRS Issues

> Chapter 26 Trail Route
> - Business activities with a loss that can be scrutinized as a possible hobby
> - Characteristics of a business operated for profit
> - How to document your business is "for profit" using the 9 characteristics listed in the chapter

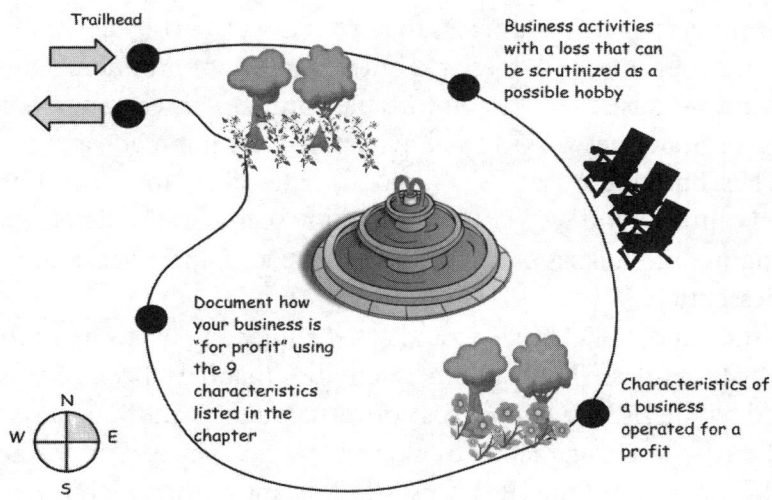

Business Activities with a Loss That Can Be Scrutinized as a Possible Hobby

Buck started a rock band, wrote clever songs, and they perform once in a while at various small venues. Buck is having a ball being in the band, and so are his friends, but having a band is expensive. The sound equipment, instruments, and the van to haul it all in has added up. "Thank goodness it saves me taxes," Buck tells his friends. From knowing Buck, I wonder if he has the energy and drive to push to make the band a financial success. Buck is retired, and suffers from health issues.

Tim loves horses, and would rather spend time with Molly, his best horse, than with his wife. Tim breeds the horses and sells the offspring. Tim's goal is to have one of his horses win a major competition or show, so he can sell the offspring at crazy high prices, like his father did before him. He just needs a big win at a competition. The travel and upkeep on the horses are taking every last dollar Tim has. "At least I don't pay any taxes," he mutters. I fear, having Tim tell me of how long he's been trying to make a go of it and seeing that he's operating on a shoestring budget, he doesn't have the resources to compete with the big players in the game, or to make the venture a success.

Kim is an artist, and refers to herself as "a starving artist." Her attorney husband doesn't mind that she's not producing any income, because they are comfortable living on his earnings. Kim advertises and networks to sell her art, but has not made a profit yet. Her husband quips, "She's a good write-off for me." Kim's art is very unique and well done, and I enjoy seeing it. But it's a rough economy, and folks are not spending large amounts of cash on nonessentials.

The band, horse breeder, and artist all need to be aware of the hobby loss rules. There are other activities that have been scrutinized by the IRS for hobby loss concerns, such as craft businesses, vineyards, and drag racing, to name a few. So, why is it important to show a profit to the IRS? This is important so that the business deductions will not be disallowed. The IRS assumes a business is operated with a profit motive if the business is profitable in at least 3 out of 5 consecutive years, and for horse-related businesses, the IRS assumes the business is operated with a profit motive if it is profitable 2 out of 7 consecutive years.

> *The IRS assumes a business is operated with a profit motive if the business is profitable in at least 3 out of 5 consecutive years, and for horse-related businesses, 2 out of 7 consecutive years.*

Characteristics of a Business Operated for Profit

The owner of a business subject to scrutiny over hobby loss rules needs to determine if their business is operated for the primary purpose of making a profit. Does the owner possess a sincere profit motive? The IRS issued this list to help folks determine if their business is a hobby, which is what the IRS uses to make their own determination of whether the business is a hobby.

1. The manner in which the taxpayer carries on the activity. Do you keep thorough business records, including thorough documentation of all revenue and expenses? Do you have a manual or computerized bookkeeping system? Do you keep the financial records of the activity separate from your personal records, keeping separate checking and credit card accounts? Have you obtained insurance and necessary licenses to operate this business?
2. The expertise of the taxpayer or advisors. Do you have the experience necessary to operate this business, or have you hired third parties that do? Have you researched the market and tecÛology enhancements in the industry in which you operate?
3. The time and effort spent by the taxpayer in carrying on the activity. Do you work at this business on a regular basis? Or do you work in this business only on an occasional basis? Do you have the endurance needed to run the business? Do you spend time evaluating the business results and have written plans for improvements, if needed?
4. The expectation that assets used may appreciate in value. Does the business exist to increase value of assets or inventory?
5. Taxpayer's success in other similar or dissimilar activities. Have you been successful at other ventures and have a proven track record at managing and operating a business? Or, have you owned a string of failed businesses in the past?
6. Taxpayer's history of income/loss with respect to the activ-

ity. Can you show you have made a profit at this activity in the past? If yes, how recently have you shown a profit?
7. Amount of occasional profits, if any. Are you making any money at this activity? Have you ever made money at this activity?
8. Financial status of the taxpayer. Do you have other financial means that support you, where you aren't dependent on making this activity a success? Without other financial support, would you still be operating this business?
9. Elements of personal pleasure or recreation. Is your participation in this activity for pleasure or recreation? Do you keep a log of business and personal use of business assets?

All of the above points are important because hobby expenses are only deductible 👆 to the extent of hobby income. So, in the case of the rock band above, let's take a look at their revenues and expenses for a recent year:

Revenue (6 shows)	$1,600
Travel expenses	(2,100)
Equipment and van depreciation	(4,800)
Supplies	(600)
Total expenses	(7,500)
Net loss	$(5,900)

In the above example, if the IRS audits and then deems the rock band to be a hobby, we would only be able to deduct $1,600 of the expenses, an amount equal to the revenue. The remainder of the expenses would not carry forward to offset revenue in the next year, so the deduction for the excess expenses is permanently lost.

On a positive note, hobby income is not subject to self-employment tax. So, if the hobby is profitable in some years, it escapes the 15.3% self-employment tax that other businesses must pay.

Chapter Summary

Document your business as one with a true profit motive, so that the IRS will not deem your business to be a hobby and disallow your expenses. If you record (on computer, paper, video, etc.) how you are meeting or exceeding the expectations in the list of 9 issues listed in this chapter that indicate profit motive, that will assist in a potential IRS audit for the hobby loss issue. By taking these steps, you will be more likely to keep your business Income Tax Deductions 👍, and thus you will lower your income tax, and keep more of your money.

> IRS Form 8949 is used to calculate Hobby Income from sale of Capital Items, such as art or other collectibles.

> IRS Form 1040, Other Income line, is used to record Hobby Income from rendering personal services and other noncapital sales.

Chapter 27
Muscle Up With the Right Hammer to Deduct Medical Expenses
(Health Savings Accounts & Flexible Spending Accounts)

> Chapter 27 Trail Route
> - Health Savings Accounts (HSAs)
> - HSAs-unlimited accumulation and carry over to future years
> - Flexible Spending Accounts (FSAs)
> - FSAs-$500 carry over to the following year

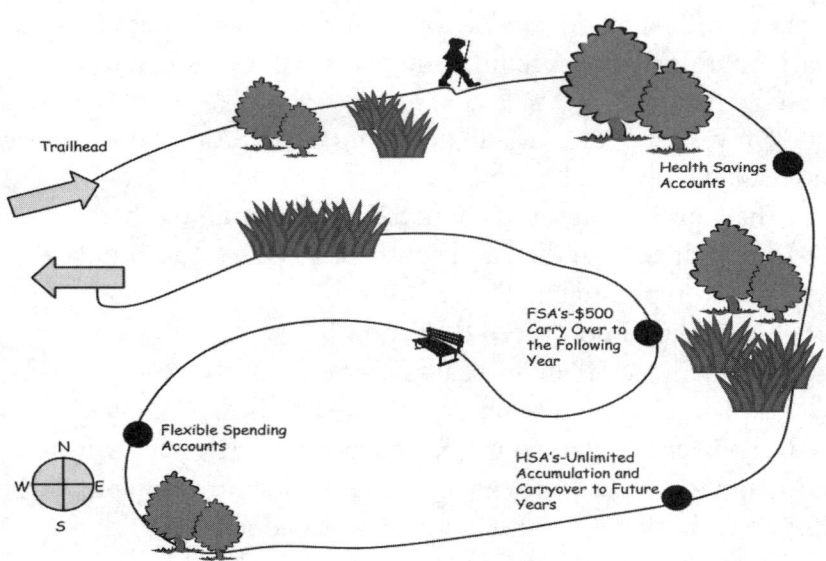

Most folks are unable to deduct medical expenses 👍 because they don't exceed the required threshold. Medical expenses aren't deductible unless they exceed 10% ✈ of total income (Adjusted Gross Income). (For folks over age 65, the threshold is 7.5% ✈ of total income for now.) For example, if your total income is $200K, only medical expenses over $20K are deductible. In my CPA practice, I've found the only middle-income folks that are deducting medical expenses are some folks in nursing homes, and those that are critically ill. But there a couple of tools that you may be able to use to help you deduct Qualified Medical Expenses (expenses incurred to assist the body to operate properly).

Health Savings Accounts 👍

A Health Savings Account (HSA) is a great solution to this issue of medical expenses that are otherwise not deductible. These accounts have been around for several years, but are becoming more common, as health insurance plan deductibles are increasing.

Last year, several of my clients covered all of their medical expenses with Health Savings Account distributions, and here is how my discussion went with one of them.

I asked, "Darla, do you have a lot of medical expenses for this year? Anything worth accumulating, to see if it's enough to deduct?"

"Oh yes," she said, "we finally set up our HSA for $6K, and we had $5,500 of medical expenses."

"That's great! You saved about $2K in tax by doing that!"

Darla rallied with that, and continued. "OK, I'll accumulate the expenses by type and email them to you."

"That's okay, I don't need them now."

"Well, why not?! You just said I'd save $2K."

I explained, "If you reimbursed yourself for the $5,500 in medical expenses from your HSA, then you don't get a further deduction for those same expenses. But I'll for sure put your $6K HSA contribution on your tax return as a deduction."

Say in 2015, you contribute to a HSA 👍 in the amount of $6,650 and take an Income Tax Deduction for the $6,650, and then you take an HSA distribution also in 2015 to pay for your teen's orthodontic bill, your and your spouse's eyeglasses, and prescriptions totaling $6,650. Because of the income tax savings of using the money from the Health Savings Account to pay these Qualified Medical Expenses, the after-tax cost of these expenses is only $4,389 (assuming you are in the 28% Federal income tax bracket and a 6% state income tax bracket). That's a savings of $2,261!

Health Savings Account (HSA) Specifics
- You can contribute $6,650 for 2015 for family coverage into a HSA, & you get an Income Tax Deduction 👍 for the contribution
- You can contribute $3,350 for 2015 for a single plan only, & you get an Income Tax Deduction 👍 for the contribution
- If you are age 55 or older, you can contribute an additional $1K annually to your HSA & deduct it on your income tax return
- As you incur out of pocket Qualified Medical Expenses, you can pay for them out of your HSA
- You can set up a HSA at a bank or at an on-line financial institution
- If your employer contributes to your HSA on your behalf, then the employer gets the Income Tax Deduction instead of you (This will be denoted as Code W on your annual Form W-2)
- If your employer allows you to contribute to the HSA via payroll deduction 👍, & you are contributing with pre-tax dollars, then there is no further Income Tax Deduction 👍 for the HSA contribution on your income tax return, but you still got the tax break because you were able to contribute on a pre-tax basis (This will also be denoted as Code W on your annual Form W-2)
- To participate in a HSA, your health insurance plan must be a High-Deductible Health Plan (defined later in this chapter), you can't be covered by any other non-High Deductible Health Plan
- You can't be claimed as a dependent on anyone else's income tax return & still participate in a HSA
- If you are eligible for a Flexible Spending Account or a health reimbursement account through your employer, you are ineligible to contribute to a HSA
- Once you are on Medicare, you can no longer contribute to a HSA

See below for the 2015 definition of a high-deductible plan.

✈	Single plan	Family plan
Minimum annual plan deductible	$1,300	$2,600
Maximum annual plan deductible (including out of pocket copays and other expenses)	$6,450	$12,900

My Favorite Income Tax Savings Point on the HSA

If in a given year, you don't use all of the funds in your HSA for Qualified Medical Expenses, the account accumulates and can be used in the future. There is no limit to the amount you can carry over to a future year, and there is no limit to how large your HSA can grow, other than making sure you stay in compliance with the maximum annual contribution limits. If you and your family are very healthy, and don't use the funds in the HSA, it's a great idea to let them accumulate (or even pay medical expenses out of pocket), so the HSA accumulates even more. At age 65, the funds in the HSA can be used to pay your health insurance premiums, other than Medicare.

At the present time, one can take money out of a HSA beginning at age 65 for anything, without penalty. Because of this current rule, the HSA can act as an additional IRA. However, rules change, and if you aren't at the threshold of becoming age 65, make sure you check the income tax law when you are age 65 to see if you can still withdraw from your HSA for any purpose.

My client, James, has a high-deductible health plan with family coverage and a HSA. James annually contributes the maximum allowable to his HSA. Each year as his family incurs medical expenses, he does NOT pay those expenses out of his HSA. Instead, James lets his HSA accumulate and thinks of the account as an additional IRA. To date, his HSA has accumulated to $32K, and he expects it will grow to $52K before he retires!

Flexible Spending Accounts 👍

Another type of hammer to use for medical expenses is the Flexible Spending Account (FSA). An employer can allow employees to contribute up to $2,550 for 2015 into this plan, for use in paying medical expenses. Previously no carry-over of funds provision existed with the FSA, but with the Affordable Care Act ("Obamacare"), employers can now amend their FSA plan documents to allow $500 to be carried over for every plan participant, if the participant has the funds in their account to carry over.

The FSA benefit plan is very similar to the HSA, just a smaller hammer. If one spouse is eligible for a FSA, and the other spouse is eligible for the HSA, forego the FSA, and contribute to the HSA instead. It's a better move to contribute to the HSA. Why?

- The unused HSA contributions carry over and accumulate without limit; and
- You are allowed much higher contributions into an HSA account in comparison to a FSA account.

One can pay for over-the-counter drugs with a FSA, whereas they cannot with a HSA. However, the employer is supposed to accumulate the over-the-counter medicines paid with FSA dollars, and add that to taxable income on the employees' W-2's. Given that over-the-counter medicine purchases are added back to the employee's W-2 as taxable income, there is no benefit to using the FSA for over-the-counter medicines.

Chapter Summary

A Health Savings Account (HSA) is a great tool to use to deduct medical expenses: contributions are income tax deductible 👍 (unless made by the employer), medical expenses can be paid out of the HSA, and the balance of the HSA can accumulate without limitation. Some folks let funds in their HSA accumulate, and think of the account as an additional IRA account. A Flexible Spending Account (FSA) is also a great tool to be able to deduct medical expenses. Only $500 of unused FSA funds can be carried forward to a new year. While HSAs are superior to FSAs, both are a good ways to be able to deduct medical expenses, and this will save you income tax dollars.

Chapter 28
Minimize Income Tax Even in Divorce

> ### Chapter 28 Trail Route
> - Final joint income tax return
> - Head of household
> - Dependency exemptions
> - Release of dependency exemptions
> - Child Tax Credits
> - Alimony
> - Child support
> - Retirement plans
> - College education tax benefits
> - Withholding allowances for future years
> - Cost basis
> - Legal fees

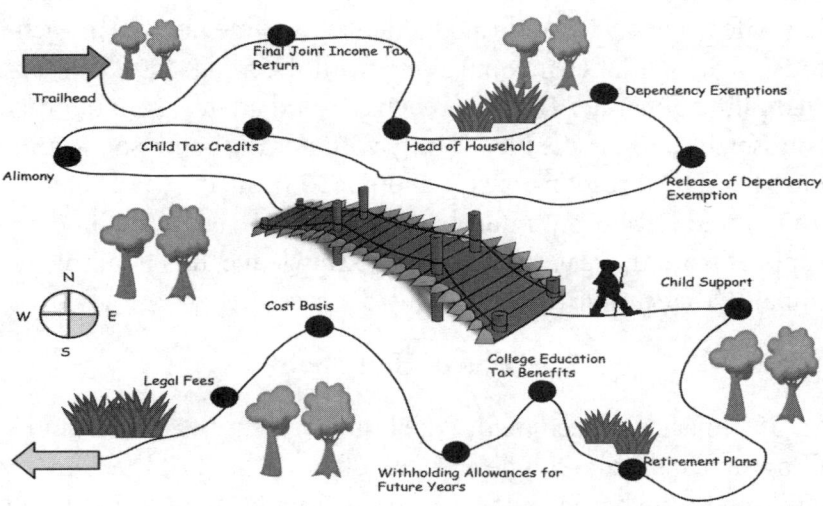

Make lemonade out of lemons they say. No one wants to be divorced before they marry, of course, but if you are in the process of divorcing or are divorced, as I am, you need to think about the income tax implications, so you don't over pay Uncle

Sam. As a single person, you likely need to hang on to every dollar possible. So let's see if you can find some helpful ideas in this chapter in minimize income tax related to your divorce, if applicable.

Final Joint Income Tax Return

Perhaps you were still married on the last day of a year, and divorced in the next year, before your previous year's income tax return was filed. Usually, your joint income tax liability will be smaller if you file jointly, but that's not always the case. If you do file jointly, both parties are responsible for the tax liability, so if you are unsure if your ex-spouse is going to pay their fair share, you should consider filing as Married Filing Separate. Lastly, if you are estranged, and cannot communicate with your ex-spouse, you likely must file as Married Filing Separate. See Chapter 9 for a full discussion of Married Filing Jointly vs. Married Filing Separate.

I worked on a case referred by a tax attorney a couple of years ago, and in that case, after we prepared all past due income tax returns, the husband owed over $350K for a seven-year period. His wife proved wise and timely filed an income tax return each of those years, with her income alone, with the filing status of Married Filing Separate. The wife received good advice from her own counsel, because if she filed jointly with her husband, she would have been held responsible for a joint $350K income tax liability. This would have been unfair because she received no income or support from those earnings. To my knowledge, this liability is still unpaid! That couple did eventually divorce.

Head of Household

If you are divorced before the last day of the year, then your filing status is either Single or Head of Household (if there are children in the home and you meet the requirements). The Head of Household filing status is often used by one or both of the divorcing parties, if there is more than one child. See Chapter 10, which is exclusively about Head of Household status. Essentially, when using Head of Household status, you get to avail yourself to more favorable income tax brackets, as compared to the income tax brackets for the Single filing status. The resulting income tax liability is lower, when applying the Head of Household income tax brackets than the Single income tax brackets. However, if you don't qualify for Head of Household status, you must file as a Single taxpayer.

Dependency Exemptions

The custodial parent is the parent with whom the child spends more nights during the year, and that is the parent with whom the dependency exemption lands. For joint custody situations, the divorce decree will usually name which parent is the custodial parent for each child. When there is more than one child, one spouse may be the custodial parent of some of the children, and the other spouse may be the custodial parent of the other children. If your divorce is not yet final, you may want to look at Chapter 11, to review all of the dependency tests, to see who is eligible for the dependency exemption prior to any court document finalizing that point.

Too many times to count, I've witnessed clients receive an IRS notice stating someone else has already taken one or more of their children as an exemption on an income tax return that has been filed earlier than theirs. In the most recent years, the IRS system doesn't even accept an efiled income tax return that has dependents listed, if someone has already claimed them. In all of these cases, the ex-spouse took the children's exemptions, regardless of whether they proved eligible to based on the dependency tests. Every time this happens, the conversation goes something like this:

The IRS will not accept an efiled income tax return or issues a notice to paper filers, if the taxpayer claims the dependency exemption for a child that has already been claimed on someone else's income tax return.

"I attempted to efile your income tax return," I explain, "but the IRS has rejected it. It appears someone else has already taken Tommy as an exemption on their income tax return."

"That rotten scoundrel, he (ex-husband) took Tommy to get a bigger refund, but the divorce papers say I'm supposed to take him."

When this happens, I mail in a paper copy of the income tax return, and attach a copy of the divorce decree, highlighting the language that allows my client to take the given exemption. At that point, the ex-spouse is issued an IRS notice that the exemption they placed on their income tax return has been disallowed, and they are billed for the additional income tax, penalty and interest.

Release of Dependency Exemption

A custodial parent can release the dependency exemption of one or more children to the noncustodial parent (for one year or all future years), which allows the noncustodial parent to:
- take the dependency exemption(s) 👍 ;
- take the Child Tax Credit(s) ❖ ; and
- take any college education benefits 👍.

This is a good move in cases where the custodial parent cannot use the dependency exemptions or Child Tax Credits ❖ (discussed below) due to high income. Also, the custodial parent may be unable to use the dependency exemptions if he or she is subject to the Alternative Minimum Tax (AMT). See Chapter 23 for a discussion of AMT.

When the custodial parent releases a dependency exemption to the noncustodial parent, the custodial parent is still eligible to:
- Take the Child and Dependent Care Credit ❖ (see Chapter 14 for details);
- Exclude from income any employer-provided Dependent Care Benefits 👍 ;
- Take the Earned Income Credit ❖ ; and
- Use Head of Household status (see Chapter 10 for details).

My ex-husband (also a CPA) and I strategize annually to see how we can minimize overall income tax. Nothing like two CPAs beating it up to get the best result! The divorce was amicable, so we cooperate without any major issues. Our divorce decree states that each of us is the custodial parent for two of our four children. Because his income proved higher than mine for a number of

> IRS Form 8332 is used to release a dependency exemption to the noncustodial parent.

years after the divorce and he failed to be eligible for the Child Tax Credit ❖ or the dependency exemptions (due to Alternative Minimum Tax), each year he would release his dependency exemptions to me. I would then place those exemptions on my income tax return. Lastly, we would calculate the total benefit of that move, and I would gift half of that back to him. For several years, we saved $4K per year by cooperating!

Child Tax Credit ❖ and Additional Child Tax Credit ❖

Parents receive the $1K Child Tax Credit ❖ for qualifying children under age seventeen. When you are considering the dependency exemption, either in the writing of your divorce decree or if you are considering signing a release of dependency exemption, consider these Income Tax Credits ❖ as well. The parent receiving the dependency exemption also gets the Child Tax Credit ❖. The Child Tax Credit ❖ phases out for 2014 at $110K ✈ of AGI for Married Filing Joint taxpayers, $75K ✈ for Head of Household and Single taxpayers, and $55K ✈ for Married Filing Separate taxpayers.

If you do not qualify to take all of the Child Tax Credit ❖ due to low or no income tax liability, you may still be able to take the Additional Child Tax Credit ❖, and the combined maximum for both credits is $1K per child. The Child Tax Credit ❖ is not refundable, but the Additional Child Tax Credit ❖ is partially refundable.

Alimony

Alimony (also called maintenance) is income tax deductible to the payer, and income taxable to the receiver. Many times alimony is a big negotiating point in a divorce, and the income tax effect of the alimony needs to be considered whether you are the payer or receiver. Say you and your soon to be ex-spouse will be in differing income tax brackets, look at the example below, that is very typical of divorce situations I've seen in my tax practice:

	Colin	Paula
Annual alimony paid	($48,000)	
Annual alimony received		$48,000
Federal marginal income tax rate after divorce	25%	15%
After tax cost of alimony paid	($36,000)	
After tax alimony received		$40,800

So in this example, Colin needs to know that his true cost of the alimony is actually 75% (100% less his Federal marginal income tax rate of 25%) of the total. Paula needs to know that she is actually only receiving 85% (100% less her Federal marginal tax rate of 15%) of the alimony, after income taxes are paid. If Colin and Paula live in a state where there is an income tax (most states have income tax), that should also be considered.

If alimony is set for life, don't forget the inflation-adjusted value of alimony will lessen over time. If you are paying the alimony, this is good news. If you are receiving the alimony, plan so that you have enough cash in future years.

Child Support

Child support is not an Income Tax Deduction for the payer and is not taxable income to the receiving spouse. In most states, child support is statutorily set, and usually not much of a negotiating point during divorce proceedings.

Retirement Plans

There's often a property settlement between the parties to the divorce. Consult your attorney to make sure the transfer of retirement accounts is carried out in accordance with the guidelines, to avoid income tax and also the 10% early withdrawal penalty if you are under age 59½. If the retirement account is an IRA, any required transfer should be done directly to the IRA of the other party to avoid the income tax and any early withdrawal penalty. If the entire IRA is being transferred, then the name and Social Security number on the IRA account could simply be changed.

For non-IRA retirement accounts, a transfer can be made with a Qualified Domestic Relations Order (QDRO). Under the QDRO rules, if the receiving spouse does not roll the retirement plan over, but instead keeps the money, there is no 10% early withdrawal penalty.

A forty-year-old gal I worked with that was going through a divorce was unable to force her now ex-husband to leave the home they shared. She kept the children with her in an apartment, while the ex-husband retained the large home. During divorce negotiations, the husband refused to turn the house over to the wife. In the end, her attorney obtained a $40K QDRO distribution for her, penalty free, for a down payment on a new suitable home for her and her children.

College Education Tax Benefits

You must take your child as a dependent on your income tax return in order to take the Tuition & Fees Deduction ☝ or the Education Tax Credit ❖. The cost of foregoing their exemption includes the cost of lost college education tax benefits. See Chapter

16 for a full discussion of college education tax benefits.

Withholding Allowances for Future Years

The Form W-4, Employee's Withholding Allowance Certificate, should be updated with your employer if the number of dependency exemptions has decreased due to your divorce. This is important because you will want to make sure the correct amount of withholding for income taxes is taken out of your wages. This issue has snuck up on even the smartest of taxpayers, especially when they divorce towards the end of the year, and lose exemptions for the whole year.

Bruce and Debbie divorced in December and Debbie is the custodial parent, so she is allowed the two children's dependency exemption. The couple usually received an income tax refund in the past, but Bruce ended up owing income tax for the year of the divorce, because he no longer was eligible for the children's dependency exemptions or Child Tax Credits ❖. This caused a swing in tax from a refund to a balance due of $4K. After completing his income tax return, we requested he update his W-4 Form with his employer, so this issue wouldn't recur for the following year.

Cost Basis

In the division of property related to the divorce, the cost basis of assets is transferred to the spouse that receives the related asset. This is important because whenever assets are sold, the higher the cost basis, and the lower the gain. Gain on sale of personal assets (such as vacation homes or cars) is taxable, but a loss on the sale of personal assets is not tax-deductible.

When securities, rental properties, and other investments are sold, whether at a gain or loss, the transaction is reportable on your income tax return. You will need the cost basis to reduce any resulting gain and income tax, or to increase your Income Tax Deduction on the loss.

Barbara and Nick divorced, and I prepared Barbara's income tax return for the year of the divorce. They owned a condo in Florida she sold subsequent to the divorce, so I inquired about the cost basis. Barbara informed me that her ex-husband held that information, and we were unable to obtain it from him. In the end, I called the accountant that previously served as their income tax preparer during their marriage, and after he received a release from Barbara, he provided me the cost basis information that Barbara needed for her income tax return. Without this information, I could not have prepared an accurate income tax return for Barbara, and she would have ended up paying too much in income tax.

Legal Fees

You likely incurred legal fees to obtain the divorce, but only the portion of these legal fees that your attorney specifies as tax planning fees are deductible ♠. Many times the deductible portion is zero, and even if a part is considered deductible ♠, that's a Miscellaneous Itemized Deduction, and those must exceed 2% of total income (AGI) before they are deductible ♠. In about 3 decades as an accountant, I've never seen legal fees pursuant to a divorce be deductible, for the portion related to tax planning, because those fees, along with the client's Miscellaneous Itemized Deductions, have never exceeded 2% of AGI.

Chapter Summary

If you are going through a divorce, the income tax implications are numerous. Which filing status ♠ should you use for the final tax return before the divorce is finalized? Which children's exemptions ♠ should you take, or should you release the exemptions to a noncustodial spouse? Which child(ren)'s Child Tax Credit ❖ are you eligible for and which college education tax benefits ♠ ? Alimony is a Tax Deduction ♠ for the payer and taxable income for the receiver; should you agree to alimony? Does a retirement plan need to be split? Have you updated your withholding allowances for the New Year to reflect the correct number of exemptions you will be taking? Have you documented cost basis ♠ of capital assets you retained? Which legal fees are income tax deductible?

With all of these variables, you will need to study how each will affect you, and how you should proceed on each item. You will see that this summary asks more questions than it answers; each person's answers will differ. You will need to find the best path for you to save the most income tax dollars.

Chapter 29

Think Green to Save Some Green

> **Chapter 29 Trail Route**
> - Energy savings for your home
> - Your car as an energy saver

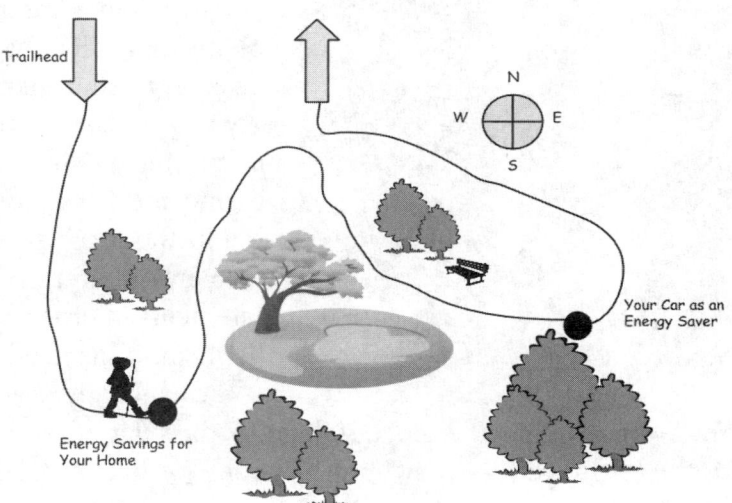

Energy Savings for Your Home

The earth's resources are not infinite. Many are searching for new energy sources, and conserving energy where possible. If you are environmentally conscious and want to save income tax, you may want to consider these home improvements which include Income Tax Credits ❖:
- Solar electric;
- Solar water heating;
- Fuel cells for heating;
- Geothermal heat pumps; and
- Wind energy.

The Income Tax Credit ❖ for all of these items is 30% of the total cost (including installation, piping and wiring), with no maximum, except the fuel cells have a maximum of $1K per kilowatt of capacity. So, if your solar energy panels, system and installation cost you $20K, for example, then you earned a $6K Income Tax Credit ❖ (a dollar-for- dollar offset of income tax liability)!

The manufacturer or salesperson will know if the energy- efficient property you are considering purchasing qualifies for the Income Tax Credit ❖ or not, and you can rely on the manufacturer's written statements in order to take the Income Tax Credit ❖.

I can already hear one of my favorite clients, Joe, gloat, "Oh good, the solar water heating is the way to go for my swimming pool." Joe likes to take advantage of every income tax planning point possible, sometimes pushing the envelope a bit, until I straighten him out. He also owns every toy imaginable.

"Sorry Joe," I'll say like a big sister. "These credits are not applicable to swimming pools or hot tubs."

Keep in mind that if you sell the home that you have installed any energy equipment in, and you received an Income Tax Credit ❖ for these, your cost basis in the property is reduced by the Income Tax Credit ❖ received. (See Chapter 22 for discussion on escaping tax on the sale of a personal residence.) Also, to qualify, all of these improvements must be installed in your US personal residence, includ-

> "I'd put my money on the sun and solar energy, what a source of power! I hope we don't have to wait until oil and coal run out, before we tackle that.
> --Thomas Edison

ing new construction, except the fuel cell property, that must be installed in your principal residence, and also includes new construction. (A personal residence, such as a vacation home, is different from your principal residence.)

The Energy Savings Income Tax Credits ❖ offset both regular tax and Alternative Minimum Tax, and if you cannot use the credit in the year of installation of the equipment, you can carry forward the Income Tax Credit ❖ to the next year.

Some utility companies offer generous rebates for the installation of solar energy equipment in your residence. Those rebates (a) reduce your cost of the solar equipment, thus reducing the Income Tax Credit ❖; and (b) reduce your cost basis in the equipment and home.

You may want to research your electric provider's website or give them a telephone call to see if they are offering rebates for solar energy installation. Also note that the Energy Tax Credits ❖ discussed in this chapter relate to residences only; businesses have differing tax treatments for Energy Tax Credits ❖ and rebates, and that discussion is outside the scope of this book.

Plug-In Vehicles Credit ❖

A friend and I escaped to a get-away weekend to Michigan City, Indiana, and we saw some unusual receptacles at the front of some of the parking spaces at the outlet mall.

"What are those parking meters doing at an outlet mall?" I asked.

"Those are electrical charging stations for electric cars."

I wonder if sometime in the future, those will be prevalent throughout most communities.

When President Obama took office, regular gasoline cost $1.85 a gallon as quoted on www.Oilprice.com. Since then, gas prices have been as high as $4 per gallon, and have bounced up and down. Many are searching for ways to cut their expenditure for automobile gasoline. You may want to buy a plug-in (electric) car if you are environmentally conscious and hope to save on the purchase of gasoline.

The Income Tax Credit ❖ for purchasing or leasing a plug-in

vehicle ranges from $2,500 to $7,500 (a dollar-for-dollar offset of income tax liability), depending on the battery capacity (which must be at least four kilowatt hours), and of course you want to know which vehicles qualify. After each manufacturer sells a total of 200K plug-in vehicles (no limit at this time to the number of years this could take), the Income Tax Credit ❖ will no longer be allowed for that manufacturer's vehicles. To learn which vehicles qualify and how many of each have sold so far, go to www.IRS.gov, and then use their search engine to look for "Plug-In Electric Drive Motor Vehicle Credit Quarterly Sales." The chart on that webpage will show how many vehicles have been sold to date by each of the

manufacturers, so you know which vehicles are still eligible for the Income Tax Credit ❖. The IRS updates this chart each quarter.

Golf carts and other recreational toys are not eligible for this Income Tax Credit, because they are not intended to be used in regular traffic on public roads. The vehicle must weigh less than 14K pounds to qualify for the Income Tax Credit ❖. If you purchase one of the otherwise eligible vehicles that was pre-owned (used), you are not eligible for this Plug-In Vehicle Credit.

One observation I have on the plug-in vehicles is that they are very expensive, in comparison to the similar makes of automobiles that run on gasoline. I would have hoped the purchase price of the plug-in vehicles less the related Income Tax Credit ❖ would approximate the cost of (or be at most 10% more than) the same vehicle that runs on gasoline. I don't want to discourage anyone from purchasing a plug-in vehicle if your goal is to do the right thing for our environment; I just want to warn you that it isn't as cost effective as you may hope at this time. Perhaps the cost of electric cars

> *For Fans of the Dallas TV Show (on TNT):*
> *Demonstrating the new alternative energy story line when the show made a 2012 comeback, Christopher Ewing, son of Bobby Ewing, drives an electric Tesla Roadster.*
> *And his once-fiancé, Rebecca, drives a plug-in Chevy Volt.*

will decrease over time.

Another concern I have is that the battery life of some of the plug-in vehicles isn't very long, so it's not practical to depend on the car for any travel outside of the immediate area where you live or where you can charge the vehicle. This concerns me because I already worry about my three teenage daughters, who are all inexperienced drivers. I sure wouldn't want them stranded somewhere without enough battery power to return to the safety of home.

Chapter Summary

There are Income Tax Credits ❖ for energy-efficient products installed in your home for wind, solar and geothermal systems, and also for plug-in electric vehicles. Make sure you follow the guidelines if you are hoping to use the Income Tax Credits ❖ on your income tax return. These Income Tax Credits ❖ can help pay for the purchase of the energy efficient home systems or plug-in electric car.

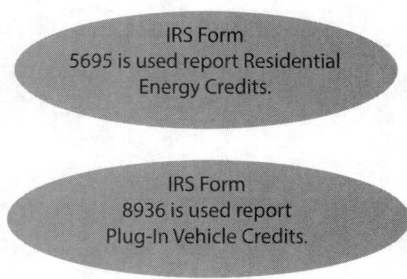

Chapter 30
What Action to Take in High-Income Years

> Chapter 30 Trail Route
> - Postpone income
> - Accelerate deductions
> - Avoid paying tax at the highest income tax rates

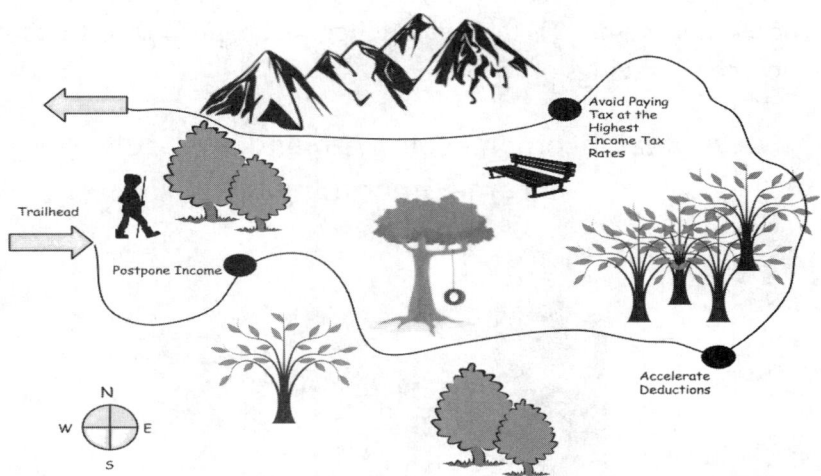

In some years, you hopefully have the enviable issue of having higher income in comparison to your previous years' incomes. Perhaps you have a major commission or sale of appreciated real estate, and you have money falling out of your pockets. Regardless of the source of the high income, you should take additional steps to minimize the income tax effect of the high-income year. With careful planning, you will keep more of your money instead of paying it in income tax.

Income Smoothing, according to Investopedia.com, is "the use of accounting tecÚiques to level out net income fluctuations from one period to the next." This concept is applicable when considering both high-income years and low-income years.

In the chart on the next page, first look at the darker columns. The taxpayer lands in the 28% income tax bracket for 2015, and then in the much lower, 15% income tax bracket for 2016. If the taxpayer earned $40K less in taxable income in 2015 and $40K more in taxable income in 2016, the taxpayer would remain in the same tax brackets for both 2015 and 2016. Now look at the lighter columns in the chart that show the effect of moving $40K in taxable income from 2015 to 2016.

In each of the years 2015 and 2016, the taxpayer stays in the same income tax bracket, but by moving the $40K in taxable income from 2015 to 2016, it's taxed at 15% for Federal income tax purposes, instead of 28% for Federal income tax purposes. That's an income tax savings of $5,200!

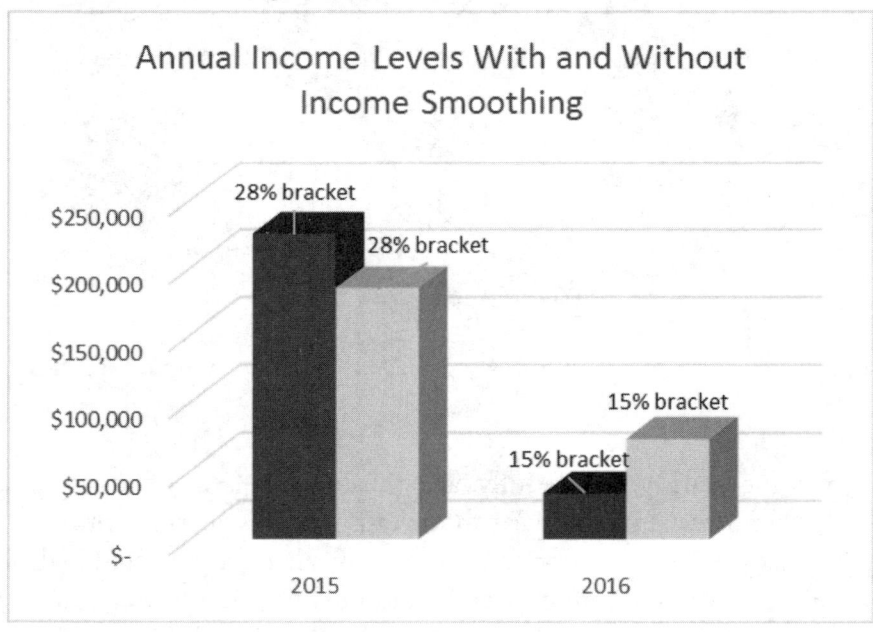

Now let's explore ways you can defer income tax to a lower-income-tax-bracket year to use the Income Smoothing concept. The first thing to consider is how you could defer income until the following year. Here are some examples:

Postpone Income

Postpone Bonus Until Next Year

Many folks are awarded an annual bonus, and they accept the

bonus check as the boss hands out the envelopes. If your income level for the current year is especially high, you can consider asking the employer to hold off until the following January to give you the bonus.

If, in the following year, your income is expected to be back to a more normal level for you or lower, then moving the bonus will lower income in the high-income year and increase income in the following income year. If you can pay income tax on the bonus in a year when you are in a lower-income tax bracket, income tax savings will result.

Participate In A Deferred Compensation Plan

You are likely used to accepting all of your income as earned. Cash is king, right? However, you may want to ask your Human Resources Department if your employer has a Deferred Compensation Plan and you are eligible to participate. You could then postpone receipt of income until a lower-income year. The company may be appreciative of a postponement in paying wages, if they are managing a tight cash flow. If your employer has no Deferred Compensation Plan, perhaps they will consider implementing one, based on your suggestion. They will need the help of a professional in the Employee Benefit Plan area to set up a Deferred Compensation Plan.

Time The Exercise And Sale Of Incentive Stock Options

Very similar to the above discussion about Deferred Compensation, you can consider postponing the exercise and sale of Incentive Stock Options if you are in a high-income year, and instead exercise and sell the options in a lower-income tax year, when you are in a lower tax bracket. (However, if your employer's stock price is attractive, you may want to exercise and sell anyway if you are afraid you won't get the higher price later. Consult your investment advisor on the issue of timing your sale to harvest the best price.) See Chapter 23 for additional discussion of how the exercise of Incentive Stock Options can trigger Alternative Minimum Tax if not sold in the same year they are exercised.

Qualified Incentive Stock Options and Nonqualified Incentive Stock Options have differing tax treatments, so make sure you know which type you have. See the chart below for a brief summary of tax treatments of Incentive Stock Options and definitely discuss the particulars of your Incentive Stock Options transaction with your CPA.

	Qualified Incentive Stock Options	Nonqualified Incentive Stock Options
Grant date (when employee receives an option to exercise in the future)	No tax effect on grant date.	No tax effect on grant date, unless the stock has a readily ascertainable value (publicly traded, for example)
Exercise date (when the employee chooses to exercise the option to purchase the stock)	No regular tax effect on exercise date, but there may be Alternative Minimum Tax from exercising.	Taxable for regular and Alternative Minimum Tax purposes for the amount that fair market value exceeds the option price on the exercise date, assuming fully vested
Fully vested date (when the employee no longer has any restrictions on transactions related to the options)	No tax effect on fully vested date.	No tax effect on fully vested date
Sell date (date the shares are sold)	Taxable when the stock is sold, and there may be a reversing effect for AMT (see Chapter 23).	Taxable for the difference between the stock sale price and the amount included in income at exercise date
Nature of income and taxability	Qualifying disposition* = Long Term Capital Gain. Disqualifying disposition** = Ordinary income for the difference between exercise price and Fair Market Value on exercise date; Capital Gain/Loss for any remaining income or loss.	Exercise date income is treated as ordinary income. Sell date income is treated as Capital Gain income.

* Not disposed within 2 years of grant date or within 1 year of exercise date and continuously employed by grantor until at least 3 months before exercised
** You fail to meet holding requirements above

Delay Sale Of Securities With Appreciated Value

Similar to the above items, you may want to postpone the sale of securities with appreciated value (unrealized gain), which will generate significant Capital Gain income upon a sale. However, note that the long-term Capital Gain rate will not push you into a higher regular income tax bracket. When your Federal income tax is calculated, the Capital Gain is peeled off first, and subjected to the Capital Gain rates. It is the remainder, after Capital Gains are otherwise taxed, that are subject to the regular income tax brackets. However, Capital Gain rates are now on a semi-graduated scale, similar to the regular income tax rates.

The Capital Gain rates are based on your total taxable income and for 2015 are at:

	0% Capital Gain rate (for those in the 15% tax bracket or lower)	15% Capital Gain rate (for those in the 25% - 35% tax brackets)	20% Capital Gain rate (for those in the 39.6% tax bracket)
Single filing	$0-37,450 of taxable income	$37,451-$413,200 of taxable income	$413,201+ of taxable income
Married Filing Joint	$0-$74,900 of taxable income	$74,901-$464,850 of taxable income	$464,851+ of taxable income
Married Filing Separate	$0-37,450 of taxable income	$37,451-232,425 of taxable income	$232,426+ of taxable income
Head of Household	$0-50,200 of taxable income	$50,201-$439,000 of taxable income	$439,001+ of taxable income

There are intermittent discussions in Congress to eliminate the more favorable Capital Gain income tax rates for the middle class. Check www.irs.gov or my website, www.LisaBcpa.com for updates if you want to know if and when the Capital Gain rates are changing or being eliminated.

See Chapter 4 for more discussion of Capital Gain matters.

Understand Concept Of Constructive Receipt

This definition of Constructive Receipt from the IRS, as quoted by Samuel A. Donaldson, Federal Income Taxation of Individuals:

Cases, Problems and Materials, 353 (2nd Ed. 2007), as reprinted on the Wikipedia website: "Income although not actually reduced to a taxpayer's possession is constructively received by him in the taxable year during which it is credited to his account, set apart for him, or otherwise made available so that he may draw upon it at any time, or so that he could have drawn upon it during the taxable year if notice of intention to withdraw had been given. However, income is not constructively received if the taxpayer's control of its receipt is subject to substantial limitations or restrictions."

More simply stated, if you have legal control of the income (or an account that is holding the income) but not physical control, you have constructively received the income, and it is taxable at the moment of constructive receipt.

If you receive a check for rental (or any) income before the end of the year, then that income is supposed to be reflected on your current year income tax return. However, if renters pay their December rent in January of the New Year, this may postpone constructive receipt of the income until the following year if you held no control over the funds. This also moves the income out of the high-income year into the lower-income year.

This same constructive receipt concept could be used to postpone other types of income, such as farm sale of grains or cattle, interest income from private parties (such as a seller financed mortgage), and sale of goods (but you are required to record the Cost of the Goods in year you record the sale), just to name a few examples.

Accelerate Deductions

The second action to consider in higher income years is to accelerate deductions 👍. This, like deferring income, will help you keep more of your money instead of paying more in income tax.

Induce Labor On December 31 👍

This seems extreme and isn't really an actionable item, but it makes the point. If you and your spouse are having a baby due around the end of the calendar year, hopefully that baby makes her appearance before midnight on December 31. If the birth happens before year-end, you will get an income tax exemption for the baby for the whole year. There are more doable examples of ways folks can increase deductions in a high-income year, though.

Clean Out The Closets 👍

If you itemize your deductions, noncash charity continues to be a great source of deductions, and it doesn't cost money to earn this deduction. You should attempt to earn this income tax income deduction in a high-income year, to get the overall income tax down. See Chapter 19 for more information on non-cash charity.

Get Charitable 👍

Cash charitable donations save more income tax in high-income years when you are in a higher income tax bracket, then when you are in lower-income years. See Chapter 19 for a more thorough discussion of charitable donations.

Maximize Retirement Plan Contributions 👍

Maximize your company 401(k), 403(b), or other retirement plan contributions to the highest allowable level. Some folks mistakenly believe putting the maximum allowable into their retirement plan means to put in the amount necessary to earn the maximum employer match, which is often 3-4% of wages. However, I suggest putting in more than that, the maximum allowable by the Internal Revenue Service, which is considerably more than 3-4%. See Chapter 5 for a more thorough discussion of retirement plans and for contribution limits for the most common retirement plans.

If you have a job as an employee, and at the same time you are self-employed, make a SEP IRA contribution on your self-employment income (must do the same for any employees) to increase your total annual retirement savings.

Contribute to IRAs 👍

If your income is within the allowable range, make a contribution to your and your spouse's IRA accounts. A nonworking spouse is eligible for a Spousal IRA, within certain income limitations. See Chapter 6 for more information on IRAs.

Participate in a Health Savings Account 👍

Put the maximum allowable into the plan each year, especially in high-income years. (See Chapter 27 for more information on Health Savings Accounts.)

Pay State & Local Income Taxes 👍

Paying your state and local income taxes before year-end will allow them to be deductible 👍 on your Federal income tax return in the current year, instead of waiting to deduct them the next year. But if you are subject to Alternative Minimum Tax, this will not be helpful because state and local income taxes are an add-back to Alternative Minimum Taxable Income, thus reversing the effect of any deduction of same.

In some cases, if you are having a high-income tax year, you may not be subject to AMT, because your marginal income tax rate may be higher than the AMT tax rate. In this case, you may be subject to AMT only in a low-income tax year. You likely would need to discuss this matter with your CPA in order to determine if paying your state and local income taxes will be helpful to you. See Chapter 23 for more discussion on Alternative Minimum Tax.

Prepay Deductible Expenses 👍

Prepaying deductible expenses could include charity pledge commitments 👍, college expenses 👍 (if you don't lose the education tax benefits due to high income, see Chapter 16 for discussions of education tax benefits), and health insurance for self-employed persons 👍.

Chapter Summary

In years when your income is relatively high, you will want to postpone income and accelerate deductions in order to smooth income, and move income to the next year.

Examples of postponing income may include:
- Postponing a bonus;
- Participating in a deferred compensation plan;
- Postponing the exercise and sale of incentive stock options;
- Delaying sale of securities with appreciated value; and
- Delaying constructive receipt of income.

Examples of accelerating deductions may include:
- Increasing charity (cash and noncash);
- Maximizing retirement plan contributions;
- Contributing to an IRA, if income level is low enough for deduction;
- Participating in a Health Savings Account plan;
- If you are not subject to AMT, paying state and local income taxes before year end; and
- Paying college expenses for the January semester in December, if your income isn't too high where you'll lose the education tax benefits.

Moving taxable income to a lower-income year will save income tax, if you are able to pay income tax at a lower rate. Saving income tax dollars will allow you to keep more cash for meeting other family needs.

Chapter 31
What Action to Take in Low-Income Years

> Chapter 31 Trail Route
> - Accelerate income
> - Postpone deductions
> - May be eligible for increased education credits & deductions due to lower income

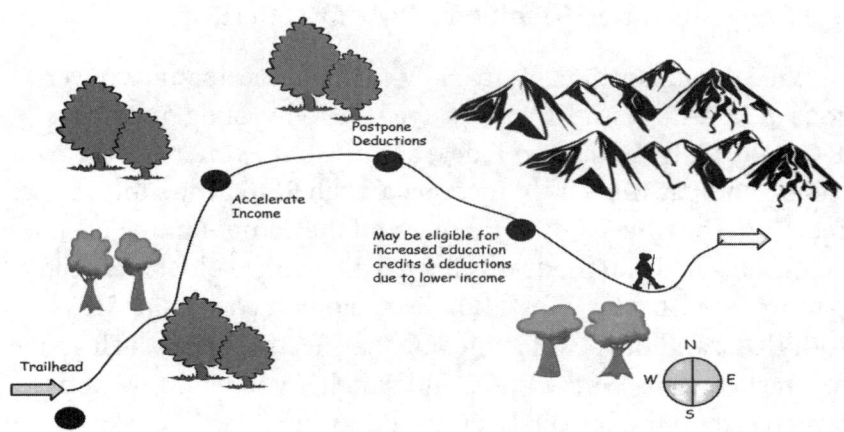

As discussed in the previous chapter, Income Smoothing, according to Investopedia.com, is "the use of accounting techniques to level out net income fluctuations from one period to the next." This concept is applicable when considering both high-income years and low-income years.

Accelerate Income

Unfortunately, most of us have years in which our income is lower than our average annual income. First, you might try to accelerate income in a down income year:

Request January Payments be Sent to You in December

Accelerating income to the current year could include rental income, farm sale of grains or cattle, interest income from private parties (such as seller financed mortgage), sale of goods (but you have to record the Cost of the Goods in year you record the sale), just to name a few examples. Remember the Constructive Receipt discussion from the previous chapter. The same Constructive Receipt concept applies to low-income years; you pay income tax on income when you constructively receive it.

Convert Traditional IRAs to Roth IRAs

Take the income tax hit in a low-income year for any conversions of IRAs to Roth IRAs. If you're relatively young, moving IRAs to Roth IRAs is a good idea, because once you make the conversion and pay the related income tax, the Roth grows forever tax free. With the time value of money, and the compounding effect, you will be glad you made this move when you're older and ready to retire. See Chapter 7 for a full discussion on converting IRAs to Roth IRAs, and the possible income tax effect. (Factors such as age, tax bracket, plans for the funds and whether you have the funds to pay any tax on the conversion must be considered. The resulting answers for folks will differ.)

Exercise And Sell Incentive Stock Options

If it makes sense based on market price, you may want to exercise and sell your Incentive Stock Options in a low-income year. (See Chapter 30 for a summary of taxation of Incentive Stock Options. Also, if you do not sell options in the same year exercise them, it could trigger Alternative Minimum Tax, see Chapter 23 for a more thorough discussion of Alternative Minimum tax on Incentive Stock Options.)

Close The Deal Before Year-End

Commissioned salespeople, work to close deals before year-end, in order to earn the commission in the down year.

Postpone Deductions

Postpone Charitable Giving

Many folks gift most of their charity dollars in December each year. In a down-income year, you likely want to postpone those charitable donations until January, when the donation will have more impact on your income tax liability.

Two cousins who are clients came to my office one day to discuss their tough financial year. They shared the task of running their finances, because they owned nearly identical investments, and shared a lifelong friendship.

"We have had such a down year," Lynette began. "The farm hasn't done too well."

Arlene chimed in. "The grain prices are terrible too, and we haven't received much income from our investments in the rental partnerships."

My recommendation was clear. "Sounds like you should not do your annual charitable gifts this December, and wait for January."

"Oh," Arlene replied, "but the church office needs our money, and they'll think we don't care about the church."

"You could call the Reverend, or meet with him after services on Sunday, and explain you need to postpone your annual gift until January, upon the advice of your CPA. That way he'll understand it's just a matter of timing on when the gift will be received."

"Oh Arlene," Lynette said, "it's a gift, they'll be happy to take it whenever we can get it there."

So the cousins postponed their charitable gift, so as to not further lessen their income for the year that already performed poorly for them. And the following year ended up being a very good year for each of them, so the charity deduction helped much more in the higher-income year.

Consider Your Medical Needs

Medical expenses are only deductible once they exceed 10% of total income ☙. (This threshold lowers to 7.5% of total income for folks age 65 and over.) In a down-income year, you may want to move forward with elective procedures, such as Lasik eye surgery, knee replacement, eyeglasses replaced, or orthodontics for the kids. In a low-income year, the threshold you must meet in order to deduct medical expense will be lower. (This is tricky, because if your income is down, you will have fewer funds available to do elective medical procedures.)

In talking to a potential client, Joan, she "corrected" me and said their former tax preparer always deducted the medical expenses, not limiting the medical expense deduction to the amount that exceeds 7.5% of total income (the limitation was previously 7.5% of total income through the end of 2012). Joan explained that she gave the itemized medical information to the tax preparer each year without fail. I then showed Joan where the total medical was indeed entered onto her Schedule A Itemized Deductions, but that it didn't exceed 7.5% of total income, and thus not deducted. Joan felt disappointed her tax preparer didn't tell her the final result of her medical deduction.

Take Advantage Of College Education Credits ❖ & Deductions ☝

A family is more likely to be able to take College Education Tax Credits ❖ or deductions ☝ in a down-income year. See Chapter 16 that shows the income limitations of all education tax benefits. Many families borrow to be able to send their children to college, but in the end, the college tax benefits help pay back the loans.

My CPA firm does an annual Income Tax Projection in early December for a client named Joe, and once we know his taxable income and income tax bracket, he finds additional income to maximize his current income tax bracket. Joe usually finds some inventory or unused fixed assets to sell from his business before year-end to maximize his income tax bracket.

Chapter Summary

In years when your income is relatively low, you will want to accelerate income and postpone deductions in order to smooth income, move income into the current year, and pay income tax at the lower rates.

Examples of accelerating income may include:
- Requesting January payments owed to you be sent in December of the low-income year;
- Converting IRAs to Roth IRAs;
- Exercising and selling incentive stock options; and
- Closing deals before year-end, for commissioned salespeople.

Examples of postponing deductions may include:
- Postponing charitable giving; and
- Delaying payment of real estate taxes and/or state income taxes.

You may also consider accelerating medical expenses for elective procedures, because they are more easily deductible in a down income year, when the threshold is easier to meet.

Moving income to a lower-income year will save income tax over the two-year period, if you are able to pay income tax at a lower rate on some of the income. The resulting income tax savings will likely be put to good use by you and your family.

Chapter 32

Penalties Are a Waste of Your Money

Chapter 32 Trail Route
- Failure to file penalty
- Failure to pay penalty
- Penalty upon early withdrawal from retirement plans
- IRS matching program

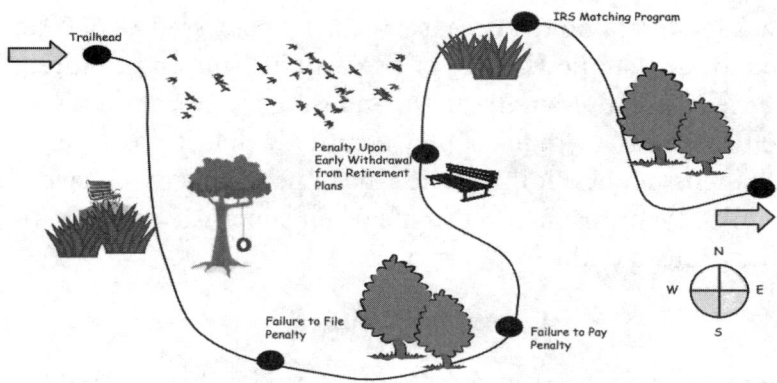

When my son, Troy, was a toddler, he used to go into the kitchen, open the dishwasher and step onto the open dishwasher door. He would slide out the top rack and stack the clean cups onto the counter for me to put away. Once in a while, Troy would unload dirty dishes, but I never corrected him, because I didn't want to discourage him and he was so good at figuring out how to do things at his young age. Troy unloading dirty dishes presented no big problem, obviously very fixable. The IRS doesn't consider income tax mistakes as adorable or as easily forgivable, as Troy was, unloading dirty dishes.

Many folks owe penalty and interest each year when they file their personal income tax returns. This is avoidable, so let me tell you how to keep penalty and interest money in your own pocket. That money will be put to much better use by you, than if you continue to pay penalty and interest to Uncle Sam.

A couple years ago, a new client, Mark, came to me because he and his wife failed to file income tax returns for the most recent 6 years! He displayed confidence that failure to file was of little consequence because he expected refunds for all 6 years. My staff prepared the returns, and I reviewed and issued them, with two big surprises. First, refunds on income tax returns filed greater than three years late are not refunded to the taxpayer, due to the statute of limitations. Second, despite not owing on most of the six years of tax returns filed, the failure to file penalties for the six years totaled $8,600.

Mark felt disappointed because, while he possessed $8,600, he planned to use that money for a cruise with his wife and children. Losing the cruise hit Mark harder than losing money, and I see that's often the case with folks; they identify with lost privileges more than lost money. If this is the type of personality you have, then think of your lost niceties in life when you waste money on penalties, instead of the lost money.

Common Penalties

There are many types of penalties that can be charged, and I've included the more common penalties in the following pages, and how to avoid them.

Failure to File Penalty

The example I started this chapter with demonstrated a Failure to File Penalty. It's such an easy fix: FILE YOUR INCOME TAX RETURNS ANNUALLY, ON TIME. If your CPA or tax preparer calls or emails you for your income tax data needed to prepare your income tax return, they aren't nagging you for personal benefit; they understand you will have to pay penalties if you fail to file an income tax return on time (which includes an additional 6 months if an extension is filed). The failure to file penalty is 5% of the unpaid income tax balance for each month or partial month the return is late, for a maximum of 25%.

Failure to Pay Penalty

The most common penalty type is Failure to Pay Penalty, and this comes about when a person doesn't have enough income tax withholding, or they don't pay in enough with their quarterly estimated tax payments. Most of the time, folks are just not aware of their progress, or lack thereof, in paying in their income taxes during the year.

In some cases, folks extend their income tax return, but an extension is for the deadline to file the income tax return, not the deadline to pay the income tax due. The balance of the income tax due is due with the extension of time to file, on or before April 15 each year. Those underestimating their balance due often have Failure to Pay Penalty.

To avoid the Failure to Pay Penalty, also called the Underpayment Penalty, one must meet one of these thresholds:

- PRIOR YEAR METHOD. Pay in 100% ✈ of your prior year income tax liability through withholding and/or estimated tax payments (this percentage increases to 110% ✈ if your total income (Adjusted Gross Income) exceeds $150K for the previous year); or
- CURRENT YEAR METHOD. Pay in 90% ✈ of your current year income tax liability through withholding and/or estimated tax payments.

You also need to know that if you make quarterly estimated income tax payments, the IRS expects you to make 4 equal quarterly estimated tax payments, unless you complete Form 2210 that demonstrates that your income fluctuated by quarter.

The failure to pay penalty is 0.5% of the unpaid balance per month or partial month, up to a maximum of 25%. This penalty is reduced by 50% for any and all months in which a formal Installment Agreement is in place with the IRS.

To avoid the Failure to Pay Penalty, my CPA firm recommends either of two solutions.

1. Prepare an adequacy of withholding calculation, using the

prior year method. For those that have jobs from which they receive W-2s, we prepare an adequacy of withholding analysis. In this calculation, we review the prior year return (including the state return, where applicable), and document the total tax liability. If the total income (Adjusted Gross Income) is greater than $150K, we multiply the Federal income tax liability by 110%. The next thing we do is request the most recent paycheck stubs from the client (from both spouses, if married), and we take the withholding to date, and add the estimated withholding that will occur between the date of the pay stub and year end. We compare this total to the prior year liability, to make sure the withholding exceeds the goal of 100% (or 110%) of the prior year liability. An example of this calculation for Josh and Heather is on the following page. If you are required to file income taxes in more than one state, add additional columns to this chart when you create it for yourself. (Don't forget to allow for the Credit Paid to Other States ❖ on your home state income tax return.)

2. Prepare an income tax projection using the current year method. For this solution, we use software in which we can prepare draft income tax returns before the end of the tax year. This is helpful in cases where income has changed drastically from that of the prior year. If income has significantly decreased, it doesn't make sense for you to pay 100% (or 110% for those with higher income) of the prior year tax liability because the actual tax will be much less. If income is significantly increased, the client still may want to just pay in 100% (or 110%) of the prior year income tax, but at least they will have a warning on how much additional tax will be owed when they file their income tax return by April 15 of the following year.

	Federal	State
2014 income tax liabilities	$32,108	$6,101
2014 total income (Adjusted Gross Income)	$150,100	
2015 Federal required withholding and/or estimated income tax payments, based on Prior Year Method.* This line is our Federal Goal.	$35,319	
2015 State required withholding and/or estimated income tax payments, based on Prior Year Method.** This line is our State Goal.		$6,101
Josh's income tax withholding to date + estimated withholding through end of calendar year	$16,100	$2,400
Heather's income tax withholding to date + estimated withholding through end of calendar year	$14,700	$2,100
Josh & Heather's estimated tax payments that they intend to make during 2015	$6,000	$1,000
Sum of income taxes paid in (sum of previous 3 lines)	$36,800	$5,500
Sum of Federal income taxes paid in (previous line) less Federal Goal. ***	$1,481	
Sum of State income taxes paid in (previous line) less State Goal. ***		($601)

* If 2014 total income exceeds $150K, multiply 2014 Federal income tax liability by 110%, otherwise, place 2014 income tax liability here.
** Most states require only 100% of the prior year income tax liability be paid in through withholding, but you should check on your state's income tax website to be sure.
*** A positive number indicates an adequate amount will be paid in by year end; a negative number indicates more income tax needs to be paid in.

> IRS Form 2210 is used to calculate Underpayment Penalty and to document income by quarter, in cases of income fluctuations.

Penalty Upon Early Withdrawal From Retirement Plans

I've seen quite a bit of this Penalty Upon Early Withdrawal From Retirement Plans in the tough economy these past few years. Many times folks take out retirement money for use for non-retirement purposes, and if they are under age 59½, that retirement plan distribution will likely have a 10% penalty affiliated with it, unless you meet special requirements. Additionally, if your Early Withdrawal is from a SIMPLE IRA received within 2 years of when you started participating in the SIMPLE IRA plan, the penalty increases to 25%.

On the following page are the more common allowable distributions that escape the 10% early distribution penalty, and note that some of the exceptions relate to both qualified retirement plans and IRAs, some of the exceptions relate to only qualified retirement plans, and some of the exceptions relate only to IRA plans.

Early Distributions from qualified retirement plans **and** IRAs that avoid 10% penalty	Early Distributions from qualified retirement plans that except 10% penalty	Early Distributions from IRAs that except 10% penalty
Distribution is a rollover to another IRA or qualified retirement plan	Distribution is after employment has ceased, if at least age 55	Distribution is to pay for health insurance for certain unemployed folks
Distribution is part of a series of equal payments over life expectancy	Distribution is related to a divorce settlement called a Qualified Domestic Relations Order (QDRO)	Distribution is used to pay for qualified college or trade school expenses of taxpayer, spouse, child, or grandchild
Distribution is made due to permanent and total disability		Distribution is for a first time homebuyer up to $10K (can't have owned a home in past 2 years, $10K lifetime limit)
Distribution is made at account owners death, to beneficiaries		
Distribution is used for qualified unreimbursed medical expenses that exceed 10% of total income (Adjusted Gross Income). Percentage decreases to 7.5% for folks aged 65 or older.		
Distribution due to an IRS levy (but not to avoid a levy)		
Distribution is to a military reservist that's been called to active duty for at least 180 days		

IRS Matching Program

The IRS receives copies of your W-2s from the Social Security Administration that your employers file, and they receive 1099s for interest, dividends and security sales from your banks and brokerage houses (these are only some of the documents the IRS receives to match to your income tax return). If you fail to include an income item on your income tax return, and the IRS received the document from an employer, brokerage house, or bank, you will receive a notice from the IRS asking about the item. You will be charged income tax, penalty and interest on the omitted item(s), unless you have a very good explanation. You likely need the assistance of a CPA to answer such a notice from the IRS.

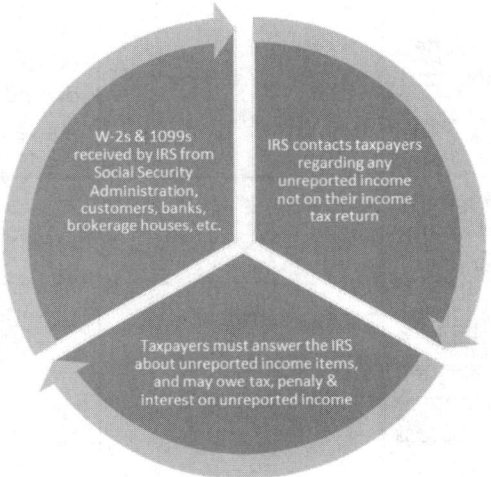

Don't cheat on your income tax preparation; you can easily get caught. If it's a black and white issue, get caught doing it right. Sure, there are times when a complicated tax issue doesn't have a clear-cut answer, and then you may need to make a judgment call on how to complete your income tax return. But if it's a clear-cut issue (and it usually is), then take the high road, and prepare an accurate and thorough income tax return. Murphy's Law may sneak up and bite you, in the form of an IRS audit, and that could include penalties if you have not accurately and thoroughly prepared your income tax return.

There is a very small segment of folks who refuse to file or pay income taxes, based on religious beliefs or their interpretation of the US constitution. Many of these folks are being prosecuted and finding themselves in prison cells or with electronic monitoring devices on their ankles. Taking a frivolous position isn't going to work in the long run, and there will be penalties for those actions.

Two cousins who were clients in my office for a number of years, came to us from a different accountant, and led me to believe the other accountant retired and possessed an "old school" style they disliked. The two cousins presented nicely enough and were quite easy to work with. They provided requested information, followed instructions and always signed the efile authorization forms. They were hard-working family men, from what I could determine.

Then the FBI subpoenaed me, wanting information on the cousins. By the end of the case, and upon hearing their confessions, my opinion of the cousins dropped faster than the New Year's Eve ball in Times Square. The cousins, while always having their income tax returns prepared by their prior accountant, failed to file their income tax returns with the IRS and failed to pay the income taxes due. They only requested the income tax returns be prepared in order to have income tax return copies to turn into the bank that held the loans on their business. These cousins are in prison for fraud and various other charges. It's doubtful they will ever to able to pay their accumulated tax and penalties.

A former client of mine, Don, received what appeared to be a routine IRS audit notice, and brought it to me. Since Don is a rebel at heart, and likes to be sarcastic, just for fun, I requested Don not attend the IRS audit meeting with me, thinking he may make the ordeal more difficult.

I went to the IRS audit meeting, with all of my tax working papers prepared and arranged, and was surprised that the IRS agent's supervisor wanted to sit in the meeting. Having gone through this many times for clients, I knew this to be unusual.

The IRS agent said, "Are there any other sources of income that should have been reported on this income tax return?"

"No", I replied.

The IRS agent pressed on, "What other kinds of activities does this taxpayer participate in that would generate income?"

"None that I'm aware of." I felt sure there was no other income.

"What other kinds of income can you think of that maybe should be on this taxpayer's income tax return?" the IRS agent inquired, for the third time.

Finally it dawned on me. I didn't have all of this client's income on his income tax return! I definitely included all income that he told me about, but…what if he didn't give me all documents or tell me about an additional source of income? I said, "OK, so you've asked three different ways about unreported income. Are YOU aware of unreported income that I'm unaware of?"

The agent said, "Yes." She slid a report over to me that showed $955K of security sales for the year under audit. I did not have these reported on my client's income tax return. My shoulders slumped with frustration.

Of course I called Don the minute I walked out of the IRS office. "Oh yeah," he said. "That's right, but it was all a breakeven deal. I was trying to be a day-trader for a while."

I explained, "Don, that activity still needs to be reported on your income tax return."

We worked hard to report the huge quantity of sales, and the cost basis of the security purchases. With the final calculations complete, the cost basis of the securities of $995K exceeded the sales proceeds of $955K, and Don ended up with a $40K capital loss. I documented all of this for the IRS agent, and the audit ended. Had Don not been audited, he would have lost out on a $40K Capital Loss, $37K of which had to be carried forward to the following year.

Chapter Summary

Be aware of the actions you need to take to avoid income tax penalties. The Failure to File penalty happens when you don't file your income tax return by the due date or extended due date. The Failure to Pay penalty happens when you fail to pay your income tax by the due date (extensions increase your time to file your income tax return, but not the time to pay your income tax). The penalty for early withdrawal from a retirement plan may apply if you take a distribution from a retirement plan if you have not yet attained age 59 ½. The main way the IRS determines a taxpayer has not reported all applicable income on their income tax return is through the IRA matching program, where employers (and other payers of income) send W-2s (and 1099s) to the government for matching against your submitted income tax return. You need your money for your own priorities; there is no need for you to give it away without good reason. You can and should comply with the IRS rules to avoid all penalties.

Chapter 33
Tax Savings Quantified

> Chapter 33 Trail Route
> - Plan so you can save income tax
> - Confirm tax savings ideas with CPA to make sure they fit your situation
> - Implement tax savings ideas in accordance with the tax rules
> - Document on "tax savings quantified" template
> - Repeat, for life

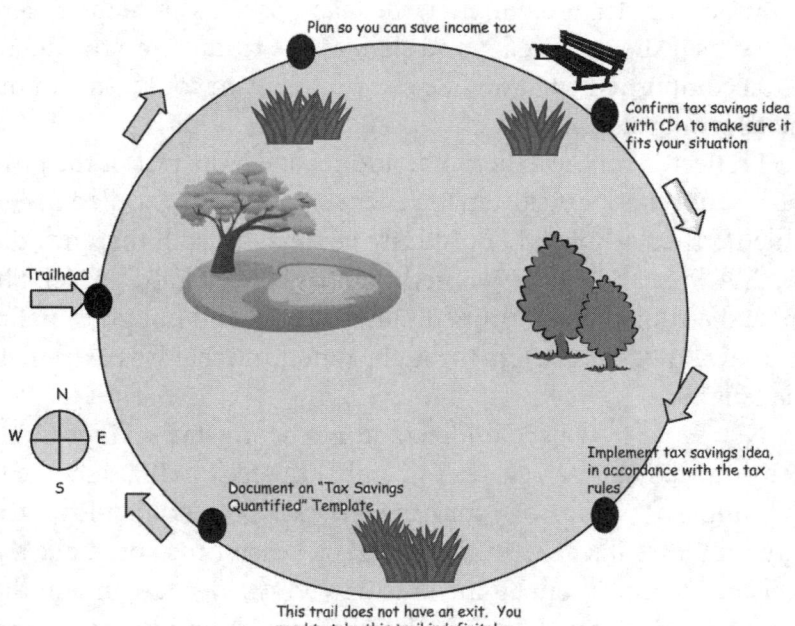

My niece, Emily, has my total respect. She has a learning disability, but she gives life her personal best. She muddled through a difficult time learning to read, but now, at age 19, she's an avid reader, consuming about three adult novels each week, and a high school graduate! Emily is shy, and stays to herself, but she can speak up when needed. She has always tried very hard at school.

One summer in her early teens, Emily played on a softball team. The team played in an important game, and the opposing pitcher shot bullets at the batters. No one on the team could hit the pitches, and her team felt down and stressed. Emily batted at the bottom of the batting order, and there were two outs. Everyone feared Emily would make the third out, and I didn't want her to feel the pressure of being responsible for ending the inning.

Emily stepped into the batter's box with a determined look. I had seen that expression on her face before. My hopes rose. Emily took a ball, then on the second pitch she swung and missed. And then the third pitch: Emily hit the ball to shallow left field, and she made it to first base! Despite the next batter striking out, and Emily getting stranded on first, the team, parents and fans cheered for her as if she had hit a grand slam as she trotted into the dugout. She accomplished what no one else on the team could; she hit off the opposing star pitcher.

I reflected on the experience and realized, the rest of the girls learned at school quickly, made friends easily, and excelled in athletics their whole life. But Emily possessed a skill that they did not. She knew how to try something that proved hard for her. She knew she could be determined in her efforts, and not give up. Emily knew how to persevere through something that was extremely challenging.

No matter how hard understanding income tax savings points is to you, you can persevere. To combat the feeling that income tax planning isn't worthy of your time, because of the difficult yet dry nature of the subject, turn it into a game: each time you make a decision to implement an income tax savings idea, document the idea and quantify it. Try to reach $5K in tax savings for your first year, and then each year, try to beat your prior year results.

Below is an example of a "Tax Savings Quantified" worksheet completed for a real client in my office, the Watsons, who are married and have three children, for 2013 and 2014:

	2014-income tax savings	2013-income tax savings
Qualified Dividends and Capital Gains, paid income tax at the Capital Gain rates instead of the ordinary (higher) rates	$1,100 (Calculated as Qualified Dividends & Capital gains, multiplied by the excess of the ordinary rates over the Capital Gain rate.)	$1,250 (Calculated as Qualified Dividends & Capital gains, multiplied by the excess of the ordinary rates over the Capital Gain rate.)
Both husband and wife contributed the maximum allowable to 401(k) plans	$13,600 (Calculated as total retirement plan contributions multiplied by combined Federal and state income tax rate.)	$13,600 (Calculated as total retirement plan contributions multiplied by combined Federal and state income tax rate.)
Dependent Care Benefit for their youngest child	$1,700 (Calculated as $5K maximum Dependent Care Benefit multiplied by the combined Federal and state income tax rate.)	$1,700 (Calculated as $5K maximum Dependent Care Benefit multiplied by the combined Federal and state income tax rate.)
College Credit❖ for their oldest child	$2,500 (Maximum allowable for the American Opportunity Credit❖.)	$0
Mortgage Deduction	$2,720 (Calculated as mortgage interest multiplied by combined Federal and state income tax rate.)	$2,950 (Calculated as mortgage interest multiplied by combined Federal and state income tax rate.)
Health Savings Account	$2,200 (Calculated as maximum allowable HSA contribution multiplied by combined Federal and state income tax rate.)	$2,100 (Calculated as maximum allowable HSA contribution multiplied by combined Federal and state income tax rate.)
Total income tax savings	**$23,820**	**$21,600**

Annual income tax savings in excess of $20K is huge for any family! And then consider earning that savings every year! And there are many more income tax savings ideas in this book that could be included, if applicable to you. You undoubtedly will put these funds from income tax savings to better use than Uncle Sam.

May you save a lot of income tax, and may you feel confident about your income tax knowledge! I sincerely hope you have enjoyed and learned from this book.

If you would like to be on my email list, please send me a note saying so at www.LisaBcpa.com

Appendix A
What to Gather for Your CPA for Tax Preparation Time

When gathering information for your CPA to prepare your annual income tax return, if you are unsure regarding whether to include a document or explanation for your CPA, or not, then include it. Your CPA would rather have too much information, than miss seeing a relevant document or knowing about a key income tax matter. This questionnaire/checklist will guide you in gathering appropriate information for the preparation of your income tax return.

To complete this form, please circle YES or NO as directed, describe or explain in lines provided, and place a checkmark beside each item in the circle as you complete them. Asking these detailed questions will allow your CPA to prepare a thorough and accurate income tax return for you. Even if your CPA provides some kind of checklist, they will be happy to receive another from their clients, especially if new items of income and deductions are located.

If a permanent-type form or document is requested below, and you provided it in a previous year, it's not necessary to include the document again.

Income items:

- ¤ *Did you work as an employee during the tax year? Circle YES or NO. If yes, please provide Form W-2(s).*

- ¤ *Are you eligible to participate in a retirement plan through your employer? Circle YES or NO.*

- ¤ *Did you receive distributions from a retirement account during the tax year? Circle YES or NO. If yes, please provide Form 1099R(s).*

- *If you received any Form 1099Rs for retirement plan distributions, were any of the distributions rolled over to a different Qualified Retirement Plan or IRA?*
  Circle YES or NO. Quantify and explain.

  _____
  _____
  _____

- *Did you receive Social Security benefits? Circle YES or NO. If yes, please provide Form SSA-1099.*

- *Did you receive Jury Duty pay? Circle YES or NO. If yes, please provide earnings statement or 1099.*

- *Did you retire or change jobs during the tax year? Circle YES or NO. Describe.*

  _____
  _____
  _____
  _____

- *Did you participate in any bartering transactions? Circle YES or NO. Describe and quantify.*

  _____
  _____
  _____
  _____

- *Did you receive an income tax refund on your prior year state income tax return(s)? Circle YES or NO. If yes, please provide Form 1099G from applicable state(s).*

- *Did you receive unemployment compensation? Circle YES or NO. If yes, please provide Form 1099G.*

- Did you receive any gambling winnings?
  Circle YES or NO. If yes, please provide Form W-2G(s).

- If you had gambling winnings, did you incur gambling losses at least equal to the gambling winnings?
  Circle YES or NO.

- Did you receive alimony?
  Circle YES or NO. If yes, please quantify.
  _____
  _____

- Did you receive any prizes or awards?
  Circle YES or NO. If yes, please quantify and describe.
  _____
  _____

- Did you receive any scholarships or fellowships?
  Circle YES or NO. If yes, please quantify and describe.
  What was the portion used for room and board?
  _____
  _____

- Do you have a farm, no matter how small?
  Circle YES or NO.
  If yes, do you have a profit and loss statement for the tax year? If not, would you like assistance in preparing it? Explain.
  _____
  _____

Portfolio & investments:

- Did you earn any interest income during the tax year?
  Circle YES or NO. If yes, please provide Forms 1099INT(s) and/or 1099OID(s).

- *Did you earn any tax exempt interest income? Circle YES or NO. If yes, please provide statement from bank or brokerage house.*

- *Did you earn any dividend income during the tax year? Circle YES or NO. If yes, please provide Form 1099DIV(s).*

- *Did you sell any stock, bonds or mutual funds during the year? Circle YES or NO. If yes, please provide Form 1099B(s).*

    - *If the cost basis for the securities sold is not on the Form 1099B, please provide. Describe any additional details on cost basis, such as if any of the securities were inherited, getting a step-up in cost basis.*

    _____
    _____
    _____
    _____
    _____

- *Did you have any matured U.S. savings bonds that you cashed in during the tax year? Circle YES or NO. Please provide 1099INT(s) or other tax document.*

- *Did you have any foreign income or pay any foreign tax during the tax year? Circle YES or NO. Please provide tax document.*

- *Did you receive any loan payments on notes held by you from property sold in the current year or a prior year (installment sale)? Circle YES or NO. Describe. Do you have an amortization schedule for the loan?*

    _____
    _____

¤ Are you the beneficiary of a trust or estate? Circle YES or NO. If yes, please include Form K-1. Or do you need assistance preparing the trust or estate income tax return, from which the Form K-1 comes? Describe.
_____
_____

¤ Did you sell any art, classic cars, or other collectibles at a gain during the year? Circle YES or NO. If yes, please quantify and describe.
_____
_____

¤ Are you a signatory on any foreign bank accounts? Circle YES or NO. Do you have an interest in any foreign bank accounts? Circle YES or NO. If yes to either, what is the maximum amount in the account during the tax year?
_____
_____

¤ Are you the grantor or beneficiary of a foreign trust? Circle YES or NO. If yes, please describe.
_____
_____

¤ Did you incur investment interest expense?
Circle YES or NO. Please quantify and include supporting documentation.
_____
_____

- Did you incur any penalties for early withdrawal of savings? Circle YES or NO. If yes, please quantify and attach statement if available.

  _____
  _____

Businesses:

- Did you start or acquire a small business during the year? Circle YES or NO. If yes, what is the entity type? (If a sole proprietor or single member LLC, the business activity is reported directly on your personal return.) Describe. If you acquired a business, please include copy of purchase agreement.

  _____
  _____

- Do you have a profit and loss statement for this business activity and/or any business activity owned by you last year? Circle YES or NO. Or do you need assistance preparing a profit and loss statement? Circle YES or NO. Explain.

  _____
  _____

- Did you receive any 1099MISC or 1099K Forms for your business? Circle YES or NO. If yes, please provide.

- If you own a small business, did you pay for services that would require you to send out 1099MISC forms (Did you pay >$600 to any service provider that isn't incorporated? Circle YES or NO. Did you pay any attorneys, in any amount? Circle YES or NO.) Did you send out the required 1099MISC forms? Circle YES or NO. Do you need us (your income tax preparer) to complete the 1099MISC forms? Circle YES or NO. Explain.

  _____
  _____

- Did you acquire an interest in a partnership or S corporation during the year? Circle YES or NO. If yes, please provide form K-1 for any new entities and for any entities you owned last year. Or do you need assistance preparing the partnership or S Corporation income tax return, from which the K-1 comes? Circle YES or NO. Explain.

  _____
  _____

- Did you sell a business during the year? Circle YES or NO. If yes, please describe. Please include a copy of the sales agreement.

  _____
  _____

- Did you have self-employed health insurance during the tax year? Circle YES or NO. Please quantify.

  _____
  _____

- *Does your business have employees? Circle YES or NO. If yes, do you provide health insurance for the employees? Circle YES or NO. And if yes, do you need assistance in determining if you qualify of the small business health insurance credit? Circle YES or NO.*

- *Is your business in the construction industry? Circle YES or NO. Do you need assistance in determining if you qualify of the Domestic Production Activities Deduction? Circle YES or NO.*

Real estate:

- *Did you buy, sell or trade any real estate during the year? Circle YES or NO. If yes, please provide closing statements and Form 1099S, if received. Describe.*

  _____
  _____

- *Do you rent real estate to any individuals or businesses? Circle YES or NO. If yes, provide 1099MISC for rental income, or quantify.*

  _____
  _____

- *Do you have your rental income and expenses accumulated? Circle YES or NO. If yes, please provide. If no, do you need assistance in compiling your rental income and expenses? Circle YES or NO. Explain.*

  _____
  _____

Deductions and Credits:

- Did you finance or refinance a principal residence during the tax year? Circle YES or NO. If yes, please provide closing statement and Form 1098. Also provide Form 1098 for any mortgage loans in existence last year.

- Were all of the loan proceeds from your current home loan(s) used to purchase or improve your main home? Circle YES or NO. Describe.
  _____
  _____

- Did you take out a home equity loan on your main residence during the tax year? Circle YES or NO. If yes, please provide closing statement and Form 1098. Also provide Form 1098 for any home equity loans in existence last year.

- Were all loan proceeds from your equity loan(s) used to purchase or improve your main home? Circle YES or NO. Describe.
  _____
  _____

- Did you incur mortgage insurance premiums for the tax year? Circle YES or NO. If yes, please provide amount paid, if not shown on Form 1098(s) requested above.
  _____
  _____

- Did you incur a theft or casualty loss (hurricane, fire, tornado or earthquake for example) during the tax year? Circle YES or NO. If yes, did insurance proceeds cover your loss? Circle YES or NO. Describe.

  _____
  _____

- Did you pay real estate taxes for the tax year? Circle YES or NO. Please list and quantify, or include paid receipts.

  _____
  _____

- Did you pay personal property taxes for the tax year? Circle YES or NO. Please list and quantify, or include paid receipts.

  _____
  _____

- Do you have evidence to support your charitable cash donations? Circle YES or NO. Please list the charitable organizations you donated cash to, and the amount given:

Charitable Organization	Cash Amount Donated

¤   Do you have evidence to support your noncash charitable donations? Circle YES or NO. If >$500 in total, please provide details of items donated, in addition to the amount.

Charitable organization	Value of goods donated	Description of goods donated

¤   Do you have unreimbursed employee expenses? Circle YES or NO. Please describe and quantify.
_____
_____

¤   Did you pay union dues for your job? Circle YES or NO. If yes, please quantify, and provide last paystub of year detailing the total union dues, if available.
_____
_____

¤   Did you pay safe deposit box fees for the tax year? Circle YES or NO. If yes, please quantify.
_____
_____

¤   Did you incur investment advisor fees for the tax year? Circle YES or NO. If yes, please quantify.
_____
_____

- Did you incur legal fees related to tax planning or estate planning? (For estate planning fees, break out the portion related to tax planning and asset protection.) Circle YES or NO. If yes, please quantify.

  _____
  _____

- How much did you pay for income tax preparation fees for the tax year (for preparation of your previous year's income tax return)?

  _____
  _____

- Did you use your automobile for your job, other than commuting? Circle YES or NO. If yes, please provide year, make, model of your automobile.

  _____
  _____

  Also provide mileage as follows:
  Commuting miles to/from work _____
  Personal miles _____
  Business miles _____
  Total miles _____

- Did you pay premiums for Long Term Care insurance during the tax year? Circle YES or NO. If yes, please quantify separately for both spouses.

  _____
  _____

- Please quantify out of pocket medical and/or dental expenses for you and your dependents (if you believe you will be over the threshold to be able to deduct):
    - Doctor copays _____
    - Deductible paid _____
    - Hospital bills _____
    - Prescriptions _____
    - Physical therapy _____
    - Lab fees _____
    - Dental bills _____
    - Orthodontic bills _____
    - Eye care and eye glasses _____
    - Miles incurred related to medical care _____

- Did you incur any unreimbursed moving expenses to take a new job during the tax year to move you, your family and your belongings? Circle YES or NO. If yes, what is the distance between your old home and your old job? What is the distance between your old home and your new job? What is the date of your move? Please quantify your costs and describe.

    _____
    _____

- Did you pay any alimony during the tax year? Circle YES or NO. If yes, please quantify and provide legal name and social security number of recipient.

    _____
    _____

- Did you incur dependent care expenses while working or looking for work? Circle YES or NO. If yes, please provide Daycare provider name, Federal ID#, address, and amount paid to them for the tax year.

    _____
    _____

- Did you pay any student loan interest during the tax year? Circle YES or NO. If yes, please provide Form 1098E.

- Did you incur college expenses for you, your spouse, or your children? Circle YES or NO. If yes, please provide Form 1099T(s) and statement from education institution, if available, that shows the portion of fees paid that are related to room & board.

- Did you make any significant purchases (such as an automobile or boat) during the year and pay sales tax? Circle YES or NO. If yes, please describe and quantify the sales tax paid.
  _____
  _____

- Did you incur any costs related to searching for a new job? Circle YES or NO. If yes, please describe and quantify.
  _____
  _____

- Did you contribute to an IRA, Roth IRA, SEP IRA, SIMPLE or any other retirement plan during the year, other than contributions via your employer, shown on your W-2(s). Circle YES or NO. If yes describe and provide amount.
  _____
  _____

- Did you make any energy efficient improvements to your home during the year? Circle YES or NO. If yes, describe and quantify.
  _____
  _____

- ¤ If you are a teacher, did you incur any educator expenses during the tax year? Circle YES or NO. If yes, please quantify.
  _____
  _____

- ¤ Did you incur any adoption expenses during the year? Circle YES or NO. If yes, when was adoption finalized? Quantify.
  _____
  _____

Personal information:

- ¤ Please provide your full legal name and date of birth.
  _____
  _____

- ¤ Please provide your spouse's full legal name and date of birth.
  _____
  _____

- ¤ Please provide the full legal name and date of birth for all dependents, including any newly born children.
  _____
  _____
  _____
  _____

Filing status & exemptions:

- ¤ Did your marital status change during the year? Circle YES or NO. If yes, explain.
  _____
  _____

- Can you be claimed as a dependent on your parents' or someone else's income tax return? Circle YES or NO. Explain.

  _____

  _____

- For any children listed above that are over age 18, were they a full-time student for the tax year? Circle YES or NO. Provide separate answer for each child that is over age 18.

Estimated tax payments:

- Please list the estimated tax payments and extension payments you made for the tax year, and the date paid:

Federal estimated tax payments		
	Amount	Date
1st Quarter		
2nd Quarter		
3rd Quarter		
4th Quarter		
Extension pmt		

State estimated tax payments		
	Amount	Date
1st Quarter		
2nd Quarter		
3rd Quarter		
4th Quarter		
Extension pmt		

- Do you expect a change in your income for next year, that should be considered in setting your estimated tax payments for the New Year? Circle YES or NO. If yes, please describe.

  _____
  _____

Other matters:

- When complete, would you like a paper copy of the income tax return, an electronic copy of the income tax return, or both?

  _____
  _____

- If this is the first year using this CPA, please include a copy of your prior year Federal and state(s) income tax returns.

- Is your mailing address the same as what was reported on last year's income tax return? Circle YES or NO. If not, please provide new address.

  _____
  _____

- Please provide your email address and phone number.

  _____
  _____

- If you will be receiving an income tax refund, do you want the refund direct deposited to your bank account? Circle YES or NO.

- If you do want any refund direct deposited, is your banking information the same as last year (routing number and account number)? Circle YES or NO. If your bank information is new, please include a voided check, or include name of bank, routing number and account number below.

  _____
  _____

- Do any of your children have unearned income of $2,100 or more? Circle YES or NO. If yes, please provide the children's Form 1099INT, 1099DIV, 1099B, etc.

- Do you have any college students in your family that will need to prepare a FAFSA for financial aid? Circle YES or NO. If yes, please make that known so your income tax return can be prepared as early as possible in the tax season, so you can meet your FAFSA deadline. Also, please document your FAFSA deadline below.

  _____
  _____

- Did you make any out-of-state purchases and not pay sales tax? Circle YES or NO. Have you determined if you need to pay Use Tax to your home state? Circle YES or NO. Describe.

  _____
  _____

- Did you make any gifts to an individual >$14K during the tax year? Circle YES or NO. If yes, a gift tax return should be prepared. Please list recipients name, social security number and amount of gift.

  _____
  _____

- Did you make any contributions to a college savings account? Circle YES or NO. If yes, please list account owner, account beneficiaries, amounts contributed and type of plan (529 plan, Coverdell, etc.).

  _____
  _____

- Did you take any distributions from a college savings account? Circle YES or NO. If yes, were the proceeds used for Qualified Education Expenses? Describe, and include statement.

  _____
  _____

- Did you make any contributions to a Health Savings Account, other than with pretax dollars paid via payroll deduction and amounts contributed by employer? Circle YES or NO. If yes, quantify.

  _____
  _____

- Did you take any distributions from a Health Savings Account? Circle YES or NO. If yes, please include statement from provider. And if yes, were all distributions to pay for unreimbursed Qualified Medical Expenses? Circle YES or NO.

- *Have you paid domestic help during the tax year? Circle YES or NO. Has their Form W-2 been prepared? Circle YES or NO. Or do you need assistance in preparation of the Form W-2? Circle YES or NO. Have you paid in Federal or state employment payroll taxes for the domestic employee for the tax year? Circle YES or NO. Explain.*

  _____
  _____

- *Have you contributed to an IRA in any previous year and NOT taken an Income Tax Deduction for it? Circle YES or NO. If you are a new client, do you have a calculation of your basis in IRAs? Circle YES or NO. Describe.*

  _____
  _____

- *What school district do you live in?*

  _____
  _____

- *Have you received any notices from the IRS or any state departments of revenue during the tax year? Circle YES or NO. If yes, please include.*

- *Would you like $3 to go to the Presidential election campaign? Circle YES or NO.*

Appendix B
Home Office Deduction Information Collection Sheet

Annual Home Expenses:
Mortgage Interest: _____
Real Estate Taxes: _____
Rent Paid: _____
Utilities: _____
Home Owner's Insurance: _____
Subdivision Assessments: _____
Housecleaning: _____
Security Monitoring: _____
Repairs & Maintenance: _____
Casualty Losses: _____

Home Information:
Date Placed in Service: _____
Original Cost of Home including land: _____
Cost of Land (based on actual cost of lot, or county assessed % of land to total real estate value): _____
Square footage of Office: _____
Total square footage of Home: _____

Major Improvements to Home:
Date: _____
Cost: _____
Description:
_____
_____
_____

Appendix C
Mileage Reporting Form

Commuting Miles _____
Personal Miles _____
Business Miles _____
Total Miles _____

Ending odometer _____
Less:
Beginning odometer _____
Total miles (s/ equal Total Miles above) _____

Vehicle Year, Make, Model
_____

Date placed in service
_____

Owned or leased?
_____

Employer reimbursements for mileage
_____

Glossary

401(k) plan 👍
Retirement plan used principally by for-profit corporations, partnerships and others for their employees. Both employees and employers can contribute to this plan.

403(b) plan 👍
Retirement plan used principally by public education organizations, 501(c)(3) non-profit organizations and certain cooperative service hospitals for their employees. Both employees and employers can contribute to this plan.

457 plan 👍
Retirement plan used principally by state and local governments for their employees. Both employees and employers can contribute to this plan.

529 College Savings Plan 👍
See Qualified Tuition Program.

72(t) election
Withdrawals from a retirement plan that are a part of a series of substantially equal periodic payments made over the life expectancy of the account owner and beneficiary. The withdrawals must continue for at least 5 years, or until the account owner attains age 59½. If the requirements are met, these withdrawals escape the 10% early withdrawal penalty.

Additional Medicare Tax
An additional .9% Medicare tax, that began in 2013, on wages and self-employment income in excess of certain limits, based on filing status.

Adjusted Gross Income
: Total income received, including (but not limited to) wages and business income after business expenses, less IRA contributions and self-employed health insurance deductions.

Adoption Credit ❖
: Dollar for dollar offset of income tax for Qualified Adoption Expenses incurred up to the per child allowable maximum for the adoption of a Qualifying Child.

After-Tax Dollars
: Refers to money on which income tax has already been paid, such as net pay from an employee's paycheck that has already had income tax withholding taken out.

AGI
: Adjusted Gross Income.

Alternative Minimum Tax
: An additional income tax system in the U.S. whereby certain deductions that are allowed for regular income tax are disallowed. A taxpayer must pay the higher of their regular income tax liability or their Alternative Minimum Tax liability.

Alternative Minimum Tax Permanent Adjustments
: For certain items included in the AMT calculation, you cannot go back in a later year and reverse that lost deduction; it's a permanent non-deductible item for AMT purposes. Examples include State & Local income taxes paid and mortgage interest not used to purchase or improve your home.

Alternative Minimum Tax Timing Adjustments
: For certain items included in the AMT calculation, you may be able to reverse this effect on your AMT calculation in a future year, by taking a Credit ❖ for Prior Alternative Minimum Tax Paid and offset future AMT obligations. Examples include Incentive Stock Options and depreciation.

American Opportunity Credit ❖
   Tax Credit (dollar for dollar offset of income tax) for the first four years of college education, that is partially refundable, limited in amount. Disbursements must be used for Qualified Education Expenses.

Appreciated Value
   Increase in fair market value of an asset over time, that is in excess of the original cost of the asset. Income tax is not owed on appreciation, until the asset is sold.

Bartering
   The trading of goods in your possession or services you can provide to someone in return for their goods or services. No money exchanges between the parties in a bartering transaction.

Basis
   See Cost Basis.

Before-Tax Dollars
   Also called Pre-Tax Dollars. Refers to money on which no income tax has been paid. This could refer to an employee benefit that is deducted from an employee's paycheck before the taxable wages subtotal is calculated and before the income tax withholding is calculated on the taxable wages.

Capital Asset
   A security, fixed asset used in business or real estate that when sold, creates Capital Gain income or loss. Also called Capital Gain Property. Inventory sold in the normal course of business is not a capital asset.

Capital Gain
   Sales proceeds in excess of cost basis on the sale of securities, real estate or other investments. If the asset was held more than

one year, the Capital Gain is Long Term, and subject to the lower Capital Gain income tax rates.

Capital Loss
Cost basis in excess of sales proceeds on the sale of securities, real estate or other investments.

Cash Basis
Method of accounting where income is recognized and expenses are recorded when cash changes hands between the parties. Generally, all individuals are on the cash basis of accounting.

Cash Flow Planning
Using strategy to make sure adequate cash levels are maintained to meet financial commitments.

Casualty Losses 👍
Personal losses from catastrophes such as fire, tornado, hurricanes, etc. Casualty losses are only deductible once they exceed 10% of Adjusted Gross Income.

Catch-Up Contributions 👍
Additional IRA or employer retirement plan contributions allowed to be made by a taxpayer, once the taxpayer reaches age 50.

Childcare Credit ❖
See Dependent Care Credit ❖.

Constructive Receipt
A taxpayer is deemed to have received income when they have possession of the funds, or when they have the legal ability to obtain the funds with no barriers or restrictions.

Cost Basis (of a capital asset such as real estate or a security) 👍
Your purchase price of a security or other capital item. Cost basis of a capital asset can be "stepped up" to Fair Market Value if inherited, as of the decedent's date of death. Cost basis is de-

ducted from sale proceeds in order to calculate the gain or loss upon the sale.

Cost Basis (of an IRA) 👍
Refers to the portion of IRAs for which the taxpayer took no Income Tax Deduction, used in determining the taxable portion of IRA distributions or rollovers to Roth IRAs.

Daycare Credit ❖
See Dependent Care Credit ❖.

Deferred Compensation Plan 👍
A pay arrangement offered by some employers where an employee can select an amount of current year compensation that they will not receive until a future year, in order to postpone paying income tax on that income.

Degree Program
Refers to a college curriculum that when studied and successfully completed, will lead to a college degree.

Dependency Exemption 👍
An allowance deducted from income for your spouse and children, before arriving at taxable income (each person listed on your income tax return is eligible for an exemption). (The taxpayer's exemption is referred to as his or her Personal Exemption.) A taxpayer may also be eligible for the exemption of others besides the spouse and children, if certain conditions exist. As income increases, exemptions can be phased out. If a taxpayer is subject to Alternative Minimum Tax, the exemptions are not allowed.

Dependent Care Benefit 👍
Funds deducted from an employee's pay on a pretax basis, and set aside in an employer account to reimburse for or pay dependent care costs. This benefit is a Tax Deduction because the

funds reduce taxable income that is shown on an employee's Form W-2 issued after each year end.

Dependent Care Credit ❖
Also called the Daycare Credit ❖ or Childcare Credit ❖, this is an Income Tax Credit ❖ for dependent care (daycare) costs paid. The credit is 20% (for middle-income households) of the daycare costs paid on up to $6K for 2 children. If the parents make less than $6K per year, the Daycare Credit ❖ is calculated on the lesser-earning parent's income. Since this is an Income Tax Credit ❖, this is a dollar-for-dollar offset of Federal income tax.

Depreciation 👍
Expensing of a fixed asset over time, as the useful life of the asset diminishes.

Distance Test
One of the requirements one must meet in order to take the Moving Expense Deduction 👍. The distance between your new job and former home must be at least 50 miles more than the distance between the old job and former home.

Earned income
Cash inflow from performance of labor, such as wages, commissions, or self-employment income.

Education Savings Account 👍
Savings account for which earnings are income tax free if used for Qualified Education Expenses. There are annual limits to the amount you can contribute and there is no Federal Income Tax Deduction for contributions. Distributions can be used for Kindergarten through college. Participation is subject to high-income phase outs.

Effective Tax Rate
> A taxpayer's average income tax rate, generally calculated as the tax liability divided by Adjusted Gross Income.

Employer Education Assistance 👍
> Funds provided by an employer for an employee to attend college classes. The benefit is income tax free to the employee up to annual limits.

Employer-Provided Adoption Benefits 👍
> Income tax free benefit from an employer for reimbursement of or paying for Qualified Adoption Expenses incurred up to the per child allowable maximum for the adoption of a Qualifying Child.

Energy Saving Tax Credit ❖
> Income Tax Credit ❖ for installation of solar, wind, or geothermal energy products. Very specific rules apply to be eligible for the Income Tax Credit.

Estate
> The entirety of a person's net assets at their death, including personal effects, investments, real estate, businesses owned, among many other types of assets that can be owned.

Exemptions 👍
> See Dependency Exemption.

Failure to File Penalty
> IRS penalty imposed for failure to file your income tax return by the due date, or extended due date.

Failure to Pay Penalty
> IRS penalty imposed for failure to pay your income tax due by the due date. An extension of time to file your income tax return does not extend the time to pay the income tax due.

Fair Market Value
: Current value of an asset in an efficient economy; the price at which a willing seller will sell an asset, and a willing buyer will buy it.

FICA Tax
: Social Security tax paid by employees and employers to the Social Security Administration of the Federal government to provide retirement benefits to retirees.

Filing Status
: Classification of a taxpayer to determine the applicable income tax bracket and taxation of various items on their income tax return. Includes Married Filing Joint, Married Filing Separate, Single, Qualified Widower, and Head of Household.

Filing Status Optimization Report
: Calculation prepared in order to determine whether Married Filing Jointly or Married Filing Separately/Head of Household produces the least amount of overall Federal and state income tax.

Flat Tax
: A tax system where everyone pays the exact same percentage of their total income in income tax. The U.S. does not have a flat taxing system because numerous Income Tax Deductions and Income Tax Credits are allowed, and because of the graduated tax scale.

Flexible Spending Account (FSA) 👍
: Employer benefit plan where an employee can pay for medical or daycare expenses with pretax dollars. Only $500 can be carried over to a new year, so a person with an FSA will want to make sure they spend almost all of the account balance each year.

Gift Tax
A Federal tax owed by donors for gifts that exceed the lifetime gift tax exclusion.

Gift Tax Exclusion
An annual per recipient threshold that if gifts exceed, a gift tax return is supposed to be filed. And there's a lifetime exclusion that is tracked on the annual Gift Tax Return. Both the annual and the lifetime exclusions change almost annually.

Gifting Limit
Also called annual gift tax exclusion. This is an annual limit a person can gift to another, and if the annual limit is exceeded, a gift tax return should be filed.

Hardship Withdrawal
Distribution from a retirement plan by an employee due to extreme financial need, as defined by the retirement plan document. The distribution does not automatically qualify to be relieved of the 10% early withdrawal penalty, just because of the hardship.

Head of Household
Filing status of a person who is unmarried or considered unmarried that provides more than half of the cost of maintaining a home for themselves and at least one child.

Health Savings Account (HSA) 🌢
Savings account for which contributions are income tax deductible, and if used to pay Qualified Medical Expenses, are tax free upon distribution. These funds can accumulate without limitation.

Hobby Loss
Loss generated from activities that lend themselves to personal recreation that may lack a profit motive.

Home Equity Debt 👆
    Additional home indebtedness, in additional to a traditional mortgage, that is based on the equity in the home.

Home Office Deduction 👆
    An Income Tax Deduction for use of your home office for work. You must use the home office regularly and exclusively for work purposes.

Incentive Stock Options
    Awards in the form of options to purchase stock in the employer/company at favorable prices, generally for middle and top management only.

Income Shifting
    Movement of income from those in higher income tax brackets to those in lower income tax brackets, often from parents to children.

Income Smoothing
    Process by which you attempt to stay in a consistent income tax bracket each year so as to not experience large spikes in income and have to pay income tax in a higher income tax bracket on those spikes in income.

Income Tax Bracket
    Level of taxation based on income. The U.S.A. has a graduated income tax system, where income is first taxed at the lower income tax rates, and only marginal income is taxed at the rate of the taxpayer's highest bracket.

Income Tax Planning
    Thoughtful strategies designed to decrease income tax burden.

Independent Contractor
    Work arrangement where worker is a contractor of the employer, instead of a traditional employee. The independent contrac-

tor is responsible for payment of his/her own income taxes and benefits, among other things.

IRA 👍

Individual Retirement Account. Funds placed in a retirement account, and if taxpayer is under certain income tax thresholds, they are eligible to take an Income Tax Deduction for the IRA contribution, and the growth on the funds in the IRA are tax deferred.

IRA Rollover

The movement of IRA funds from one qualified IRA account to another. A direct transfer can be made, or the account owner can request the funds, and then reinvest them into another IRA account within 60 days. Rollovers other than direct transfers are supposed to have withholding taken out.

IRA Rollover Loan

An undocumented "loan" where an owner of an IRA requests funds from the IRA account, uses the funds for up to 60 days, and then re-deposits the funds into an IRA before 60 days have elapsed. If the funds are not returned to an IRA account within 60 days, this will be considered a taxable distribution. And if the account owner has not yet attained age 59½, the 10% penalty for early withdrawal will likely apply. When returning funds to the IRA account, the account owner must also deposit funds that were originally applied to income tax withholding when the distribution was received.

IRS Matching Program

IRS initiative to match various income documents from employers, banks and customers to a person's income tax return, to ensure taxpayers are reporting all income received on their income tax returns.

Itemized Deductions 👍
  Personal expenses that are deductible from Adjusted Gross Income to obtained Taxable Income (personal exemptions are also deducted before arriving at Taxable Income). Itemized Deductions include Medical Expenses (after limitations), Real Estate taxes, Personal Property Taxes, State & Local Income taxes or Sales Tax, mortgage interest (within limits), charity (within limits) and miscellaneous itemized deductions (that exceed applicable threshold).

Kiddie Tax
  Income tax assessed on a child's unearned income in excess of a certain limit, taxed at the parents' highest income tax rate.

Lifetime Learning Credit ❖
  Nonrefundable Tax Credit (dollar for dollar offset of income tax) for college education for an unlimited number of years, but does have annual limits. Disbursements must be used for Qualified Education Expenses.

Line Item Audit
  IRS audit where the IRS requests supporting documentation for just one line item on a taxpayer's income tax return, such as charitable donations.

Marginal Tax Rate
  The highest income tax rate to which a taxpayer is subject; every new dollar of taxable income is subject to tax at this highest income tax rate.

Married Filing Joint
  Filing status where spouses file a combined income tax return.

Married Filing Separate
  Filing status where spouses file separate income tax returns. The spouses need to have lived apart for the last 6 months of the year to use this filing status.

Miscellaneous Itemized Deductions 👍
Deductions included on a person's Itemized Deductions Schedule and most of the Miscellaneous Itemized Deductions are deductible only for the portion that exceeds 2% of Adjusted Gross Income. Examples include income tax preparation fees and unreimbursed employee expenses.

Mortgage Insurance Premiums 👍
Amounts paid to your mortgage company to cover premiums on an insurance policy that will cover the unpaid balance of the loan, if borrower becomes disabled or passes away. If income is below certain levels, these premiums may be income tax deductible.

Mortgage Points 👍
Additional "interest" charge on a residential mortgage, stated as a percentage of the loan. For example, one point = one percent of original loan proceeds. These points are deductible either over the life of the mortgage loan or in the year loan was taken out, if not rolled into the total loan.

Municipal Bonds
Debt instruments issued by a state or local government in order to raise funds for a project in their jurisdiction. The interest from municipal bonds is Federal income tax free, and may be state income tax free if issued by your home state.

Net Investment Income Tax
3.8% tax that began in 2013 on the lessor of net investment income or income in excess of applicable thresholds based on filing status.

Non-Deductible IRA
IRA purchased that is not income tax deductible likely because taxpayer's income is above the allowable thresholds to be able to deduct the IRA contribution. Non-deductible IRAs are said to have "basis", and reduce the taxable portion of IRA withdrawals.

Non-Degree Program
: Refers to a college courses that when studied and successfully completed, will not lead to a college degree. Sometimes such courses are more related to one's hobby or other personal interests.

Passive Activities
: Activities where the taxpayer does not actively participate, usually generated from rental real estate or investments in partnerships.

Passive Loss 👆
: Loss from an investment in an activity where the taxpayer does not actively participate, usually generated from rental real estate or investments in partnerships. There are limitations to the amount of passive losses one may deduct, based on basis and passive income levels.

Penalty Upon Early Withdrawal of Retirement Funds
: 10% penalty imposed by IRS for a person cashing in retirement funds before age 59½, if none of the allowable exceptions to the penalty are present.

Permanent Differences
: Adjustments to regular taxable income to obtain Alternative Minimum Taxable income, whose effect will not reverse in a future year, such as state and local income taxes.

Personal Exemption 👆
: An allowance deducted from income for yourself, before arriving at taxable income (each person listed on your income tax return is eligible for an exemption). (The spouse's and children's exemptions are referred to as Dependency Exemptions.)

Phase Out
: Refers to the reduced eligibility of use of an Income Tax Deduction or Income Tax Credit as income rises. Each Tax Deduction and Tax Credit has their own phase out thresholds.

Principal residence (for residential sale gain exclusion purposes)
: The home where you live most of the time, that is closest to your job, where your spouse and children stay, address that is on your income tax returns/driver's license/voter registration, that is closest to where you bank, and that is closest to where you attend any religious establishment.

Profit Motive
: Evidence that a person is running a business for purposes of making a profit. If a person is being audited by the IRS for Hobby Losses, he/she likely will need to prove there is a profit motive in running the business.

Profit Sharing Plan
: Retirement plan used by for-profit business entities and employer contributes based on the profits of the business.

Qualified Adoption Expenses 👍
: Expenses incurred in connection with the adoption of a child that are eligible for the Adoption Credit ❖ or Employer-Provided Adoption Benefits 👍; includes adoption agency fees, legal fees, court costs, travel, meals while away from home, etc.

Qualified Dividends
: Dividend income earned on stocks that have been owned for more than one year or on mutual funds, where the mutual fund has owned stock for more than one year. These dividends are taxed at the lower Capital Gain rates, not at ordinary income tax rates.

Qualified Education Expenses 👍
Expenses eligible for Education Tax Credits ❖ or Tuition & Fees Deduction👍. The types of eligible expenses vary based on the education benefit for which you are trying to qualify. Tuition and fees are eligible regardless of which education tax benefit you are taking.

Qualified Medical Expenses 👍
Expenses eligible for a medical expense Income Tax Deduction, or for reimbursement from a Health Savings Account or Flexible Spending Account. Generally, includes expenses incurred to help the body operate properly. Cosmetic surgery and health club dues are not Qualified Medical Expenses, but some weight loss programs are, if prescribed by a doctor for an obese person, and infertility treatments are considered Qualified Medical Expenses. Visit www.irs.gov for a complete list of allowable medical expenses.

Qualified Tuition Program 👍
Income tax free savings plan for college, and participation is not phased out due to high income. Contributions are not income tax deductible for Federal purposes, but earnings are income tax free if distributions are used for Qualified Education Expenses.

Qualifying Child (for Adoption Tax Benefits)
Child that is eligible for adoption and is under age 18 when the Qualified Adoption Expenses are incurred or is incapable of caring for himself or herself.

Qualifying Child (for Dependency Exemption)
Your child that you are eligible to place on your income tax return in order to take their dependency exemption based on these tests: relationship, age, residency, support, joint return and tie breaker (if applicable).

Qualifying Relative
: Your relative or other member of household that is not a qualifying child of someone else that you are eligible to place on your income tax return in order to take their dependency exemption based on these tests: member of household or relationship, gross income, and support.

Refundable Tax Credit ❖
: A dollar for dollar reduction of income tax, that is at least partially eligible to be refunded to the taxpayer when the Tax Credit ❖ exceeds the income tax liability. Most Tax Credits are not refundable.

Release of Dependency Exemption
: When a custodial parent signs a form to allow the noncustodial parent to take the dependency exemption of their joint child. The release can be for one year, or for all future years.

Residential Sale Gain Exclusion ☙
: Excess of sale proceeds over cost basis of your principal residence that is not income taxable because you occupied the home in 2 of the 5 years prior to the sale. Maximum exclusion varies by marital status and exclusion can be pro-rated if the 2 year requirement is not met.

Retirement Plan Loans
: Loans from retirement plans to the retirement plan participant that usually must be repaid within 5 years unless proceeds were used to purchase a principal residence. Many 401(k), 403(b) and pension plans allow participant loans to the extent of participant contributions.

Roth IRA
: Funds placed in a retirement account that grow income tax free; distribution of funds from the Roth IRA are income tax free, if initial holding period obligation is met. No Income Tax Deduction is allowed for contributions into a Roth IRA.

Roth IRA Conversion
> Transferring IRA funds to a Roth IRA so that the funds will grow tax free, after applicable income taxes are paid on the transfer.

Savings Bond
> A debt security issued by the U.S. government that pays interest at maturity. Interest earned on Series EE bonds issued after 1989 and Series I bonds, used to pay for Qualified Education Expenses is income tax free if the taxpayer is below the required income threshold.

Savings Bond Interest Exclusion 👍
> Interest from Series EE bonds issued after 1989 or Series I bonds that is income tax free if used for Qualified Education Expenses, if the taxpayer is below the required income threshold.

SEP IRA 👍
> Self Employed retirement Plan, an IRA for a Self-employed person, and it has higher contribution limits than a traditional or Roth IRA.

SIMPLE IRA 👍
> Retirement plan for small for-profit employers with less than 100 employees. Both the employer and employee can contribute to the plan, within limits. The plan allows for catch-up contributions for those age 50 and older.

Simplified Home Office Method 👍
> An Income Tax Deduction for use of your home office for work. You must use the home office regularly and exclusively for work purposes. With this method, you calculate the deduction based on a flat dollar amount per square foot of the office, and there is no deduction for depreciation.

Spousal IRA 👍
: IRA purchased by a nonworking spouse of an employed person. The contribution limit is the same as the traditional IRA, including catch-up contributions, if applicable. The employed spouse must have earnings that meet or exceed the sum of both spouses' IRA and employer retirement plan contributions.

Standard Deduction 👍
: Allowable Deduction from Adjusted Gross Income, before arriving at Taxable Income. If a taxpayer itemizes their deductions, they cannot also take the Standard Deduction.

Step Up In Cost Basis 👍
: Increase in cost basis of an asset (such as real estate or securities) that is inherited, to Fair Market Value as of the decedent's date of death.

Student Loan Interest Deduction 👍
: Income Tax Deduction for the payment of interest expense on a qualifying student loan. This deduction is subject to income phase out.

Tax Anxiety
: Feelings of anxiety brought on by contemplating income tax and preparation of same.

Tax Bracket
: See Income Tax Bracket.

Tax Credit ❖
: A dollar for dollar reduction of income tax for an allowable expenditure.

Tax Deduction 👍
: A reduction before arriving at taxable income for an allowable expense. The tax savings is calculated as the amount of the Tax Deduction multiplied by the marginal income tax rate.

Tax Deferred Income 👍
  Refers to when income tax is not currently due on income, such as growth within an IRA or employer retirement plan.

Tax Free Income 👍
  Refers to when income is not taxable at all, such as growth within a Roth IRA, or from bartering personal services for personal services.

Tax Simplification
  A goal of the U.S. Government, that so far has been unattainable, to make the U.S. income tax system easier with which to comply.

Taxable Income
  Amount on which Federal income tax is calculated. Calculated as Adjusted Gross Income less Itemized Deductions (or Standard Deduction) less personal exemptions.

Time Test
  One of the requirements one must meet in order to take the Moving Expense Deduction 👍. The employee must work at least 39 weeks at the new job in order to take the Moving Expense Deduction and 78 weeks for a self-employed person.

Timing Differences
  Adjustments to regular taxable income to obtain Alternative Minimum Taxable income, whose effect may reverse in a future year, such as for depreciation expense.

Tuition and Fees Deduction 👍
  An Income Tax Deduction allowed for college education costs, subject to limitations and high-income phase out rules.

Unearned Income
  Cash inflow from portfolio investments, such as interest, dividends and Capital Gains.

Unrealized Gain
Potential gain (income) from securities in your portfolio that if sold would result in a Capital Gain, and if held more than one year, would be eligible for the more favorable Capital Gain rate.

Unrealized Loss
Potential loss from securities in your portfolio that if sold would result in a Capital Loss.

About the Author

Lisa Bushur, CPA writes about income tax savings ideas. Lisa started her career at a Big 4 accounting firm, then worked as a Controller of a medium-sized transportation company, then opened her own CPA firm. And now Lisa focuses on writing and speaking about the income tax ideas she's learned in about three decades of being a CPA.

If you would like to be on Lisa's mailing list, contact her or buy additional copies of this book, go to **www.LisaBcpa.com**.

Notes:

Notes: